BRAXFIELD

BRAXFIELD

the hanging judge ?

The Life and Times of
Lord Justice-Clerk
Robert McQueen of Braxfield

BRIAN D OSBORNE

First Published 1997
Argyll Publishing
Glendaruel
Argyll PA22 3AE
Scotland

Subsidised by the Scottish Arts Council

THE SCOTTISH ARTS COUNCIL

British Library Cataloguing-in-Publication Data.
A catalogue record for this book is available from
the British Library.

ISBN 1 874640 03 3

Origination
Cordfall Ltd, Glasgow

Printing
ColourBooks Ltd, Dublin

LIST OF ILLUSTRATIONS

The illustrations from Kay's *Original Portraits* are by courtesy of Midlothian Council Library Service

CONTENTS

List of Illustrations

Acknowledgements

A Note on Names

ACKNOWLEDGEMENTS

It is my pleasure to be able to thank many people who have most kindly and generously assisted me in the writing of this book.

I owe a particular debt of gratitude to a number of friends who have not only coped with my enthusiasm for Robert McQueen but have read various parts of this book in draft form and have commented and made valuable suggestions and corrections. Ronald Armstrong (whose question about whether a biography of Braxfield existed certainly entitles him to be considered the godfather of this book) and Louis Stott have been particularly helpful in this regard and Kevin Goldie's legal training saved me from many errors in Chapter Three. John Gilfillan and Leila Stott provided timely assistance in the translation of passages of Latin and French respectively. The help and support of all the above is gratefully acknowledged, although responsibility for any mistakes and shortcomings, of course, rests with the author.

The resources of Edinburgh City Archives, Edinburgh University Library, The Faculty of Advocates, The Mitchell Library, Glasgow, The National Library of Scotland, The Scottish Record Office, and South Lanarkshire Libraries have been of great value in the preparation of this book and the efficiency and courtesy of the staffs of these institutions is most gratefully acknowledged, as is the assistance received from the Court of the Lord Lyon King of Arms and the College of Heralds in London. A special word of appreciation is due to my former colleagues in East Dunbartonshire Libraries whose excellent collections and service and their proximity and familiarity made them a frequent and uncomplaining target for my demands.

I must acknowledge permission received from Major John J Graham for permission to quote from the Graham of Fintry papers. I would also wish to thank Mr E R McCosh, Hardington, for his assistance.

Brian D Osborne, April 1997

71

I. KAY del.ᵗ & ſculpt 179?

Robert McQueen of Braxfield

John Kay's caricature of the Lord Justice Clerk dates from 1793,
the year of Thomas Muir's trial for sedition.

A Note on Names

There is a certain inevitable confusion about the names of many of the characters in this book, including the central figure of Braxfield. His family name of McQueen can be, was and is spelled variously McQueen, M'Queen, Macqueen and MacQueen. His own autograph spelling in various letters and legal documents is McQueen and this form has been adopted throughout, except in quotations when the form used there has been adopted – even, as in the case of an entry in the Books of Sederunt of the Lords of Council and Session recording his admission to the Court of Session, when two different forms are used in one document.

After McQueen's elevation to the Bench his formal title was Lord Braxfield, even though the custom was for judges still to sign documents with their Christian and Family names. In the chapters discussing McQueen's private and family life and career as an advocate he has been referred to as McQueen while in the chapters discussing his judicial career, he has been referred to as Braxfield, except in quotations when the form used in the original source has been adopted. Elsewhere McQueen and Braxfield have been used as seems most appropriate in the context.

There are other, minor, name problems. Three Court of Session judges in McQueen's period changed their judicial titles – Lord Barskimming becoming Lord Glenlee and Lords Tinwald and Barjarg successively changed their titles to Lord Alva. The seemingly endless supply of Campbells, Dalrymples and Dundases gracing the Scottish Bar and Bench would present fewer problems had there been a slightly more generous supply of Christian names to help distinguish between them. The two David Dalrymples on the Bench simultaneously are fortunately capable of being distinguished by one being formally known as Lord Hailes and one as Lord Westhall. The Dundas family produced two Lord Presidents – Robert Dundas, Lord Arniston in 1748 and Robert Dundas, Lord Arniston in 1760. Both these Robert Dundases had previously been Lord Advocates – a third Robert Dundas was appointed Solicitor General in 1784 and Lord Advocate in 1789. Ilay Campbell, Lord Succoth and his contemporary John Campbell, Lord Stonefield also require to be distinguished from each other and from Archibald Campbell, Earl of Ilay, an Extraordinary Lord of Session from 1708–1761.

CHAPTER 1

Braxfield the Myth

*"to entertain a sneaking kindness
for any unpopular person"*

The dark figure of Robert McQueen, Lord Braxfield, Lord Justice-Clerk, scourge of the Scottish radicals, the transporter of Muir, Skirving and Margarot glowers down through the centuries from the Bench of the High Court of Justiciary – execrated by liberals, patronised by sophisticated commentators, pilloried in popular legend. But the image, or the myth, still has considerable power. Why?

Robert McQueen (1722–1799), better known by his judicial title as Lord Braxfield, alone of all the legal talent to grace Scotland's Court of Session and High Court of Justiciary in the second half of the eighteenth century, still presents a vivid and recognisable image today. Braxfield, whether monster, crude bully, reactionary or not, is the only name from that period still to have any degree of popular resonance. Some of Braxfield's fame or notoriety is undoubtedly due to the inspired re-creation of him by Robert Louis Stevenson as the central figure of Lord Hermiston in *Weir of Hermiston*:

> You're a young man that doesna approve of Caapital
> Punishment . . .

Hermiston says to his well-intentioned liberal son, Archie:

> Weel, I'm an auld man that does. I was glad to get Jopp

haangit, for what would I pretend I wasna? . . .
I'm a man that gets through with my day's business, and let
that suffice. (1)

Which seems a reasonably accurate account of Braxfield's philosophy.
Elsewhere in the unfinished novel Stevenson adds to his portrait of
Braxfield/Hermiston, and again, perhaps not unjustly:

> But Hermiston was not all of one piece. He was, besides, a
> mighty toper; he could sit at wine until the day dawned, and
> pass directly from the table to the bench with a steady hand
> and a clear head. Beyond the third bottle, he showed the
> plebeian in a larger print; the low, gross accent, the low, foul
> mirth, grew broader and commoner; he became less
> formidable, and infinitely more disgusting. (2)

Too much should not be made of this, however. Stevenson re-created
Braxfield – he did not invent him. Nor is Stevenson's portrayal entirely
negative – besides the "low gross accent" and the "low foul mirth" he
writes memorably of Hermiston, displaying a very Roman (and very
Scottish) *gravitas* and *severitas*: '. . . on he went up the great, bare staircase
of his duty, uncheered and undepressed.' (3)

The man Braxfield was already in the public domain, indeed in
the public imagination; a dominant figure, imposing, commanding,
looking sharply at the world out of his Raeburn portrait. The Raeburn
painting was also commented on by Stevenson in "Some Portraits by
Raeburn" published in his collection of essays, *Virginibus Puerisque*,
and Stevenson's remarks do indicate something of the abiding power
of the Braxfield image and name. It is worth noting that the essay was
written in 1876, almost two decades before RLS started work on *Weir
of Hermiston*. He writes:

> So sympathetically is the character conceived by the portrait-
> painter, that it is hardly possible to avoid some movement of
> sympathy on the part of the spectator. And sympathy is a thing to
> be encouraged, apart from human considerations, because it
> supplies us with the materials for wisdom. It is probably more
> instructive to entertain a sneaking kindness for any unpopular
> person, and, among the rest, for Lord Braxfield, than to give way to

perfect raptures of moral indignation against his abstract vices. He was the last judge on the Scottish bench to employ the pure Scotch idiom. His opinions, thus given in Doric, and conceived in a lively, rugged, conversational style, were full of point and authority. Out of the bar, or off the bench, he was a convivial man, a lover of wine, and one who "shone peculiarly" at tavern meetings. He left behind him an unrivalled reputation for rough and cruel speech; and to this day his name smacks of the gallows.(4)

Braxfield did not lack for distinguished contemporaries on the Bench, contemporaries who might well have been expected to live quite as vividly down the years in the public imagination. A Supreme Court whose members included James Burnett, Lord Monboddo, a Darwinian before his time; who wrote learnedly if somewhat erratically on man's kinship to the apes, and who earnestly believed that humans were born with tails and attributed the inconvenient fact that we fail to display these appendages to a midwives' conspiracy to remove them at birth; cannot be said to want for human interest. The fancy of Francis Garden, Lord Gardenstone, to keep a pet pig, as others might keep a dog or cat, and to allow it to share his bed, might, in an animal-loving nation have been thought quite likely to help ensure his survival in popular legend. The "Fifteen" of the Court of Session in Braxfield's years on the Bench from 1776 to 1799 included eccentrics, learned jurists, scholars, and workaday plodders. Braxfield, however, then and now, outshines his contemporaries and, in a curious way, has been seen to swallow them all up in his personality with collegial decisions being attributed to him alone and a wealth of stories and legends surrounding his name.

Perhaps Braxfield's involvement with the criminal cases of the Justiciary Court contributed both to his contemporary, and to his posthumous, fame or notoriety. In his day the Lord President and the other fourteen Senators of the College of Justice sat as the Court of Session, the supreme Scottish civil court. The country's most serious criminal cases were dealt with by six of these judges who received additional appointments as Commissioners of Justiciary, sitting under the presidency of the Lord Justice-Clerk.

There was in addition a sinecure office of Lord Justice-General, held normally by a politically favoured nobleman. The Court of Session sat only in Edinburgh while the High Court of Justiciary met there and, by delegation of one or two judges, on twice-yearly circuit in nine

towns and cities throughout Scotland. The most memorable cases of
late eighteenth century Scotland were, with perhaps the exception of
the Douglas peerage inheritance cause, criminal cases and Braxfield's
involvement in many of them did much to ensure both his contemporary fame and his lasting reputation or notoriety.

The dramatic nature of criminal cases meant a greater degree of
public interest and, perhaps inevitably, more opportunity for judicial
comment and the introduction of personalities. Opportunities of which,
it would seem, Braxfield was never slow to avail himself of. The stories
of Braxfield's coarseness, his contempt for the accused, his rough
treatment of advocates, his unseemly levity are all well known. Remarks
like his: 'Ye're a vera clever chiel, man, but ye wad be nane the waur o' a
hanging' (5) and 'Hang a thief when he's young, and he'll no steal when
he's auld' (6) are the staple of many a collection of Scottish anecdotes.
Some of them may even be accurate, and indeed one hopes that the tale
of his rebuke to two drunken advocates is one of the true ones:

> Gentlemen, ye maun jist pack up yer papers and gang hame,
> for the tane o' ye's riftin' punch, and the ither's belching
> claret, and there'll be nae gude oot o' ye the day. (7)

It is interesting to see how other men's remarks were early on attributed
to Braxfield, and despite correction and refutation still attach to his
name. Perhaps the most striking example of this mythic quality of
Braxfield is the "checkmate" story. Braxfield, so the tale runs, was in
the habit of playing chess with an acquaintance when on the Western
Judiciary Circuit. One day however his acquaintance, Donald, appeared
before him charged with the capital crime of forgery. The jury having
returned their verdict Lord Braxfield pronounced for doom and then,
addressing the prisoner, said: 'And now, Donald, my man, I think I've
checkmated you for once.' (8)

A splendid and colourful story, confirming all that has been said
of the heartlessness of the man described as "Scotland's Judge Jeffreys"
– splendid but untrue, even if, according to John Gibson Lockhart, no
less an authority than Sir Walter Scott told it to the Prince Regent.
However the tale was comprehensively rebutted by Charles Hope, Lord
President Granton, who secured the withdrawal of the story in
subsequent editions of Lockhart's *Life of Scott*. Even the critical Lord
Cockburn who was, as we shall see, no friend to Braxfield, attributes

the checkmate story to Lord Kames, sets it in another town, with another criminal and another crime. Alexander Young, whose unpublished *Memoir of Robert Macqueen of Braxfield: Lord Justice-Clerk* (9) provides a useful corrective to much of the Braxfield mythology, confirms that the author of the "checkmate" quip was in fact Henry Home, Lord Kames.

Whether Scott confused the story, or as seems more likely it was erroneously reported to Scott's biographer and son in law, Lockhart, by William Adam, is not of the first importance. What is surely significant is that this remark – so quintessentially "Braxfieldian" – could so readily be attributed to Braxfield. Scott knew Braxfield well, dedicated his thesis on entry to the Faculty of Advocates to Braxfield, was a neighbour in Edinburgh's George Square, shared many of Braxfield's concerns about the dangers of radicalism and the threat to the established order of society: in short Scott was not likely to be a hostile witness. But Scott, and those of a like mind could easily assume that Braxfield had made the "checkmate" remark, and could happily dine out on it at Carlton House. In any event Lockhart, in response to protests, altered his story in later editions, cautiously attributing the remark to "a certain judge".

The "checkmate" story is also interesting in that it reveals something of the style and manner of the Scottish bench at this time. After all, the same Lord Kames, anticipating his death, and on what he felt would be his last attendance at the Court of Session, bade farewell to his fellow Senators of the College of Justice with the memorable phrase: 'Fare ye a' weel, ye bitches!' (10) If Kames could thus apostrophise his fellow judges and make remarks such as the "checkmate" one to condemned men, behaviour unthinkable and indefensible by the standards of modern judicial propriety, then perhaps Braxfield needs to be seen not as a unique monster but as a man occupying an identifiable place in a spectrum of manners and behaviour, manners and behaviour that are alien to us but not necessarily so remote from the prevailing mores of his time. Stevenson comments on Lord Braxfield's role in the Muir and Skirving trials that: ' . . . his appearance on these occasions was scarcely cut to the pattern of today' (11) which is true, but men must surely be judged, as Stevenson implies, by the standards of their own day as well as by later, objective or absolute standards.

Braxfield has been painted in such unrelievedly dark colours that an observer might be forgiven for wondering how such an evidently unsuitable and improper man became head of the Scottish criminal justice system. Henry Cockburn (1779–1854), who himself became a Court of Session judge in 1834, wrote of Braxfield that he was: ' . . . like a formidable blacksmith . . .' (12) and that he was:

> Illiterate and without any taste for refined enjoyment,
> strength of understanding, which gave him power without
> cultivation, only encouraged him to a more contemptuous
> disdain of all natures less coarse than his own

and furthermore concluded that: 'It is impossible to condemn his conduct as a criminal judge too gravely, or too severely.'

In fairness to Cockburn he does also say that Braxfield was: ' . . . the giant of the bench . . .' and that he was a ' . . . profound practical lawyer . . .' (13) and speaks of how:

> . . . having worked out a principle, he followed it in its
> application, fearlessly and triumphantly, dashing all
> unworthy obstructions aside, and pushed on to his result
> with the vigour and disdain of a consummate athlete. And he
> had a colloquial way of arguing, in the form of question and
> answer, which, done in his clear abrupt style, imparted a
> dramatic directness and vivacity to the scene. (14)

Subsequent writers on Braxfield have followed Cockburn's line – often following Cockburn's very words, while in some cases omitting a number of Cockburn's significant qualifications and reservations. For example in describing the trial of Thomas Muir of Huntershill Cockburn states that Mr Horner, a juror in the case, told him that Braxfield seeing him passing by the bench on his way to the jury box whispered: 'Come awa, Maister Horner, come awa, and help us to hang ane o' thae daamned scoondrels.' (15) Cockburn appends a footnote to state that "hang" was Braxfield's phrase for all kinds of punishment – later writers have been less scrupulous. W Forbes Gray, in *Some Old Scots Judges* (1914) takes Cockburn's story, repeats it with the bowdlerisation of "d-----d" for "daamned" and omits the crucial explanation of Braxfield's idiosyncratic use of the word "hang".

In this instance Cockburn's account is based on a clear line of evidence – he was told the story by Horner, the father of a school-friend. Whether such hearsay evidence would have been acceptable in Cockburn's court is another matter, and one which need not detain us – biography fortunately requires a somewhat lower evidential standard than does the criminal justice system.

However there do remain very major problems with Cockburn as a source of evidence on Braxfield. Despite the fact that Cockburn is so widely cited as a reliable contemporary source he is only this in the most narrow and technical of senses. When Robert McQueen died, aged seventy seven, in May 1799, Henry Cockburn was only nineteen and would not be admitted to the Faculty of Advocates until December 1800. His picturesque stories of Braxfield on the bench are thus not based on first hand evidence – as he admits himself: 'Of the fifteen judges of those days, some of course were "heads without name." Of the others Monboddo, Swinton, and Braxfield had left the scene shortly before I entered the Faculty.' (16)

Perhaps more significant from the evidential standpoint than Cockburn's "hearsay" status is his total political and cultural antipathy to Braxfield. McQueen was an arch-Tory, a reactionary and bigoted defender of the established order, a heavy drinker, and an impassioned adherent of the Scots tongue. Braxfield it was who memorably remarked of the advocate Francis Jeffrey, educated at Oxford, and beginning his career at the Scottish Bar, that: 'The laddie has clean tint his Scotch and fund nae English.' (17) In short he was a not untypical figure of that spirit in Scotland in the mid-eighteenth century which resisted the changes coming from the South. Braxfield was most assuredly not one of those Edinburgh Enlightenment figures who hired elocution teachers to drill the Scotticisms out of their writing and speech. His religious duties would seem to have sat lightly on him – as they did to many others who followed in the tradition of eighteenth century Auld Kirk Moderatism.

Between McQueen and Cockburn lies the gulf of fifty seven years – and it might be accepted that it is always going to be difficult for a young man at the start of his career to rightly and fairly judge an old man at the end of his. But more than a generation gap separates McQueen and Cockburn – they are divided by language, by political ideology, by religious conviction, by social custom, by manners. McQueen was an anachronistic survivor of a fast-vanishing Scotland – a mid-eighteenth century figure, rough, perhaps even gross, in manner.

Cockburn as a nineteenth century Whig was emotionally and intellectually opposed to much that McQueen represented. Even in language Braxfield was an offence. Surprisingly perhaps when one considers that Cockburn himself ' . . . retained his Scottish accent and was fond of Scotch allusions.' (18) Perhaps less surprisingly when one recollects that Cockburn was an Edinburgh man, and of the Edinburgh establishment, while McQueen's accent was learned in his Lanarkshire childhood. The gulf between the East and the West of Scotland has not quite disappeared even in our own day. Cockburn wrote of Braxfield that: 'His accent and his dialect were exaggerated Scotch' (19) and, indeed, his portraits of the other judges of the period similarly make play with their subject's linguistic peculiarities and idiosyncrasies of manner.

The Scottish Bar in Braxfield and Cockburn's time was highly politicised – this aspect of legal life will be dealt with in Chapter 3 – but it is appropriate here to remark that the Tory administration – symbolised by the Dundas hegemony – and supported by Braxfield had established a monopoly of power and preferment and Whig advocates like John Clerk of Eldin, Henry Erskine and Cockburn himself were very much excluded from office. Cockburn's distaste for Braxfield thus owes something to personal dislike, something to a generation gap, something to a sea-change in manners and behaviour and a significant amount to irreconcilable political differences.

That Braxfield was a reactionary and bigoted defender of the established order is a truth which it would be futile to attempt to deny. His comments at Thomas Muir's trial are rightly remembered and rightly held against him. In his charge to the jury Braxfield observed that it required no proof for them to accept that: ' . . . the British constitution is the best in the world' and advised that:

> A Government in every country should be just like a corporation; and, in this country, it is made up of the landed interest, which alone has a right to be represented. As for the rabble, who have nothing but personal property, what hold has the nation on them? What security for the payment of their taxes? (20)

While it is fair to comment that not dissimilar arguments were adduced at the time, and later, in favour of the practice of purchasing commissions in the Army, to ensure that only those with a stake in Society occupied such positions, Braxfield's view of the state is hardly likely to commend itself to democrats in any age and was certainly anathema to the Whig reformer Cockburn.

Nor were these comments isolated or unconsidered, or even excusable by being provoked by the excitement and stresses of the trial. In September 1794, a year after the Muir trial, Braxfield went on the Northern Justiciary Circuit and opened the Justiciary Court at Inverness, where, on this occasion, there was no criminal business to be dealt with. The Lord Justice-Clerk, addressing the assizers and sheriffs of the eight Highland counties covered by the Inverness sitting of the Justiciary Court, took the opportunity to observe:

> . . . that although the constitution and laws of this country were the most perfect that ever yet existed, in so much, that we were envied by all the surrounding nations for the liberty we possessed, and the absolute security of our lives and properties which we enjoyed; yet strange as it may seem, it now appeared, by incontestable evidence, that there had existed a dissatisfaction, very unaccountable, amongst a number of persons in various parts of the united kingdoms; and that many of them had proceeded to measures of the most dangerous tendency, not with the view of obtaining redress in a constitutional manner, of grievances which had a real existence, but with the intention of subverting our blessed constitution, and overturning the laws of our country. (21)

Braxfield's defence of the existing order, as not only perfect but unarguably perfect, and probably unimprovably perfect, undoubtedly led him to excess, as similar sentiments led others to excess. While Braxfield, as Lord Justice-Clerk, presided at the Edinburgh trials of the radicals Muir, Margarot and Gerrald, the trial for sedition of Thomas Fyshe Palmer was heard on Circuit at Perth in September 1793 by Lords Eskgrove and Abercromby, and resulted in Palmer's transportation to Australia for a term of seven years. It should not be overlooked that in all of these cases there was a clear breach of the law to answer – however repressive the law, or laudable the intentions of the reformers and however excessive the punishment.

Why these judges reacted in the way that they did to the radical proposals of Muir and his contemporaries in favour of universal suffrage cannot be evaluated without reference to the contemporary international situation. Muir's trial took place in August 1793. The year had already seen the outbreak of war between Britain and revolutionary France, the execution of Louis XVI, the rise of the Committee of Public Safety in Paris and the Reign of Terror.

War panic and a perceived threat from alien ideas and influences frequently produce official over-reaction. During the 1914–18 War anti-German sentiment in Britain took on such manifestations as attacks on dachshund dogs and such prejudices made the Battenberg family Anglicise their name to the somewhat less Germanic Mountbatten and the Royal House of Saxe-Coburg and Gotha re-invent itself as the picturesquely English House of Windsor. During the 1939–45 War, a round-up of "enemy aliens" interned Italian ice-cream sellers and German Jewish musicians. The United States, after Pearl Harbour, moved swiftly to intern thousands of inoffensive Japanese-Americans, who were envisaged as presenting a threat to national security.

States have a natural, if not always laudable or dignified, tendency to defend themselves against threats, real or imaginary. Britain, faced not only with war with France, which was a common enough experience, but with an opponent committed to a revolutionary ideology, which was a novelty, could predictably be expected to clamp down on internal dissent. The Government and its supporters in the official classes could, equally predictably, be expected to see links between domestic reform agitation and the events in France. Earlier wars, even the American War of Independence, had not carried the extra dimension of threat that must have been perceived from a war against a revolutionary government, a government that had executed the King and would shortly execute Marie Antoinette. The mob action in Paris, the Terror, the massacres in the prisons, the overthrow of the monarchy were all profoundly alarming to the established order. Such alarm does not justify the reaction of the State or of Braxfield and his fellow judges – but it does, to an extent, explain it.

Braxfield's alleged dictum to Robert Dundas, the Lord Advocate, on possible difficulties over political prosecutions: 'Let them bring me prisoners, and I'll find them law' (22) is perhaps no more than a blunt and honest version of a widespread tendency on the part of states down the ages to use the criminal justice system for their own ends.

It is indeed Braxfield's bluntness and his coarseness that has made him particularly memorable – if Lords Eskgrove and Abercromby were happy to see Palmer transported, and the whole Bench concurred in the sentences on Muir, Margarot & Skirving, it would seem that the additional obloquy attaching to Braxfield springs not only from his dominant position as Lord Justice-Clerk, but from his inability or unwillingness to act in an appropriately refined manner – or perhaps his inability or unwillingness to resist a *bon mot*.

Cockburn reports that during the trial of Joseph Gerrald the accused remarked that all great men had been reformers: ' . . . even our Saviour himself.' Braxfield's response, which Cockburn felt was too profane to be given in detail in his *An Examination of the Trials for Sedition in Scotland* (1851), but which later he felt able to quote in the posthumously published *Memorials of his Time* (1856), was allegedly to respond: 'Muckle he made o' that, he was hanget.' (23) The twentieth century legal historian William Roughead argued, convincingly and at some length in an essay "The Bi-Centenary of Lord Braxfield" published in his collection *Glengarry's Way and other studies* that this, perhaps the most famous "Braxfieldism", was in whole or part a fabrication. Roughead cites a contemporary reviewer of Cockburn's *Trials for Sedition* who noted that:

> . . . we find that the words put into the judge's mouth were known in Edinburgh to be a mere invention, a jest that passed current at the time and was by all who heard it known to have – most men said – no foundation at all, while some few believed, or affected to believe, one part of the dictum, saying that Lord Braxfield might have muttered, 'Muckle he made o' that'; but all, without exception, utterly denied the grossly indecent addition . . . what is well known to all who lived at the time, that the speech was universally treated as a mere jocular invention, by way of very gross caricature of the chief. (24)

Cockburn in his *Memorials* gives not only Braxfield's supposed words but also the manner in which the Justice-Clerk delivered them, thus: '. . . chuckled Braxfield in an under voice . . .' (25) – a touch which is certainly the type of convincing detail which helps ensure the circulation of such a colourful tale. However it is worth remembering that in March 1794, when Gerrald was being tried and Braxfield was supposedly scandalising public decency with such remarks, Henry Cockburn was a youth of fourteen and a half, in his first session at Edinburgh University. Just how did he know that Braxfield chuckled "in an under voice"?

Cockburn must be convicted of being a bad witness – if justly to be praised as a first rate teller of stories – because of the divergences between his accounts in *Trials for Sedition*, where he directly quotes the court report which gives Gerrald as saying: 'Christianity itself was an innovation' (26) and that in *Memorials* where he says, without producing substantiation, that:

> The reporter of Gerald's case could not venture to make the prisoner say more than that "Christianity was an innovation". But the full truth is, that in stating this view he added that all great men had been reformers, "even our Saviour himself". (27)

The *Scots Magazine*, not a pro-radical journal, in its account of the Gerrald trial is silent as to any claims for Christ as a reformer or any reference to the Lord Justice Clerk's heterodox views on the Crucifixion. It might also be added that if Cockburn is to be believed on Braxfield's use of the word "hanged" for any form of punishment, the comment, if made, may not have been a direct reference to Christ's execution.

One might feel disinclined to condemn Braxfield on Cockburn's rather contradictory evidence and agree with Roughead in accusing him of: '. . . party prejudice and partiality for telling good stories.' (28) But what must be admitted is that the currency that the story had enjoyed suggests that even if Braxfield did not say the words in question they were seen as being, at least, not uncharacteristic of the man. Had such a story, with its blasphemous connotations, been attached to a less "colourful" figure than Braxfield, then surely in an age of orthodox religious observance it would certainly not have gained credence.

The charges levelled by Cockburn against Braxfield are that his conduct as a criminal judge was, in Cockburn's phrase: '. . . a disgrace to the age' and that his undoubted ability combined with:

> . . . a passion for rude predomination, exercised in a very discretionary court, tended to form a formidable and dangerous judicial character. This appeared too often in ordinary cases; but all stains on his administration of the common business of his

court disappear in the indelible iniquity of the political trials of 1793 and 1794. In these he was the Jeffreys of Scotland. He as the head of the Court, and the only very powerful man it contained, was the real director of its proceedings. (29)

It is possible to feel that Cockburn is somewhat over-egging his pudding here. W Forbes Gray, a later follower of Cockburn, feels obliged to say that the comparison with Judge Jeffrey hardly does Braxfield justice. Braxfield, he concedes: ' . . . was a sound and able lawyer, which Jeffreys was not, and he was no sycophant, which Jeffreys was.' (30)

The trials which Cockburn refers to will be examined in more detail in Chapter 7 but it is worth noting at this point that Braxfield's fellow judges took similar decisions, as in the Palmer case, when he was not on the Bench, and it is worth noting that in a number of criminal cases, juries, in the face of very clear direction from Braxfield, displayed their independence by acquitting the accused. One of the key points in the Cockburn case against Braxfield is that he, as the presiding judge, had control of the selection of juries. As he says in *Sedition Trials*:

> The jurymen were filtered into the box by a process which
> made them very much the creatures of the court. When a trial
> was to be in Edinburgh, each of the sheriffs of the three
> Lothians sent a list of forty-five names to the Justiciary office.
> The names put on these lists depended entirely on the sheriffs'
> discretion. Out of these three lists the Justiciary-clerk selected
> in certain fixed proportions from each county forty-five, who
> alone were ordered to attend on the day of trial. The clerk,
> though not removable, was appointed by the Lord Justice-
> Clerk, who was under no open control in his selection. (31)

However if even such allegedly packed juries could, in quite a number of cases under Braxfield's control, turn out to be of an alarmingly independent cast of mind and reject the Lord Justice-Clerk's guidance this does tend to cast some doubt on the picture of the all-powerful Braxfield. It is also arguable that Cockburn's picture of a subservient Court is over-drawn:

> Over the five weak men who sat beside him, this coarse and
> dexterous ruffian predominated as he chose. He had the skill

to conceal his influence by making what he wished, be said or done by his brethren; but everybody who understood the scene knew whose mind was operating. (32)

The first sentence asks the reader to accept that the entire Scottish criminal Bench, other than Braxfield, were weak nonentities, dominated by Braxfield even when he was absent; while the second sentence might be seen as embracing conspiracy theory just a little too enthusiastically for comfort. Quite how Cockburn reconciles his earlier description of four of the judges (Henderland, Dunsinnan, Swinton and Abercromby) as: '. . . personally, mild, respectable men, and as judges, perfectly honest.' (33) with their presumed subordination to the untrammelled will of a dominant Braxfield is not clear. He suggests that these four, whose legal abilities, incidentally, he roundly criticises: '. . . though meaning well, and perfectly unconscious of doing ill, had no experience of political trials, or of such times, and were sincerely under the influence of fear.' The fifth judge, Eskgrove, Cockburn acknowledges to be superior to these four in his expert knowledge of feudal law:

But, besides having their public defects, he was an avaricious, indecent old wretch, whose habits and appearances supplied all Edinburgh with ludicrous and contemptuous anecdotes, and whose law was less connected with practical knowledge or common sense, than except for his example, could be believed.(34)

As can be seen Cockburn finds little to praise in any member of the criminal judiciary of the 1790s other than the fact, or alleged fact, that Henderland, Swinton, Dunsinnan and Abercromby: '. . . being gentle and decorous, were no friends to Braxfield privately. His mere indecency was sufficient to debar much personal intercourse . . .' (35) which may be true, or which may say as much about Cockburn's prejudices as it does about the Justice-Clerk and his colleagues. He describes Braxfield as being: ' . . . of debauched habits, and of grosser talk than suited the taste even of his gross generation' (36) and this usefully reminds us, again, that in Cockburn's account we are reading a mid-Victorian looking back more than fifty years to another age, another set of manners, almost indeed to another world.

There is a significant dimension to Braxfield's character – a particular type of Scottishness which was fast disappearing in his era. Walter Scott saw it going, regretted it, and warned of what would be lost if it went. Writing in his Journal on 14th March 1826 he spoke of the 'loosening and grinding down all those peculiarities which distinguished us as Scotsmen' and in his *Malachi Malagrowther* letters he exclaimed:

> For God's sake, sir, let us remain as Nature made us,
> Englishmen, Irishmen and Scotchmen, with something like
> the impress of our several countries upon us. (37)

Braxfield certainly had his full share of "those peculiarities which distinguished us as Scotsmen" and the "impress" of his country on him. Cockburn, however great his adherence to Scots language and concern for the survival of Scottish culture and heritage nevertheless very clearly looked back to Braxfield's age as one of a much lower moral standard – a "gross generation" – and his judgement of Braxfield is as affected by this as by his political partialities.

Braxfield, it must be admitted, would not be most twentieth century people's choice for a judge at their trial. His coarseness and prejudice cannot be denied. But still there remains some doubt – is there not more, must there not be more, to the man than the darkly monochromatic picture so skilfully painted by Cockburn and thereafter enshrined in legend?

Could a man who had enjoyed a brilliant and highly remunerative career at the Bar have been so totally "coarse and illiterate". Could a man who stood out so determinedly for old ways and the old tongue against the increasing Anglicisation of speech and manners really be no more than just a vulgar buffoon? Could a man who enjoyed a wide social circle in legal and official Edinburgh and Scotland, and one who, however humble his birth, by talent, position and family ties had come to be accepted and move easily in "good society" have really been so crude, gross, irreligious, and indecent as Cockburn paints him?

Perhaps it is impossible now, in the absence of much personal documentation and first hand knowledge, to make any sort of a definitive judgement on Robert McQueen, Lord Braxfield. The two centuries which separate us from his time make such judgements difficult but this book will attempt to look at what evidence exists and to consider the man in the context of his time and his environment.

Henry Dundas, Viscount Melville & Robert Dundas

"King Harry" and his nephew, who dominated Scottish political and legal affairs in the late eighteenth century. Robert, dressed in the Lord Advocate's robes, is depicted receiving instructions from his uncle.

CHAPTER 2

Scotland in the Age of Braxfield
1722–1799

". . . the seat of science and of good taste . . ."

McQueen's lifetime saw far-reaching and significant changes in Scotland and some appreciation of these changes, social, cultural, political, administrative and industrial helps in an understanding of his life and the influences at work on it. By the nature of his career and class most of McQueen's social and business contacts were with a small social group, although his clients, and later those appearing before him in court, were obviously more varied. The emphasis in this chapter on the governing class and the professional and intellectual elites should not obscure the fact that they represented only a tiny minority of the whole population of Scotland – the parliamentary electorate of Scotland did not exceed 5,000 male voters.

Scotland in 1722, the year of Robert McQueen's birth, was a land marked by deep division. The age-old tension between Highlands and Lowlands continued with a fair measure of suspicion and distrust on both sides. Pro- and anti-Union sentiment, the running sore of the Jacobite cause, and economic pressures all contributed to the internal divisions. The last full-scale Jacobite rising, in 1715, was a very recent memory and the Jacobite threat from some of the Highland clans had been underlined by the small-scale, ill-managed and abortive rising in 1719 – the year in which McQueen's parents married. Jacobitism would form a counterpoint to McQueen's life – by the time of the '45 Rising he was a young advocate in Edinburgh. Comprehensive evidence for McQueen's movements at this critical moment is not available but, unless he had been discreet enough to retire to his family home in rural Lanarkshire, he would have seen the triumphant entry of Charles Edward Stuart at the head of his army into the city on 17th September. The citizens of Edinburgh thereafter saw the establishment of a Jacobite court at Holyrood; observed, or joined in, the Jacobite rejoicing at the news of the Battle of Prestonpans on 21st September and watched the Highland army march off to England on 3rd November.

A tactful withdrawal to Lanark for McQueen would in fact have been the obvious course and he is recorded as being in Lanark Sheriff Court on the 3rd and 31st December 1745 and on a number of other occasions in the early months of 1746. There would have been little to do in Edinburgh, the Courts did not sit until well after the Government victory at the Battle of Culloden, in April 1746, had drawn a line under the Jacobite threat. Indeed the Books of Sederunt of the Lords of Council and Session for November 1745 reflect the problem faced by the Court of Session. Three of the fifteen judges met on 15th November and with due concern for legal procedure and precedent searched the minutes for 1715 to see what the Court did then but found that 'nothing parallel to the present situation of the Court was found there' and recorded in the Books of Sederunt their conclusion:

> ... although the rebels have abandoned Edinburgh and these Lords have repaired to it in order to proceed to dispatch of publick business, they found they cannot do so by reason the Lord President and several other of the Lords are hindered to come to town, by the continuance of the rebellion in the parts of Scotland beyond the fforth and that others of the Lords have not yet had time to repair to Edinburgh since the rebels abandoned it so that there is not a quorum of them in or about the town. (1)

McQueen's home area in Lanarkshire was one which produced few supporters for the Jacobite cause and the Faculty of Advocates, while including some Jacobite sympathisers within its ranks, was overwhelmingly on the side of the established authority. However Lowland his immediate origins may have been, as his name suggests, Robert McQueen was ultimately of Highland descent. Indeed the only other McQueen to feature at all prominently in Scotland's story was McQueen the Inverness-shire ghillie who, in 1743, killed what was believed to be the last wolf in Scotland. The Lanarkshire McQueens have been claimed as a cadet branch of the chiefly house of McQueen of Corrybrough, a minor clan within the Clan Chattan confederacy and five McQueens are recorded as serving in various regiments of the Jacobite army in the '45.

In the aftermath of the '45 the Government's determination to ensure that this would be the last Jacobite rising resulted in a very extensive programme of action. This included bans on Highland dress, the ending of the traditional heritable jurisdiction – the landowner's right to act as judge on his own estate – and the forfeiture of the estates of the attainted Jacobite leaders. The last of these resulted in a massive amount of legal business and the young McQueen, who had made something of a specialisation in feudal law, became one of the leading advocates engaged in this area of work. However these fairly remote family links and his professional engagement with work on the Forfeited Estates need not suggest that he, more than any other Lowlander, had a particularly strong interest in or sympathy with the Highlands or the Highlanders. Almost thirty years after the '45 Samuel Johnson could reflect in his *Journey to the Western Islands*:

> To the southern inhabitants of Scotland, the state of the mountains and the islands is equally unknown with that of *Borneo* or *Sumatra*: Of both they have only heard a little, and guess the rest. They are strangers to the language and the manners, to the advantages and wants of the people, whose life they would model, and whose evils they would remedy. (2)

When McQueen was a young man the Highlands were seen as a place of danger, a threat, indeed an anachronism. In the aftermath of Culloden the Highlands were to be "pacified", the traditional social system systematically broken down and the power of central authority asserted. By the end of McQueen's life the Highlands had become a place where intrepid tourists, like Pennant, Boswell and Johnson ventured. The Highlanders, from being a deadly threat to the established social order, had become recruited into the British army and won renown for their heroism and dash. The Highlands had also started on their process of romanticisation. The publication of the Ossianic legends in James Macpherson's epic version took all Europe by storm and the Highlands became a place of fantasy where heroes and warriors loved and fought.

Scotland in the year of McQueen's birth was still an essentially rural society. Indeed in 1755 in the Rev Alexander Webster's census of Scotland the two most populous counties (indeed the only two whose populations exceeded 100,000) were found to be rural Perthshire, with 120,000 inhabitants and Aberdeenshire with 116,000. A century later the centre of national gravity would have shifted to the industrial areas of the central belt. Aberdeenshire, at 212,000 had sunk to third place behind Lanarkshire at 530,000 and Midlothian at 259,000. Perthshire, which had only increased in population by 19,000 to 139,000 was now in eighth place, behind Angus, Ayrshire, Renfrewshire and Fife.

In the early eighteenth century not only did most people live on and from the land but, in an age before the full flowering of a banking and capital investment system, land was the most convenient and the safest means of investing money and a principal expression of social status. A Highland chief might gain more prestige from and take more pride in a long retinue of fighting men than of cash investments lying in a southern bank and even in the Lowlands landownership was seen as the proper means for a successful man to invest his wealth and display his stake in society. It was no accident that in almost every case when a new judge was appointed to the Court of Session he took as his judicial title the name of his landed estate and McQueen would follow in this tradition when, in 1776, he was appointed to the Court with the title of Lord Braxfield.

The influence of major landowners on politics and society was still strong. The role, for example, of the Archibald Campbell, the 3rd Duke of Argyll, as a government manager in Scotland in the immediate post-Jacobite period has been well documented. The influence of such a man went into all areas of public life – patronage was an accepted part of life and favours were openly sought and openly granted and would be for many years to come. In 1825 Alastair Macdonnell of Glengarry, admittedly a somewhat anachronistic character, wrote to the 2nd Viscount Melville, then the head of the Dundas dynasty of government managers for Scotland, seeking various favours and noting that he had 'since 1794 regarded your house as my patron which (during the lifetime of your worthy father) never failed.' (3) If such was still the case in the nineteenth century, then the role of patronage was even stronger in the eighteenth century. Appointments to both minor and major public offices were considered as a part of a wider political power play and this practice extended even to judicial appointments.

Just as a Highland chief, like Macdonnell, could profitably attach himself to the coat-tails of a political power-broker so too could an ambitious young lawyer like McQueen. His obituary in the *Scots Magazine* indeed suggests that his connection with the Dundases of Arniston, successors to the Duke of Argyll as political managers, was of long standing:

> Mr M'Queen had contracted an intimacy with Mr Dundas,
> afterwards Lord President of the Court of Session, and his
> brother, the Right Hon. Henry Dundas, at a very early period
> of life. The Lord President, when at the bar, married the
> heiress of Bonnington, an estate situated within a mile of
> Braxfield. During the recesses of the Court, these eminent
> men used to meet at their country seats, and read and study
> law together. This intimacy, so honourable and advantageous
> to both, continued through life. (4)

Robert Dundas, Lord Arniston, was some nine years older than McQueen and was admitted to the Faculty of Advocates in 1738. With the benefit of both natural talent and the not inconsiderable advantage of coming from one of the great Scottish legal and political dynasties he was appointed as H.M. Advocate – or what we should now call Lord Advocate – in 1754. This role combined great political influence with the more mundane duties of acting as Scotland's chief public prosecutor. Dundas quickly made use of the skills and abilities of his friend McQueen, and it is from this date onwards that we see Robert McQueen functioning as part of the Crown prosecution team in a variety of significant cases and becoming briefly one of the Advocates Depute. This work, in the circumstances of the eighteenth century, did not however demand McQueen's exclusive services and he was able to continue to develop a large and lucrative private practice.

The Dundas connection continued when, in 1760, Robert Dundas was appointed to Scotland's senior judicial post as Lord President of the Court of Session on the death of Robert Craigie, Lord Glendoick.

Dundas wished to recruit McQueen to the Bench but without immediate success. The *Scots Magazine* obituary narrates its outcome:

> Lord President Dundas and the Lord Advocate, (Henry
> Dundas), well knew Mr M'Queen's merit and abilities, and
> they were both desirous of testifying their sense of them, by
> obtaining for him a seat on the bench. . .
>
> In the year 1776, a Judge's gown became vacant by the death
> of Lord Coalston, upon this occasion, the solicitations of the
> Lord President and his brother, the Lord Advocate, were
> renewed, aided and seconded by the late Earl of Suffolk,
> Secretary of State.

The role of family influence and patronage in the period cannot be overstated. Towards the end of McQueen's life, in December 1798, he was to write to Henry Dundas seeking his help in gaining an official position for his second son, John. After acknowledging the assistance given by the Secretary of State, the Duke of Portland, in the matter he concludes:

> . . . yet it is upon your friendship and knowledge of me that I
> rely; and it will be a lasting proof of it to me, if I have the
> satisfaction of seeing my Son secured. . . (5)

It was precisely this careful management of patronage, the exchange of favours for political influence, the buying of votes by judicious management of appointments to posts great and small, which ensured the Dundas influence over Scottish affairs. The many governmental roles of Henry Dundas, 1st Viscount Melville, provided ample opportunities for the effective distribution of patronage and the securing of support. Melville was, variously, Member of Parliament for Midlothian, Commissioner for the Forfeited Estates, H.M. Solicitor, H. M. Advocate, Treasurer of the Navy, First Lord of the Admiralty, Secretary of State for War, Home Secretary, President of the Board of Control for India, as well as filling more decorative offices such as Keeper of the Signet, Chancellor of St Andrews University, and Lord Privy Seal of Scotland. Dundas managed to be in office during Tory, Whig and Coalition administrations, a skill which suggests both a certain political flexibility as well as underlining his indispensability and firm grasp of the principles of political power. He was said to have counselled fellow ministers:

> Beware of resignation; for when you are out, the Lord
> Almighty knows when you may get in again. (6)

The wide-ranging, almost regal power of Dundas was why he could be described by James Boswell as "Harry the Ninth". Walter Scott described one aspect of the Dundas patronage system in his comment that India, under the direction of Dundas, was:

> . . . the corn chest for Scotland, where we poor gentry must
> send our younger sons as we send our black cattle to the
> South. (7)

and the flow of younger sons of politically significant families into Indian appointments, or midshipman's berths in the Navy, was one of the essential tools of a system of control that the nineteenth century Whig ascendancy described as the "Dundas Despotism."

Later ages have in general looked on this system with contempt, seeing it as being hopelessly corrupt, inefficient and squalid. Victorian reformers of the civil service sought to establish rigorous systems of competitive examination and selection which would avoid any possibility of improper influence or imputation of corruption. However the eighteenth century was different and contemporaries would have felt it very strange, and indeed unnatural, had the old system of favours, patronage and personal loyalties not been adhered to. James Boswell once said that:

> . . . as that man was esteemed the best sportsman that brought
> down the most birds, so was he the best representative that
> brought the best pensions and places to his countrymen. (8)

Robert Louis Stevenson in *Kidnapped* gives a much later, and admittedly literary, but nonetheless valid interpretation of one aspect of this *realpolitik* of eighteenth century life. His Jacobite agent, Alan Breck Stewart, explains the facts of judicial and political life to the naive young

Lowland Whig, David Balfour. The Red Fox, Campbell of Glenure, has been murdered and Alan predicts that the trial result was a foregone conclusion. After all it will be held:

> . . . in Inverara, the Campbell's head place; with fifteen
> Campbells in the jury-box, and the biggest Campbell of all
> (and that's the Duke) sitting cocking on the bench.

David remonstrates that the Duke of Argyll (who as Lord Justice-General was the nominal head of the criminal justiciary) was a wise and honest nobleman. His more worldly-wise companion answers:

> . . . the man's a Whig, nae doubt; but I would never deny he
> was a good chieftain to his clan. And what would the clan
> think if there was a Campbell shot and naebody hanged, and
> their own chief the Justice General?

This may be an extreme example of the importance of personal loyalties, but eighteenth century political relationships were in a long-established Scottish tradition of bonds of manrent and interlocking formal systems of personal and family alliances.

What we now see as a corrupt system was in fact the political convention of the age and the skilful manipulators of the system – the Argylls, Lord Bute and the Dundases – did so in an attempt to ensure good government. It was accepted that the pick of the spoils would go to supporters of the ruling faction even if some occasional gestures were made towards a bi-partisan approach, particularly in the area of legal appointments.

If the Scotland of 1722 was still a largely traditional rural society, McQueen's lifetime would see major economic changes. Agriculture was the subject of significant changes with the enclosure of land and the introduction of improved breeds of sheep and cattle and better strains of crops. The traditional runrig system of open fields was rapidly vanishing in the face of enclosure and the growth of large farms This process was one in which McQueen, as an important landowner, had his part to play. Agricultural technology also showed considerable developments in McQueen's lifetime. James Small's development of the chain plough was just one example of a range of developments which would materially affect the way the land was worked.

Interestingly enough one of the early supporters of Small's new plough
was Braxfield's senior judicial colleague, Henry Home, Lord Kames.
Kames, a major intellectual force on the Scottish bench for thirty years,
among many other works published *The Gentleman Farmer* in 1776.

Industrialisation had also come to Scotland by the end of
McQueen's life. The foundation of the Carron Iron Works, near Falkirk,
in 1759 gave Scotland both a focus for industrial development and a
place of fascination and wonder for countless visitors. When the
Corsican patriot leader General Paoli came to Scotland in 1771 his host,
James Boswell, showed him the usual tourist sights of Glasgow,
Edinburgh and Loch Lomond, but also conducted him to Carron:

> They then viewed the iron works at Carron, which are carried
> on at so prodigious an expense and have diffused so much
> opulence and such a spirit of improvement in that part of the
> country. General Paoli had a particular pleasure in viewing
> the forge where were formed the cannon and warlike stores
> which a society of gentlemen in Scotland sent to the aid of the
> brave Corsicans. (9)

If Carron was one pole of the Scottish industrial revolution, then New
Lanark was the other. The cotton mills established near the fast flowing
waters of the Clyde by David Dale in 1785 soon rivalled Carron as a
"visitor attraction", the more so because of their founder's, and his
son-in-law Robert Owen's, remarkable social philosophy and insistence
on good quality housing, schools, and planned working conditions.
New Lanark was, in part, built on the Braxfield estate and McQueen
had a number of property dealings with Dale. Other developments,
such as the construction of the Forth and Clyde Canal between 1768
and 1790, and the dredging and widening of the River Clyde from
1770 onwards, are further evidence for the changing nature of Scotland
and a move away from an agricultural to a more industrially-based
economy.

McQueen lived through not only an industrial revolution but an
intellectual revolution in Scotland. In 1722 Scotland was undoubtedly
something of a provincial backwater – within fifty years Scotland and
Scotsmen were at the forefront of European thought. The story of the
Scottish Enlightenment has been told often enough and to establish
the reasons for this remarkable flowering of science, law, philosophy

and literature is certainly beyond the scope of this book. However a simple recitation of some of the highlights of the period does serve to show the scope of Scottish intellectual life and the nearness of many aspects of it to McQueen's day to day existence. The well-known remark of "Mr. Amyat, King's Chemist, a most sensible and agreeable English gentleman" as relayed by the Edinburgh antiquary William Smellie (the printer of the Edinburgh edition of Burns' poems):

> Here I stand at what is called the *Cross of Edinburgh*, and can, in a
> few minutes, take fifty men of genius and learning by the hand (10)

usefully emphasises both the vigour and vitality of Edinburgh intellectual life, and the intimate, close-knit, small scale character of the town. Political, scientific, legal, religious, intellectual, philosophical, academic Edinburgh all rubbed shoulders with each other. Men moved easily from one milieu to another – a country minister (William Robertson) became Principal of Edinburgh University and one of Europe's leading historians; a judge (Kames) wrote with equal facility on agriculture, law and philosophy.

The nineteenth century concept of Edinburgh as "the Athens of the North", which owed something to the physical resemblance between Edinburgh viewed from Leith and Athens seen from Piraeus and which also recognised the classical architectural inheritance of the eighteenth century Enlightenment, may be overplayed – but in one sense the popular conceit has some validity. Both Periclean Athens and Enlightenment Edinburgh were small cities with a small, inter-connected intellectual/political elite and a much larger supporting structure of unenfranchised and, in some cases, unfree workers. In the 1760s and '70s coal miners and saltpan workers could still be found existing in a state of serfdom not three miles from Mr Amyat's "Cross of Edinburgh". The final Emancipation Act freeing these workers from their bondage to a pit did not come on to the Statute Book until 1799, the year of Braxfield's death.

The work of David Hume, a philosopher of European reputation and for six years Librarian to the Faculty of Advocates, is central to the story of the Enlightenment, but Hume was only one of a group of philosophers who gave the Scottish enlightenment its special character – contemporaries like Dugald Stewart, Thomas Reid, Adam Fergusson were figures of international significance.

Part of the story of the Enlightenment is the increasing emphasis on the organisation and systematisation of knowledge. This became a particularly Scottish concern and a process which was symbolically encapsulated in the publication in Edinburgh of the first edition of the *Encyclopaedia Britannica* in 1768–71. The remodelling of the capital city by the formation of new residential areas – first of all around George Square and later in the New Town, and the erection of classically modelled public buildings such as Register House and the University is also evidence of the concern with the working out of ideas of order and system, this time in new concepts of the arrangement and ordering of physical space.

Perhaps the most outstanding work of the Scottish Enlightenment is Adam Smith's *Wealth of Nations* published in 1776. This became a book of vast influence in the development of political economy, and a text which still, at the end of the twentieth century, is bitterly fought over by political and economic theorists of the left and the right who see in Smith's seminal work support for their doctrines.

An ambitious scheme which exemplified much of the rational, systematising flavour of Scottish thought of the period was Sir John Sinclair of Ulbster's imaginative project to get each of the parish ministers of Scotland to write an account of their parish in order to accomplish, as Sinclair wrote, 'the purpose of ascertaining the quantum of happiness enjoyed by its inhabitants'. In the *Analysis of the Statistical Account* which Sinclair published in 1825 and 1826 he defined, with Scottish thoroughness, what he called 'statistical philosophy':

> Its object is, to promote the happiness of an individual state,
> by a careful inquiry into its peculiar circumstances. (11)

Sir James's *Statistical Account* not only brought a new concept to the public mind but provided an invaluable and unique description of the nine hundred and thirty eight parishes of Scotland at a period of critical industrial, agricultural and social change. This process was seen to be of immediate benefit and was repeated in the 1840s and again in the mid-twentieth century and apart from its intended contemporary uses has been blessed by historians and researchers in the two centuries since it appeared.

Physical science, as well as the social sciences, was a major concern

of the Enlightenment and the Edinburgh-born physician Joseph
Hutton's pioneering work on geology, *The Theory of the Earth*, published
in 1785, with its description of immense, slow acting geological
timespans destroyed the orthodox view, based on a literalistic
interpretation of Genesis, of the formation of the earth as a work of a
particular day in 4004 BC. Remarkably Hutton's work, genuinely
revolutionary in its impact and implications, failed to produce the
fundamentalist clamour that might have been expected from what is
often over-glibly characterised as a sternly Calvinist society and his
quiet passage probably reflects the Moderate intelligentsia's domination
of the Church. Speculative philosophy and rational enquiry were no
longer a sure road to anathema and pulpit condemnation.

Joseph Black, the pioneering chemist who established the principle
of latent heat was Professor of Medicine and Chemistry at Edinburgh
from 1766. The age of Braxfield was also the first age of steam and the
work of the Greenock-born James Watt (1736–1819) in the development
and perfecting of the steam engine would give an enormous impetus
to the development of industry, mining and transport. Before Braxfield's
death an experimental steamship would be set sailing on the Forth
and Clyde Canal and the transport revolution was underway.

The contemporary centrality of Scotland to European intellectual
life is demonstrated by two letters to contemporaries of McQueen. The
first, from Voltaire to William Robertson, Principal of Edinburgh
University, acknowledging receipt of a copy of Robertson's *History of
Charles V* attests to the great French thinker's appreciation of the
historical writing and scholarship of Robertson and David Hume:

*Il y a quatre jours que j'ai reçu le beau présent dont vous m'avez
honoré. Je le lis malgré les fluxions horribles qui me font craindre de
perdre entièrement les yeux. Il me fait oublier tous mes maux. C'est a
vous et a M. Hume qu'il appartient d'écrire l'Histoire. Vous êtes
eloquent, savant, et impartial. Je me joins à l'Europe pour vous
estimer.*

It is four days since I received the fine present with which you
have honoured me. I am reading it despite the horrible
inflamation which makes me fear to lose my sight entirely. It
makes me forget all my ills. You and Mr Hume are born to
write history. You are eloquent, scholarly and impartial. I am
at one with Europe in respecting you. (12)

As significant was a letter in 1762 from a Swiss jurist, Daniel Fellenberg, to Henry Home, Lord Kames, Fellenberg enthused to Kames:

> Édinbourg est aujourd'hui le séjour de la science et du bon goût. Ce'est dan cette ville que paraissaent depuis quelque temps les meilleurs ouvrages Anglais. Nous voudrions connaître plus particulièrement les hommes célèbre qui s'y trouvent.

> Edinburgh is today the seat of science and of good taste. For some time the best English works have been published in that town. We would wish to know better the celebrated men who are to be found there. (13)

Even the curmudgeonly Dr Samuel Johnson, who once remarked that Scottish learning was rather:

> . . . like bread in a besieged town, every man gets a little, but no man gets a full meal. (14)

for all his anti-Scottish rhetoric did not disdain to employ five Scots as his lexicographical amanuenses in the compilation of his great Dictionary.

With all these political, economic and intellectual changes came social change. Part of this was represented, in Edinburgh, by the move of the upper classes out of the crowded, towering tenement lands of the Old Town, to the planned rational housing of the new age. Developments such as George Square, to the south of the ridge of land stretching from the Castle to Holyrood which was the heart of old Edinburgh, soon attracted discerning residents.

In January 1770 Robert McQueen moved out from Covenant Court in the High Street and joined the move to the suburbs by taking a feu of:

> . . . that dwelling house and back court behind the same being the third house from the west in the north row in the great square built by James Brown in Ross Park and which is now called George Square, with the stable and coach house built in the said back court and the four vaulted cellars below. . . (15)

George Square was planned as an exclusive development and was to become home to many of the city's legal elite – a neighbour of McQueen's was Walter Scott, a Writer to the Signet, and father of Walter Scott, the poet and novelist. Young Walter, on entering the Faculty of Advocates in 1792, tactfully dedicated his admission thesis to the Lord Justice-Clerk, his George Square neighbour, Lord Braxfield.

With the completion of William Mylne's North Bridge in 1772 and the development of James Craig's ambitious design for the New Town. beyond the Nor' Loch, another area of ordered and orderly housing was made available to the lawyers, bankers, businessmen and gentry of the capital. This process culminated in Robert Adam's masterpiece of classical urbanism, Charlotte Square, designed in 1791, the year before the death of this great master of Scottish enlightenment architecture.

With the new buildings and new, planned, residential areas came new manners and new tastes. In 1745 a new industry had appeared in Scotland with an advert in the Edinburgh press for "painted paper for hanging walls". The Edinburgh publisher William Creech, a frequent juryman at Braxfield's trials, commented on some of the social changes which he had seen in his lifetime. He reflects on the move of the elites from the Old Town:

> In 1763 – People of quality and fashion lived in houses, which, in 1783, were inhabited by tradesmen, or by people in humble and ordinary life. The Lord Justice-Clerk Tinwald's house was possessed by a French teacher – Lord President Craigie's house, by a rouping-wife or saleswoman of old furniture. (16)

No more would be seen the sight of a fully-robed Court of Session judge picking his way through the filth of the High Street and entering a dark and noisome close to climb the common stairs to his apartment. George Square and Queen Street might be more elegant, more hygienic, more modern – but something of the peculiar character of old Edinburgh, and something of the enforced social integration of all social classes living in the same tenement lands had been lost for ever.

William Creech also observed that the changing times brought other social changes in their wake:

> In 1763 – People of fashion dined at two o'clock, or a little

42

after it; business was attended to in the afternoon . . . In 1783 –
People of fashion, and of the middle rank, dined at four or
five o'clock. No business was done in the afternoon, dinner of
itself having become a very serious business.

Not least of these social changes was the growing gulf between the
Scots speaking generality of the population and the social and
intellectual elite who adopted, with more or less enthusiasm and skill,
an English accent, idiom and vocabulary. One of the more engaging
tales told of Lord Braxfield illustrates his stubborn adherence to the
old style of speech. His servant James came to him and advised him
that he would be leaving Braxfield's service at the next term day. His
Lordship enquired:

> 'What's wrang noo James?'
> 'Naething, but your Lordship's temper, you are sae passionate.'
> 'Hoot man what need you mind that. Ye ken weel that it nae
> sooner on than it is aff'
> 'Very true my Lord, but then it is nae sooner aff than it's on.'(17)

The source for this anecdote, John Mowbray, a Writer to the Signet,
who knew Braxfield from first hand experience, has the Lord Justice-
Clerk and his *valet de chambre* speaking an identical Scots. Braxfield
was a confirmed adherent of the old Scots tongue – although he was
not the only one in official circles or on the Court of Session bench;
Lord Kames of "fare ye all weel – ye bitches" had clearly kept to the
older ways and Henry Dundas was another who retained his native
tongue. The Bar, too, had its enthusiastic speakers of Scots. One young
lawyer who often crossed swords with Braxfield was John Clerk of
Eldin who later in his career was arguing an appeal case before the
House of Lords. The case hinged on water rights and Clerk argued:

> '. . . the watter had rin that way for forty years. Indeed
> naebody kenn'd how lang . . .'

The Lord Chancellor, much amused by Clerk's Scottish accent asked:

> 'Mr Clerk, do you spell water in Scotland with two t's?

The fiery advocate responded:

> 'Na, my Lord, we dinna spell watter wi' twa t's but we spell
> mainners wi' twa n's. (18)

However, the Clerks, Dundases and Braxfields were increasingly seen
as isolated exceptions and polite Edinburgh society in all its
manifestations, legal, political, intellectual and ecclesiastical, took up
with enthusiasm the cause of polite speech. In 1761 the Select Society
announced the formation of "The Society for Promoting the Reading
and Speaking of the English Language in Scotland". Their regulations
opened with a clear statement of the problem, as the founders saw it:

> As the intercourse between this part of Great Britain and the
> capital daily increases, both on account of business and
> amusement, and must still go on increasing, gentlemen
> educated in Scotland have long been sensible of the
> disadvantages under which they labour, from their imperfect
> knowledge of the ENGLISH TONGUE, and the impropriety
> with which they speak it.
>
> Experience hath convinced Scotsmen, that it is not
> impossible for persons born and educated in this country, to
> acquire such knowledge of the English Tongue, as to write it
> with some tolerable purity.
>
> But with regard to the other point, that of speaking with
> propriety, as little has been hitherto attempted, it has
> generally been taken for granted, that there was no prospect
> of attempting any thing with a probability of success; though,
> at the same time, it is allowed to be an accomplishment, more
> important, and more universally useful, than the former. . .
>
> Even persons well advanced in life may be taught, by
> skilfull instructors, to avoid many gross improprieties, in
> quantity, accent, the manner of sounding the vowels, etc.
> which, at present, render the Scotch dialect so offensive. (19)

This early, if remarkably well developed, example of the Scottish cringe
had to a considerable extent been inspired by a course of lectures on
the English tongue given in Edinburgh earlier that year by Mr Thomas
Sheridan, actor and "orthoepist" – the father of the playwright Richard

Brinsley Sheridan. The first series of these lectures were attended:

> ... by more than 300 gentlemen, the most eminent in this
> country for their rank and abilities; who expressed no less
> satisfaction with the ingenuity and justness of his sentiments,
> than with the elegant and interesting manner in which he
> delivered them. (20)

Oddly enough none of the three hundred eminent gentlemen seemed to think there was anything odd about their being lectured on the proper use of English by an Irish actor. Their acceptance of this situation was reflected in the practice of David Hume, the giant of the Edinburgh Enlightenment and a scholar of European reputation, sending his manuscripts to be checked for English style to a Bristol linen-draper. The atheistic Hume, so ran the aphorism, died repenting "not his sins but his Scotticisms". He was not alone.

The Select Society planned to raise funds, considering that it:

> ... would be of great advantage to this country, if a proper
> number of persons from England, duly qualified to instruct
> gentlemen in the knowledge of the English Tongue, the
> manner of pronouncing it with purity, and the art of public
> speaking, were settled in Edinburgh; and if, at the same time,
> a proper number of masters from the same country, duly
> qualified for teaching children the reading of English, should
> open schools in Edinburgh for that purpose. (21)

What is most remarkable in this episode is that the leading spirits in this campaign, the men who felt so insecure in the use of their mother tongue, were not some "upwardly-mobile" collection of aspirants to high office, preferment and distinction. They were already there, at the top of the tree. The roll of the Ordinary Directors of the Society reads like a *Who's Who* of the Scottish establishment:

Lord Auchinleck – Court of Session judge and father of James
Boswell
Lord Alemoor – Court of Session judge
Sir Adam Fergusson, Bart.

Walter Stewart – Advocate

William Johnstone – Advocate

George Dempster – Advocate

James Ferguson tertius – Advocate

Alexander Tait – Clerk of Session

Rev Dr Hugh Blair – in 1762 appointed Regius Professor of
    Rhetoric & Belles Lettres at Edinburgh

Rev Dr John Jardine- Minister of the Tron Church, Chaplain to the
    King

Rev Dr William Robertson – Minister of Greyfriars and in 1762
    appointed as Principal of Edinburgh
    University

Dr John Hope

Professor Adam Ferguson – Professor of Natural Philosophy at
    Edinburgh

John Fordyce – Merchant

John Adam – Architect. The son of William Adam and designer of
    the Edinburgh City Chambers

James Russel – Surgeon

Perhaps the most unexpected name on this list is the first: Alexander Boswell, Lord Auchinleck. Auchinleck was a traditionalist and no mean exponent of the Scotch tongue, describing (or so records Sir Walter Scott) his son's great hero, the patriot leader, Pasquale Paoli, as 'a landlouping scoundrel of a Corsican' and much of James Boswell's stormy relationship with his father centred on the son's desire to make his name in England rather than follow his father's wishes that he should stay at home, work at the Scottish Bar and improve the family estate in Ayrshire.

Quite why these distinguished gentlemen so enthusiastically embraced the concept of linguistic assimilation is a complex issue. To a considerable extent the distinctiveness of written and spoken Scots had been under attack for centuries. The transfer of the Royal Court and its attendant patronage to London in 1603 was undoubtedly one major influence. There was a definite need for any Scots going south in the wake of James VI to adapt and conform. The adoption of the Authorised Version of the Bible after its publication in 1611 was another and, in age of faith and religious conformity, a more all-pervading blow to the survival of Scots as a literary language. The Parliamentary Union of

1707 brought increased contacts, as did the growing number of civil cases going from the Court of Session to appeal in the House of Lords.

The unpopularity of the Scots in England throughout the seventeenth and eighteenth centuries is well-attested. Scots who, for business or pleasure, wished to go to England, and in particular to London, would, perhaps quite understandably, wish to be able to pass for natives. The repeated Jacobite risings and threats of risings were hardly calculated to endear the Scottish nation to its southern neighbour – particularly when, as in 1745, they seemed to be in danger of becoming successful. The Rev Alexander Carlyle tells how he was in London with the Scottish doctor, novelist and dramatist Tobias Smollett when the news of Culloden arrived. They make their way through the streets full of exuberantly celebrating Londoners with Smollett, resident in London and presumably having lost much of his accent through service in the Royal Navy, cautioning Carlyle:

> . . . against speaking a word, lest the mob should discover
> my country and become insolent, 'for John Bull,' says he, 'is
> as haughty and valiant to-night as he was abject and
> cowardly on Black Wednesday when the Highlanders were
> at Derby.' (22)

Such anti-Scottish sentiment continued and the period of office (1762–63) of the highly unpopular Scottish Prime Minister, Lord Bute, did not make the position of Scots any easier. Nor did the increasing success of many Scots in England make them or their nation popular. One Scot who succeeded in England, William Murray, 1st Earl of Mansfield, who became Lord Chief Justice of the Court of King's Bench, was subject to bitter personal attacks – a cartoon published in 1764 *Sawney Wetherbeaten* or *Judas Iscariot* shows Mansfield as a gaunt and louse-ridden figure in Highland Dress and he is depicted as saying:

> . . . London, the only place for preferment in the land – for I
> would sell my king as my God for gold. . . (23)

The potency of popular anti-Scottish feeling is shown by an incident recorded in James Boswell's diary for 8th December 1762:

At night I went to Covent Garden and saw *Love in a Village*, a
new comic opera, for the first night . . . Just before the
overture began to be played, two Highland officers came in.
The mob in the upper gallery roared out, 'No Scots! No Scots!
Out with them!,' hissed and pelted them with apples. My
heart warmed to my countrymen, my Scotch blood boiled
with indignation. I jumped up on the benches, roared out,
'Damn you, you rascals!,' hissed and was in the greatest rage.
I am very sure at that time I should have been the most
distinguished of heroes. I hated the English; I wished in my
soul that the Union was broke and that we might give them
another Battle of Bannockburn. I went close to the officers and
asked them of what regiment they were of. They told me Lord
John Murray's, and that they were just come from the
Havana. 'And this,' said they, 'is the thanks that we get – to be
hissed when we come home. If it was the French, what could
they do worse?' 'But,' said one, 'if I had a grup o yin or twa o
the tamd rascals I sud let them ken what they're about.' The
rudeness of the English vulgar is terrible. This indeed is the
liberty which they have: the liberty of bullying and being
abusive with their blackguard tongues. (24)

One may assume that these ill-used officers of Murray's Regiment (later
to become known as the Black Watch) were unlikely to subscribe to the
Select Society or sign up for Mr Sheridan's course of lectures. But
Boswell, however much his patriotic blood might boil at this English
slight on his nation, had his share of the prevailing linguistic concerns.
In 1786, trying to make his way at the English bar, having been reassured
by Dr Johnson that his accent was not pronounced enough to cause
problems in this enterprise, he records in his diary:

Thursday 8th June. Rose sadly irresolute. Almost cried. Was
weak enough to try to get comfort from Mrs Strange. Her
vulgar Scotch disgusted me. Left her and called on Jack Lee. . .
Went again to Mrs Strange and fairly complained to her of her
speaking so broad, and got her a little refined. (25)

McQueen, we may assume, did not attend Mr Sheridan's classes and
his friend Henry Dundas retained a broad Scotch accent even though
he was much in London and rose to high Government office. James

Boswell, however, was one of the three hundred gentlemen who paid their guineas to have their "gross improprieties" corrected.

There were other changes in the period more significant than the desire to write and speak polite English. Braxfield's lifetime saw a perhaps unparalleled outbreak of revolt and revolution around the world and a increasing degree of political agitation and instability at home. In middle life he saw the revolt of the American colonies – the Declaration of Independence was signed in the same year, 1776, as he was appointed to the Court of Session. Indeed the process of his passing his trials as a Lord of Session was interrupted by the observance of a day of fasting and humiliation when prayers were offered for the success of British arms and the ending of the American rebellion. The Lords of Session 'met and went to Church.' (26)

The case of the American colonists divided opinion in Britain. Some saw them as patriots struggling for rights that every British citizen should enjoy – others as threats to an established order. James Boswell's diaries display the impact of the American Revolution on one Scots observer:

> I was rather inclined to the American side of the present
> grand dispute, notwithstanding Dr Johnson's eloquence, and
> I spoke warmly pretty often, from the spirit of opposition
> principally, I believe, as well as from a regard to what
> appeared to me just and reasonable. (27)

Later Boswell was to be concerned lest the absence of letters from Johnson meant that the Doctor had heard reports of, and been offended by, his support for the colonists.

In Braxfield's later years he witnessed the French Revolution – the Bastille fell the year after he was appointed Lord Justice-Clerk and the last six years of his life would see Britain engaged in a world-wide war with Revolutionary France. At home the age of revolutions was seen working itself out in a variety of ways and many of the most significant cases of Braxfield's later years were the trials for sedition of activists in the various reform organisations established in imitation of the French revolutionaries.

There can be no doubt that Braxfield did not respond well to the revolutionary spirit or even to what we can now see as the much more modest aspirations of the British reform organisations. His grandfather may have been the gardener on a landed estate but Braxfield had become entirely incorporated into the establishment and had, himself, become a major landowner. A conservative cast of mind, which in its more acceptable manifestations displayed itself in a stubborn adherence to the language of his forefathers and an attractive taste for sentimental old Scottish songs, was in the socio-economic and political arena to show itself in an undoubtedly reactionary attitude to the reformers and a profound contempt for the concept of universal suffrage. He was not alone in these attitudes – the support of his fellow judges for his actions and their own views and comments are indicative of the general attitude of the ruling classes. In one of the sedition trials, that of Thomas Palmer, Lord Abercromby's charge to the jury included the following notable dictum:

> Gentlemen, the right of universal suffrage is a right which
> the subjects of this country never enjoyed; and were they to
> enjoy it, they would not long enjoy either liberty or a free
> constitution. (28)

Like most men Braxfield and Abercromby were creatures of their period and class and unsurprisingly proved to be incapable of transcending these constraints. These great international and national issues were of course intensely divisive. The publication, in 1791 of Thomas Paine's *The Rights of Man* provided a text for the age; a gospel for many and a threatening tract for others. Liberal sentiment saw in the French Revolution an attack on what was undoubtedly a corrupt and morally bankrupt system. Poets everywhere sang of the political situation. Alexander Wilson, the radical Paisley weaver poet (later to win greater fame for his contribution to American ornithology) wrote:

> The *Rights of Man* is now well kenned,
> And red by mony a hunder;
> For Tammy Paine the buik has penned,
> And lent the court a lounder
> It's like a keeking-glass to see
> The craft of kirk and statesmen,
> And with a bauld and easy glee,

Guid faith the birky beats them
Aff hand this day. (29)

Wilson's greater contemporary, Burns, in *The Tree of Liberty*, celebrated the revolutionary events:

Heard ye o' the tree o' France
I watna what's the name o't;
Around it a' the patriots dance
Weel Europe kens the fame o't.
It stands where ance the Bastille stood,
A prison built by kings, man,
When Superstition's hellish brood
Kept France in leading strings, man.

Upo' this tree there grows sic fruit,
Its virtues a' can tell, man;
It raises man aboon the brute,
It maks him ken himsel, man.
Gif ance the peasant taste a bit,
He's greater than a lord, man,
An' wi' the beggar shares a mite
O' a' he can afford, man. (30)

In much the same spirit in February 1792 Burns sent four carronades, the short-barrelled cannon developed at the Carron Foundry in Falkirk, as a gift to the French National Assembly. Around this period subscriptions were raised in Glasgow and other centres to assist the French against any foreign powers that might attack them.

A growing wave of reform agitation, focused on subjects as varied as burgh reform and the abolition of slavery, swept across the nation. The intensity of political debate is testified to by the rapid growth in the Scottish periodical press. In 1782 there were only eight newspapers published in Scotland – by 1790 this number had been increased to twenty-seven. Many of the newspapers and periodicals of the period were avowedly on the side of reform.

Political societies also sprang up around the country – mostly on the reform or progressive side such as the Friends of the People but also including anti-reform societies. One of the most significant of these constitutionalist bodies was the society which met in Edinburgh's Goldsmiths Hall in 1792 and whose members were to be prominent among the jurors in some of the sedition trials. The language of much of this reform agitation took on a distinctly radical tone, even when enunciated by highly respectable organisations and addressed to ostensibly less contentious issues. Thus the Medical Society of Edinburgh, petitioning on the abolition of slavery used the following resonant phrases in its resolution:

> All men are born free and equal in rights. The first object of government is to secure to all the right which all derive from nature to civil liberty. The object of political liberty is to prevent the abuse of power in government. . . (31)

It is difficult to believe that the authors were not conscious of the echoes of the American Declaration of Independence and the French Declaration of the Rights of Man – both documents which owed much to Enlightenment concepts.

The role of bodies such as the Friends of the People, the British Convention and of activists such as Thomas Muir and Maurice Margarot will be dealt with in Chapter 7 when the series of important political trials which have so coloured later generations' view of Braxfield will be considered. However it must be realised that to the Government, and its supporters like Braxfield, the idea of a gathering of Edinburgh medical men passing resolutions in such terms was unwelcome but the outbreak of political activity among the lower orders was infinitely more threatening. In his charge to the jury in the trial of Thomas Muir, Lord Braxfield clearly showed the official concern that existed regarding political activism among the working classes. Muir was an advocate and came from a family of small landowners, indeed he was a man in many respects drawn from the same sort of family and professional background as Robert McQueen. Muir had spoken and engaged in political activities among the textile workers in Milton of Campsie, near his family estate of Huntershill, Bishopbriggs. To a passionately committed defender of the established order, like Braxfield, Muir must have seemed a particularly threatening figure. His stepping out of the expected role of a man of his class and profession to engage with weavers and artisans in political activity was a much more dangerous and destabilising action than the Medical Society's resolution – and so it inevitably brought forth the Lord Justice-Clerk's impassioned, if hardly judicial, charge to his carefully selected jury:

> I leave it for you to judge whether it was perfectly innocent or not, in Mr Muir, at such a time, to go about among ignorant country people, and among the lower classes of people, making them leave off their work, and inducing them to believe that a reform was absolutely necessary to preserve their safety and their liberty, which, had it not been for him, they would never have suspected to be in danger. You will keep this in remembrance, and judge, whether it appears to you, as to me, to be sedition. (32)

Similarly the English Unitarian preacher, Thomas Fyshe Palmer, convicted of sedition at Perth in September 1793 by Lords Eskgrove and Abercromby, was seen as a mischievous middle class figure who was leading the lower classes astray. Lord Cockburn notes:

> In proposing that the prisoner should be transported, Lord Abercromby describes his guilt as deepened by three aggravations. One of these – namely, his being a man of superior station and talents, which it was the more criminal in him to employ the influence of in order to lead poor and ignorant people into mischief – was certainly an important feature in the case, and justly operated against him. (33)

The conscious parallels between bodies such as the British Convention and their French role-models, parallels which were encouraged on both sides of the Channel, naturally increased the fear and suspicion of the authorities. The French Revolutionaries looked on the activities of the British Convention with considerable interest and favour. Henry W Meikle, in *Scotland and the French Revolution* notes that one issue (December 30th 1793) of the official French newspaper *Le Moniteur* devoted five of its twelve columns to the affairs of the British Convention – and this at a time when France was at war with Britain, Austria, Prussia, Holland, Spain, Sardinia, Tuscany and Naples and *Le Moniteur* might have been thought to have ample urgent material to fill its pages. The French saw in the political agitation in Ireland and Scotland possible, and from their standpoint, encouraging signs of the break-up of the Union. French commentators had long been aware of the proper distinctions to be drawn between England and Scotland. In Diderot's *Encyclopédie*, published in the 1770s the entry on Scotland had included these sentiments:

> *L'Écosse a été redoutable tant qu'elle n'a pas éte incorporée avec L'Angleterre; mais, comme dit M Voltaire, un état pauvre, voisin d'un riche, devient vénal à la longue; et c'est aussi le malheur que l'Écosse éprouve.*

> Scotland was to be feared as long as it was not linked to England; but as M. Voltaire says, a poor state which has a rich state as its neighbour becomes venal in the long run, and that too is the misfortune suffered by Scotland. (34)

The eighteenth century being the age that it was, poetic approval was even adduced for the development of Scottish radical activism:

> *Édimbourg ressaisit les droits sacrés de l'homme,*
> *Édimbourg s'est levée: à sa puissante voix,*
> *Albion va bientôt voir refleurir les lois,*
> *Et les François vainquers secondant son audace,*
> *Elle va des tyrans exterminer la race*

> Edinburgh is snatching back the sacred rights of man
> Edinburgh has risen: at its powerful voice
> Albion will soon see the laws flourish again
> And with the victorious Frenchmen supporting its boldness
> It will exterminate the race of tyrants. (35)

More significantly than the musings of poets, the French authorities laid plans to rescue the transported Muir and Margarot from their captivity. Muir had originally been charged with sedition on 2nd January 1793 – on being liberated on bail he travelled to France, arriving there on 20th January, the day before Louis XVI's execution. War broke out between France and Britain on 1st February and Muir found himself unable to return to face his trial, set for 11th February. Muir was declared an outlaw due to his failure to present himself at his trial and his name was struck from the roll of the Faculty of Advocates.

During his time in France Muir mixed with many of the Revolutionary leaders such as Barras, Condorcet, La Fayette. Although he was later to return to Scotland to face trial, his decision to visit France, at a time of grave international tension, and while awaiting trial on serious charges arising out of his political activity raises the gravest doubts about Muir's judgement and commonsense.

The trip, and Muir's later stay in France, does however further demonstrate the reality of the links between the Scottish reformers and the French revolutionaries – a link which existed independently of the fears and prejudices of reactionary figures like Lord Braxfield. Muir, after an adventurous escape from Botany Bay made his way back to Europe via Mexico. Reaching France in 1797 he was enthusiastically welcomed with a public banquet at Bordeaux and moved on to Paris where he was welcomed by the Directory. Muir became a prolific pamphleteer in the French republican cause, although his sufferings and his ill-health would seem to have affected his judgement. His view of the situation in Scotland and the likelihood of popular support there for a French invasion is less than balanced.

Muir was, perhaps because he told the French leadership what they wanted to hear, consistently well thought of by the French government and figured in their list of a Directory to run a Scottish Republic following a successful invasion. It is curious to think that both the French revolutionaries and the arch-conservative Braxfield viewed Muir as a significant figure.

Lord Kames, Hugo Arnott & Lord Monboddo

Three literary lawyers. Arnott, whose extreme thinness seems to have fascinated Kay, was an advocate and author of a History of Edinburgh *and* Criminal Trials. *Kames and Monboddo were senior colleagues of Braxfield on the Court of Session Bench.*

CHAPTER 3

The Law

"... the laws of this kingdom
hath attained so great perfection..."

While much else in the state was changing the last pre-Union Parliament of Scotland carefully ordained, in Article XIX of the Treaty of Union:

> That the Court of Session, or College of Justice, do after the Union, and notwithstanding thereof, remain in all time coming within Scotland, as it is now constituted by the Laws of that Kingdom, and with the same Authority and Privileges as before the Union, subject nevertheless to such Regulations for the better Administration of Justice as shall be made by the Parliament of Great Britain...
>
> And that the Court of Justiciary do also after the Union, and notwithstanding thereof, remain in all time coming within Scotland, as it is now constituted by the Laws of that Kingdom, and with the same Authority and Privileges as before the Union...
>
> And that all Inferior Courts with the said limits do remain subordinate, as they now are, to the Supreme Courts of Justice within the same in all time coming; And that no Causes in Scotland be Cognisable by the Courts of Chancery, Queen's Bench, Common Pleas or any other Court in Westminster Hall; and that the said Courts, or any other of the like nature, after the Union, shall have no power to cognosce, review, or alter the Acts or Sentences of the Judicatures within Scotland or to stop the execution of the same. (1)

Article XIX secured the continuation as a distinct entity, both in its jurisdiction, institutions and structure and, as significantly, in its philosophy, of the Scottish legal system. In the creation of an incorporating Union which saw many sweeping changes in Scottish life, the distinctive structure of Scots Law would survive, with some modifications. It was, however, not long after the Union that a new court of Exchequer was established in Scotland, with a mixed bench of English and Scottish judges. Soon too civil, though not criminal, appeals were being heard in the House of Lords – this latter seeming breach of the Union terms was accounted for by the House of Lords not being a "court in Westminster Hall". The scarcity of legally qualified Scottish peers was a source of some difficulty as the House of Lords had a very natural tendency to judge matters by English doctrine and practice. Robert McQueen, in an opinion probably written in 1773, observed, with a view to the probability of an eventual House of Lords appeal in the case under consideration:

> ... the contrary doctrine is taken from the ideas of the Laws
> of England by which I am afraid the present case does not fall
> to be decided altho' there is no doubt that as this question
> will in reality be determined by English Judges, the ideas of
> the Laws of England will have considerable influence upon
> their judgement. (2)

Scots law was, in its sources and doctrines, quite distinct from the English system, with its distinction between courts and principles of common law and courts and principles of equity. The Scottish system integrated the two and added to them the power of the Court of Session to exercise the *nobile officium* – the capacity to take extraordinary action to achieve equity where there was no statute law provision or where the ordinary procedures would have failed to produce a just result. The Scots system was based on Roman law with much input from Dutch, German and French jurists and would have sat uneasily alongside the English common law system. Even when the two legal systems arrive at broadly the same result they frequently do so from different premises and by means of a different process of reasoning. The English system is inductive, in that it depends to a large degree on precedent; the Scottish, deductive, being more concerned with a search for first principles – principles which may be buttressed by precedent but which do not rely on them. Quite apart from such philosophical distinctions there were, and remain, major differences in procedures and of course in the organisation and structure of courts.

The publication of major works such as Stair's *Institutions of the Laws of Scotland* in 1681 had given to the law of Scotland an intellectual coherence and a philosophical basis which undoubtedly reinforced its claims to a separate and protected status within the new United Kingdom. Scottish lawyers believed firmly, and with some justification, in the merits, in the excellence, or, if truth be told, in the superiority, of their legal system. Lord Stair, dedicating his work to King Charles II had boldly claimed that:

> . . . the laws of this kingdom hath attained so great perfection, that it may, without arrogance, be compared with the laws of any of our neighbouring nations. (3)

The enthusiasm of Scots lawyers for the superiority and distinctiveness of their system was matched by an enthusiasm for their language. One of Stair's distinguished contemporaries, Sir George MacKenzie, Lord Advocate, founder of the Advocate's Library, and the "Bluidy MacKenzie" of Covenanting legend wrote:

> To me it appears undeniable that the Scottish idiom of the British tongue is more fitting for pleading than either the English idiom or the French tongue; for certainly a pleader must use a brisk, smart, and quick way of speaking: whereas the English, who are a grave nation, use too slow and grave a pronunciation, and the French a too soft and effeminate one. And therefore I think the English is fit for haranguing, the French for complimenting, but the Scots for pleading. Our pronunciation is like ourselves, fiery, abrupt, sprightly, and bold. . . (4)

The continuation of a distinctive legal system and a separate national church after the Union of 1707 made, in a country without a parliament or other national institutions, the law and the Kirk significant fields of surrogate political activity. The record of debates in the General Assembly of the Church of Scotland shows that it is not just in the twentieth century that religion and party politics have been closely intertwined. In May 1782 for example, Henry Erskine, a leading Whig advocate, moved a resolution in the General Assembly congratulating the King on the recent change in Ministers which had brought in the government of Lord Rockingham.

Just as the General Assembly of the Church of Scotland became a major forum for political activity and attracted the presence as commissioners of many prominent persons, so the law also became both a career path for the ambitious and an arena for political activism. The law attracted men of property and of good family to its higher ranks and entrants to the Faculty of Advocates were in the main drawn from the sons of landowners and the upper reaches of the middle classes. In 1769 the Faculty of Advocates included in its membership three peers, Lords Belhaven, Elibank and the Earl of Hyndford as well as sixteen knights and baronets. The comparatively more modest background and the slightly lower status of the Writers to the Signet, at the same period, is suggested by the absence of any peerage or knighthood titles among their members. Despite the effective domination of the law by these elite groups the system remained, to a degree, open to talent and the rise of Robert McQueen, Lord Braxfield, demonstrates this possibility through one man's fairly rapid progression through professional life to a final position at the very summit of the legal profession. McQueen's grandfather had been gardener on a country estate and the gardener's son, John, on showing talent and promise had been encouraged by the landowner and trained in the law to become the estate's man of business. John McQueen eventually established a country practice which proved profitable enough to allow him to buy the small Lanarkshire property of Braxfield. John's eldest son, Robert McQueen was apprenticed to an Edinburgh Writer to the Signet, but never completed his apprenticeship, studied at Edinburgh University and was admitted to the senior legal body, the Faculty of Advocates – whose members had the sole right to plead before the Supreme Courts and from whose membership was drawn the senior judiciary. McQueen thus demonstrates the possibility of an entry into the higher reaches of the law in three generations – however most of his contemporaries in the Faculty and, later, on the Bench would have come from families much longer incorporated into the social, political and legal establishments.

The Faculty of Advocates played a much larger role in eighteenth century Scottish life than simply being a professional body for lawyers.

A remarkably large number of the period's writers, thinkers and politicians were also advocates. The Faculty's Library, which enjoyed legal deposit privileges under the Copyright Acts, was to be the forerunner of and the foundation for the National Library. The internal politics of the Faculty reflected the politics of the nation; in January 1796 the distinguished Whig advocate, Henry Erskine, who had been Dean of the Faculty for eleven years, was deposed from this position by the Tory majority in the Faculty as a result of his involvement in public meetings called to oppose the passing of new legislation on treason and sedition.

The law was not only a substitute for politics in a nation without many of the trappings of a state – it was politics. The very centrality of the Scottish legal system to late eighteenth century Scotland is demonstrated by the dual role of the chief law officer – the Lord Advocate or H.M. Advocate. After the office of Secretary of State for Scotland was abolished in the wake of the '45, Scottish affairs at Westminster were dealt with at Cabinet level by the Secretary of State for the Northern Department, and after the creation of the Home Office in 1792 by the Secretary of State in that Department. However these Ministers had wide ranging responsibilities, of which Scottish affairs were but one. Unless they happened, like Henry Dundas, to be a Scot they were unlikely to have any great knowledge of Scotland or the minutiae of Scottish politics. In practice much of the routine work, patronage and political fixing in Westminster and Scotland was carried out by the Lord Advocate who, sometimes uneasily, carried out the multiple duties of being Scotland's voice in Government, Government's voice in Scotland and the chief public prosecutor.

If the law was politics, politics was also the law. The electoral process revolved around a tiny number of landowning voters – but the possibility existed of creating new voters by creating fictitious or "faggot" votes by notionally subdividing properties. The establishing and challenging of electoral rolls was a fundamental part of the political process – and a large part of the work of the courts.

The law was very much a family tradition, with the same distinguished names cropping up in senior positions in succeeding generations. The Dalrymples of Stair provided advocates and judges throughout the seventeenth and eighteenth centuries and the Dundases of Arniston became famous for the number of members of their family who succeeded in the law. The great Midlothian house of Arniston and its connections provided two Presidents of the Court of Session, numerous Court of Session judges, as well as filling politico-legal posts such as H.M. Solicitor and H.M. Advocate, or, in modern terms, Solicitor General and Lord Advocate. Of the thirty-two appointments to the Court of Session between 1760 and 1800 at least fourteen of the new judges are recorded as being either the sons of advocates or of Writers to the Signet. Of the remainder, who were all drawn from landed or professional backgrounds, many had significant family connections with the higher echelons of the law – for example David Rae, Lord Eskgrove, was the son of a minister but counted a Court of Session judge as his grandfather and William Honyman, Lord Armadale, the son of a landowner, had married Braxfield's daughter.

The legal profession, in its senior ranks, was a small one. In 1769, for example, a year when McQueen was at the height of his career at the bar, the *Edinburgh Almanac's* list of the Faculty of Advocates ran to only 216 names, not all of whom were practising. The same publication also listed the 103 members of the Society of Writers to the Signet. The Court of Session and High Court of Justiciary were staffed by just fifteen judges. There was thus a certain intimacy in the system – men's failings, idiosyncrasies, abilities, peculiarities, would all be very well known. The law was a small, gossipy, club-like institution and much of the comment on Braxfield's manners, or Braxfield's comments on advocates and fellow judges needs to be read and understood in this context.

There was in Scotland, as in England, a basic division in the legal profession between advocates or barristers, who argued cases before the higher courts and gave written opinions, and solicitors, or writers as they were known in Scotland, who dealt directly with the lay client, prepared initial paperwork and instructed the advocates. The pre-eminent organisation for Scottish solicitors was the Society of Writers to the Signet – whose name came from their members' privilege of preparing legal papers to be sealed with the royal seal or signet. However writers came in several categories, a distinction which had long been recognised in social status and legal recognition. When in 1693 the Scots Parliament had passed a poll-tax measure the payments were scaled according to social status. Knights and baronets, for example, were to be assessed at £24 as were:

... all Writers to the Signet, Clerks of Soveraign Courts, all

> Advocats, Sheriffs and their Deputs, Commissars and their
> Deputs and Doctors of Physick (5)

while '. . . Notars and procurators before inferior Courts' would pay £4
and 'all Writers not to the Signet, Agents and Clerks of inferior Courts'
were assessed at £6.

The Society of Writers to the Signet had been constituted in 1594
by Sir Richard Cockburn of Clerkington, Secretary to King James VI
but this creation seems simply to have given formal effect to earlier
practice.

The Faculty of Advocates, whose origins date back to the formation
of the Court of Session when the Act decreed that:

> . . . there be ane number of advocates and procurators chosen
> and to be chosen the number of ten persons that shall be
> called general procurators of the Council, (6)

regulated the training, admission and practice of its members. Many
Scottish advocates commenced their legal training by an apprenticeship
in a Writer's office and followed this with a course of study at a
university – this was the path followed by McQueen. Others completed
their Scottish university education with a period at one of the
continental universities. The most common faculties chosen were those
of Leiden and Utrecht in Holland – a reminder of the long-established
and close links between Scots law and Roman-Dutch law. McQueen's
elder son, Robert Dundas McQueen, was one of many Scots lawyers
who over the years went to Holland to complete their studies, although
McQueen himself was an entirely home-bred product.

The Faculty preserved the Scottish tradition of free legal aid to
those whose means did not enable them to hire counsel. This tradition
can be traced back to an act of James I, dating from 1424, providing for
legal aid to the poor.

> Ande gif thar be ony pur creatur that for defalt of cunying or
> dispense can not or may not follow his cause the King for
> the lufe of God sall ordane that the Judge before quha the
> cause suld be determined purvey and get a lele and wys
> advocate to follow sic pur creatures cause . . . (7)

This tradition of providing true and wise advocates was continued by the Faculty's practice of maintaining a panel of "counsel for the poor" and the Writers to the Signet and the other leading body of solicitors, The Society of Solicitors before the Supreme Courts, maintaining a panel of agents for the poor. This provision, was in marked distinction to the English situation where, in the eighteenth century, persons accused of criminal charges had no right to counsel throughout the trial.

Other measures, such as provisions against detention without trial which obliged the Crown to commence the trial process within 110 days of the suspect's incarceration, a remarkably forward-looking provision of a Scottish Act of 1701, made the Scottish criminal justice system considerably more sympathetic to the rights of the accused than was the English system. Indeed the distinctions between the two jurisdictions are quite remarkable – for example in the late eighteenth century, the age of Braxfield, there were fewer than fifty capital offences on the Scottish statute book. The English total of capital offences peaked at around three hundred early in the next century.

One feature of eighteenth century Scottish criminal law was the possibility of a non-capital offence, such as a minor theft, being punishable by death if the accused was found to be by "habit and repute" a thief. Braxfield was to expound this point to a jury at the High Court in Edinburgh in March 1796. William Brown, a carter in Leith was charged with stealing six iron bars and being "habit and repute a thief". In his summing up Lord Braxfield said that he:

> ... thought it necessary to mention, that, by the law of
> Scotland, a person convicted of the most trifling theft, if he
> should at the same time be proved habit and repute a thief,
> would render him liable to a capital punishment; while
> simple theft, if not to a very great extent, would only infer an
> arbitrary punishment. Whatever, therefore, the opinion of the
> Jury might be, as to the stealing of the six bars of iron, which,
> of itself, was not a capital offence, he thought they must, at
> any rate, find the habit and repute not proven. (8)

In the event the jury in William Brown's case found the charge of stealing the bars of iron not proven and Brown walked free.

A case some years earlier had provided Braxfield with an opportunity to correct a mistaken impression regarding theft and its liability to capital punishment. A former soldier, William Gadesby, was being tried on five charges including one of housebreaking. Three of the charges were found not proven and his counsel argued that with only two charges remaining, neither of which were attended with aggravating circumstances, an arbitrary (that is non-capital) punishment should be inflicted. After argument between counsel Braxfield, the Lord Justice-Clerk was reported as follows:

> As to the objection, that it required three acts of simple theft to constitute a capital crime, the Lord Justice-Clerk said, that he would take this public opportunity to rectify this mistaken opinion, and he wished it to be publicly known, as he understood that such a notion prevailed in the country. The law did not say so, and although there were certain circumstances which often attended crimes of theft which induced the court to restrict the libel to an arbitrary punishment, such as the way in which the crimes were committed, and various other incidental circumstances, yet many other instances occurred where small thefts were made capital. (9)

Gadesby's prospects were diminished by one of two guilty verdicts being for a housebreaking charge, a capital charge, and he was sentenced to death.

One curious feature, to our eyes, of the eighteenth century Scottish criminal justice system was that the judges lacked the ability to imprison for lengthy periods. There were no purpose-built prisons as we know them and imprisonment for more than a year was a rarity, in part because confinement for a longer period in the disgusting conditions of a place like the Edinburgh Tolbooth would have been a virtual death sentence. Lord Henderland summed up these conditions in a comment on the disposal of the accused in one of the 1793 sedition trials:

> . . . to make them denizens as it were of that unhallowed place, which is the sink of corruption, – where everything that is vicious, base and criminal, are huddled together, – where, if they preserve their health, they cannot for a long tract of time escape the contagion of vice and more sordid criminality. . .(10)

Cases had thus generally to be disposed of by fines, by whipping, by banishment furth of Scotland, by transportation to the colonies, and by hanging. Hanging was, in fact, and despite later loose talk of Braxfield as a "hanging judge" or "Scotland's Judge Jeffreys", a comparative rarity. William Creech noted:

> In 1763, and many years preceding and following, the
> execution of criminals was rare. Three annually were
> reckoned the average for the whole Kingdom of Scotland.
> There were three succeeding years, (1774, 1775, 1776), in
> which there was not an execution in Edinburgh. (11)

He however goes on to note with regret that in 1783 there were six criminals under sentence of death in Edinburgh jail, in one week, and that thirty seven capital indictments were issued on the Autumn Justiciary circuits. In fact, even of those criminals convicted of capital offences many never suffered the extreme punishment. It was quite usual for a proposal to be made, and accepted, that a lesser punishment be imposed. A practice which this 1788 report, dating from the first months of Braxfield's period as Lord Justice Clerk, illustrates:

> On Friday March 15, Isabel Tait, indicted for child-murder,
> having petitioned for banishment, and the advocate-depute
> consenting, the Court sentenced her to be banished Scotland
> for life, and allowed her to the 1st of June to leave the
> kingdom. (12)

This case does suggest a certain degree of humanity on the part of the judicial system – not only was Isabel Tait allowed to move to England but she was given ten weeks to put her affairs in order and to get there.

When McQueen was admitted to the Faculty of Advocates in 1744 the old system of heritable jurisdictions was still in place. The owners of estates had the right to administer justice, over a wide range of charges, on their properties. This relic of feudalism would soon be swept away in the aftermath of the Jacobite rising. The country had long been divided into sheriffdoms and in the earlier part of the eighteenth century the functions of the sheriff court, both civil and criminal, had been performed by sheriffs-depute appointed by the hereditary sheriffs. These sheriffs-depute generally continued into the new dispensation and discharged an extensive range of both criminal and civil legal functions as well as miscellaneous administrative duties. Members of the Faculty of Advocates filled these shrieval posts, often as a stage on their route to a Court of Session post. Thus Lord Monboddo and before him, Lord Gardenstone had, prior to their elevation to the College of Justice, served as Sheriff-depute in Kincardineshire. Advocates less frequently appeared before these lower courts, concentrating their attention on the two supreme courts which dealt with the most important civil and criminal cases.

The Court of Session, established as a permanent supreme court in 1532, by King James V's College of Justice Act:

> Concerning the ordour of Justice and the institution of ane college of cunning and wise men for the administracioun of justice. (13)

Originally staffed by a mixture of lawyers and clerics the clerical element had disappeared after the Reformation. When the Court had been reconstituted in 1689, following the accession of William and Mary, there had been provision made for the appointment of supernumerary Extraordinary Lords of Session, who were politically significant peers of the realm. However no appointments of Extraordinary Lords was made after 1723 and the last survivor of the old order, the Marquis of Tweeddale died in 1762, so that by the period of McQueen's appointment the Court of Session had long comprised fifteen professionally qualified judges who sat without a jury for the disposal of civil cases. These judges were formally referred to, variously, as Lords of Council and Session or Senators of the College of Justice. Their legal title, Lord Arniston, Lord Braxfield, Lord Succoth etc, was generally derived from the name of their family estate. This was not a hereditary title and did not, of course, entitle the bearer to a seat in the House of Lords. Although they were recorded in the sederunt of the Courts by their judicial titles the judges signed documents with their Christian and family names and, until 1905, their wives were not allowed to use their husband's judicial title – thus the formal manner of address would be Lord Braxfield and Mrs McQueen, rather than Lord & Lady Braxfield – the views of the wives of the Senators of the College of Justice on this discrimination do not seem to be recorded.

The Court of Session met in Parliament House in Edinburgh for two sessions a year – a winter session from 12th November to 11th March and a summer session running from 12th June to 11th August, the summer sitting being altered in 1790 to run from 12th May to 12th July. This working pattern reflected the dominance of the agricultural interest – the landowning judges could be at home on their estates during the critical periods of sowing and harvesting.

During its periods of sitting the Court of Session sat each weekday, except Mondays. The Court was divided into an Outer House, an Inner House and a Bill Chamber. Proceedings were generally carried out by written pleadings. Simpler cases could be disposed of by a single Judge in the Outer House, the Lord Ordinary, and the great majority of cases were decided in this way in the Outer House. More complex cases, after their preliminary stages in the Outer House conducted by the Lord Ordinaries, were referred to the Inner House – the full panel of fifteen judges, or at least a quorum of nine of them. Each member of the College of Justice, except the Lord President, took a week-long turn sitting at the Fore Bar as Lord Ordinary. Three other judges took turns to sit at Side Bars in Parliament House, dealing with other parts of the legal process – as Lord Ordinary on Oaths, Lord Ordinary on Witnesses and Lord Ordinary on Concluded Causes. The Bill Chamber, presided over by the Lord Ordinary for the week, controlled the process of appeal from lower courts to the Court of Session.

The scene in Parliament House when the Fore Bar and Side Bars were in operation was one of great bustle and confusion – all these hearings took place in the main hall, the Outer House, with advocates, solicitors, clients milling about. A scene far removed from what is perhaps our normal image of the dignity of the law. Alexander Young, who knew the scene well from his work there as a Writer to the Signet recounts that:

> The Side Bars in the Outer House were then of a very
> singular construction, being merely an Arm Chair in a
> small recess, with a narrow shelf in front, which brought
> the Judge, Counsel and Agents in such close connection
> that they almost touched each other . . . (14)

Thomas Carlyle gives a young man's impression of Parliament House in 1809. Although this was after the 1808 reform which meant that the full bench of fifteen no longer sat together and saw the creation of a bicameral court with a permanent Outer House and appellate Inner House. However, from Carlyle's description, little had yet changed from the lively, if somewhat confusing, scene that Braxfield and Young would have known:

> An immense Hall, dimly lighted from the top of the walls,
> and perhaps with candles burning in it here and there; all in
> strange chiaroscuro, and filled with what I thought
> (exaggeratively) a thousand or two of human creatures; all
> astir in a boundless buzz of talk, and simmering about in
> every direction, some solitary, some in groups. By degrees I
> noticed that some were in wig and black gown, some not,
> but in common clothes, all well-dressed; that here and there
> on the sides of the Hall, were little thrones with enclosures,
> and steps leading-up; red-velvet figures sitting in said
> thrones, and the black-gowned eagerly speaking to them, –
> Advocates pleading to Judges, as I easily understood. How
> they could be heard in such a grinding din was somewhat a
> mystery. (15)

For the more complex cases which were sent to be dealt with by the full bench, the Court was presided over by the Lord President of the Council, the head of the Scots judiciary.

Walter Scott in *Redgauntlet* describes much of the progression of a suit through the Court:

> '. . . the client states the cause to the agent – the agent to the
> counsel –' 'The counsel to the Lord Ordinary,' '. . . the
> Ordinary to the Inner-House, the President to the Bench.' (16)

Many of Scott's novels have characters obsessed with the law and its language, like Bartoline Saddletree in *The Heart of Midlothian*, or who have long-running suits before the courts, like Peter Peebles in *Redgauntlet*. In another novel, *Guy Mannering*, Scott has a character observe that: 'a man's aye the better thocht o' in our country for having been afore the Feifteen'. This frequent use of the law is a reminder not only that Scott was himself an advocate, Sheriff-Depute of Selkirk and a Principal Clerk to the Court of Session but of the central role that the law and the institutions of the law played in the nation and the minds of its people.

Parliament House was in many ways a curiously apt location for the Supreme Courts. As the name suggests it had been the seat of the pre-Union Scottish Parliament and had been built specifically for that purpose and to accommodate the Courts in 1632–40 by the Edinburgh Town Council. With the disappearance of the Scottish Parliament in 1707 the Law, so carefully and specifically protected in the Treaty of Union, took over the whole of Parliament House as in many ways it, with the Kirk, took over from Parliament and the traditional political process the provision of a focus for national identity.

New judges, or Lords of Session, were appointed by the Sovereign on the advice of the ministers of the Crown but, before being installed, had to prove their competence:

> When any new Lords of Session shall be presented by his Majesty for tryall of their qualifications, they shall sit three days besides the Ordinary in the outer house, and shall have inspection of such processes as are carried to interloquitor, and shall make report of the points taken to interloquitor, in presence of the whole Lords. As also for completing their tryall, they shall sit one day in the inner house, and after any dispute is brought to a period, and the Lords are to advise the same in order to the pronouncing of their interlocutor, they shall resume the dispute, and first give their opinion thereanent, in presence of the whole Lords. (17)

Having passed this test members normally sat until their death – resignation and retirement were fairly uncommon in the eighteenth century Court of Session.

The personnel of the Court of Session bench was traditionally and exclusively drawn from the ranks of the Faculty of Advocates – although there was in fact authority under the Treaty of Union for Writers to the Signet to be appointed as Senators of the College of Justice, under special and stringent provisions, including public and private trial of their competence by the Faculty of Advocates carried out at least two years before they were nominated to the bench. Perhaps unsurprisingly no Writer to the Signet was appointed to the Court in this period.

Despite the provisions of the Treaty of Union that no changes would be made in the Court and that it would 'remain in all time coming within Scotland, as it is now constituted by the Laws of that Kingdom' there were various attempts made to reform it. One particularly contentious attempt was made, in 1785, to reduce the number of Court of Session judges to nine or ten in order to provide the rump with higher salaries. This measure was widely opposed throughout Scotland, with county meetings passing hostile resolutions. It also attracted the scorn of James Boswell, who with his customary gift for self-publicity, inserted a letter in the Edinburgh papers:

> To the People of Scotland
>
> I rejoice to find you are roused by the alarming attempt to infringe the articles of the Union, and introduce a most pernicious innovation by obtaining an act of parliament to alter the constitution of the College of Justice, by diminishing the number of Lords of Session, in order to give them larger salaries. I feared you were torpid. – Having called to you with so much success last year to oppose Mr Fox's East-India bill, I resolved to call to you again on this momentous occasion.
>
> My friends and countrymen, be not afraid. I am upon the spot. I am upon the watch. The bill shall not pass without a spirited appeal to the justice and honour of the Commons of Great Britain. Collect your minds. Be calm; but be firm. You shall hear from me at large a few days hence.
>
> I am ever your very faithful humble servant.
> Ja. Boswell
> London, May 12 1785. (18)

Whether the alarming news that Boswell was "upon the watch" was the determining factor or not the proposal was dropped and in 1786 an Act was passed raising the salaries for the Senators of the College of Justice. The Lord President's salary was set at £2,000 and the remainder of the Lords of Session were paid £1000.

Behind this issue was a serious difficulty. Even when raised to their 1786 levels the salary of a Court of Session judge was not particularly attractive. *The Scots Magazine's* obituary of McQueen noted that the Dundases:

> . . . well knew Mr M'Queen's merit and abilities, and they

were both desirous of testifying their sense of them, by obtaining for him a seat upon the bench. Mr M'Queen for some time resisted their importunities. Being in the receipt of much more money as a barrister, he conceived that duty to his family required his perseverance in that situation. (19)

It went on to comment that, when at last he yielded to pressure in 1776, his financial sacrifice was such that:

The late Lord Mansfield [William Murray, 1st Earl of Mansfield, Scots born lawyer and politician who became Lord Chief Justice of England] who was so sensible of the valuable addition which the bench received by this appointment, and of the disinterested conduct of Mr M'Queen on this occasion, that he spoke of it in the highest terms of approbation.

McQueen' sacrifice was considerable. In the 1760s the salary of a Court of Session judge was approximately £610. Ilay Campbell, a leading advocate of the period, who later became Lord President of the Court of Session as Lord Succoth, told James Boswell of McQueen's spectacular earnings of £1900 per annum from his legal practice and that he himself had made as much as £1600 a year in the course of his profession. This conversation, Boswell confided to his journal:

. . . excited the solid coarse ambition of making money in the Court of Session. (20)

The problem of staffing the Bench with the best available talent was one which seems regularly to have exercised official minds. In 1799, when Lord Braxfield died, the then Lord Advocate, Robert Dundas, wrote to the Home Secretary, the Duke of Portland, with the sad news and to air the serious problem of filling the vacancy on the Court of Session. He wrote:

The President [Ilay Campbell, Lord Succoth] is extremely desirous to have the vacancy filled up by some Eminent Lawyer. But the misfortune is that those high in their profession will not accept & we have been drove to the necessity of placing on the Bench men indeed of Integrity and

Honour, but not of such extensive Practice, or such profound legal knowledge, as ought always to be the case with some of the members of that Court. (21)

The other branch of the Supreme Court was the High Court of Justiciary, responsible for the trial of the most serious criminal offences and for criminal appeals from lower courts. The High Court was nominally under the direction of the Lord Justice-General, by the mid-eighteenth century a sinecure office occupied by a well-placed nobleman. From 1763 to 1778 this was the Duke of Queensberry, and from 1778 to 1796, Viscount Stormont, later the 2nd Earl of Mansfield, the nephew of the Earl whose comment on McQueen's disinterested acceptance of judicial office was noted above.

In reality the High Court was presided over by the Lord Justice-Clerk, who received, from 1786, an additional salary of £600. Apart from the Justice-Clerk, five other Court of Session judges, who received an additional salary of £300 each, were given "a justiciary gown" or additional appointments as Commissioners of Justiciary. Like the Lord President, the Lord Justice-Clerk was to some extent a government functionary, frequently consulted on various matters of Scottish government and policy. His role as an officer of state was recognised by the grant of an additional annual payment of £100 '. . . for answering the expense of correspondence on the public affairs. . .' (22)

This use of the senior judiciary, along with the law officers such as the Lord Advocate, in a quasi-political role in part arose from the abolition of the post of Secretary for Scotland and reflected some of the strains of running a Scotland, with its distinctive institutions and traditions, within the structure of the British state. Quite how far the judiciary became involved in national politics is shown by the work of Duncan Forbes of Culloden, who served as Lord President of the Court of Session from 1737 to 1748. Forbes had been a vital part of the government's response to the Jacobite rising and attempted, with limited success, a moderating influence on the Duke of Cumberland's post-Culloden repression of the Highlands. Forbes' role and influence was admittedly, in part, due to his position as a landowner on the edge of the Highlands, but he clearly also saw that his post as Lord President involved him in the executive branch of government in a way that would be quite alien to a twentieth century Lord President.

All these judicial appointments were, of course, often the subject of considerable competition and lobbying. In 1780 James Boswell writes in his diary of the machinations surrounding Braxfield's succession to the Justiciary seat his father, Lord Auchinleck, was on the point of vacating:

> Yesterday I was uneasy to think of Lord Covington's disappointment by Lord Braxfield's getting my father's Justiciary Gown, which, by the influence of the Dundases and his own prejudice against Lord Covington, he would not resign unless Lord Braxfield should get it, though Lord Covington had Lord Mansfield's promise. . . I had spoken to the Lord Advocate for him, pressing the hardship of disappointing him. My Lord gave me a very solid answer: that it would be wrong to give the gown resigned by one old man to a man even older. . . (23)

Alexander Lockhart, Lord Covington, a distinguished advocate and former Dean of the Faculty of Advocates, was eighty years of age when the forty year old Boswell interested himself in his case and, as the Lord Advocate pointed out, Lord Covington was seven years older than Boswell's father who was now retiring on the grounds that he was finding the Justiciary work over-taxing. Boswell also records a conversation between his father and his clerk, John Stobie, which gives the clerk's rather cynical view of the legal and official rat-race. Lord Auchinleck had been unwell but was recovering, Stobie visits him and is asked:

> 'Come awa', John. Are aw the Lords of Session living yet?'
>   'Ay, my Lord. But mony a ane's wishing them dead. Ony body that has a post has folk to wish them dead.'
>   'Wha are the expectants now?'
>   'Plenty of expectants my Lord.' (24)

The Boswell diaries also show one of the reasons why Judges hung on to office into extreme old age. There was no automatic pension arrangement and a retiring judge was dependent on official goodwill to be granted a pension. When Auchinleck surrendered his Justiciary post he was granted a pension of £200 per annum, to commence when his Justiciary salary ceased – a piece of good news which Lord Braxfield was able to announce to Auchinleck and Boswell over tea at Auchinleck's Edinburgh house on Sunday 5th March 1780.

Unlike the Court of Session the High Court of Justiciary sat both in Edinburgh, sitting as need dictated outwith the normal Court of Session terms, and in nine assize towns in Scotland arranged in three circuits. These were, the Northern Circuit; covering Aberdeen, Inverness and Perth, the Southern Circuit; Ayr, Dumfries and Jedburgh; and the Western Circuit of Glasgow, Inveraray and Stirling. Each circuit was covered twice a year, once in the Spring in April and once in Autumn, in September. In the sixteenth century the Lord Justice-General had been ordered to be available continually in Edinburgh to hear criminal actions.

However the centralisation of criminal justice proved to have drawbacks and a peripatetic Justiciary Court had been established by an Act of James VI in 1587 which had noted the:

> . . . grite delay in actionis criminall throw the not halding of justice airis twyis in the yeir according to the auncient and lovable ordour established be divers guid laws and actis of parliament maid of befoir . . . (25)

and ordained that "sum of the senatouris of the college of justice" who were "maist able for travell" should be appointed as deputies to the Lord Justice-General to go into every quarter of the realm in April and October. This provision was formalised in 1672 in an Act of Parliament:

> . . . That the office of Deputes in the Justice-Court be suppressed, and that five of the Lords of Session be joyned to the Justice-Generall and Justice-Clerk, and all of them invested with the same and equall power and jurisdiction in all criminall causes; that the Justice-Generall being present preside, and in his absence the Justice-Clerk. . . (26)

By Braxfield's time the pattern of three circuits outlined above had emerged and six days were spent in each town and, in theory, two judges performed each circuit and sat together to try cases. In practice a fair number of diets were conducted by one judge.

Justiciary cases, whether on circuit or in Edinburgh, were tried before a jury of fifteen. The selection of the fifteen jurors from a leet of forty-five names drawn up by the Sheriff-Clerk of the county was, unlike present practice, a matter for the presiding judge, and this was to be a source of unease during the sedition trials of Braxfield's latter years. The jurors, who could reach their verdicts by a majority vote, had the option of three verdicts, Guilty, Not Guilty and the unique Scottish verdict of Not Proven.

After hearing the evidence in the case and before being asked to reach their verdict the jury were addressed on the law and the evidence by the presiding judge. This was something of an innovation and Lord Kames is credited with introducing the notion of the judge discussing the credibility of witnesses. However even a quite forceful charge and direction was not guaranteed to be accepted by juries, who often displayed a considerable degree of independence – an independence which does call into some question the dominance of the justiciary suggested by Cockburn and other commentators – although it must be admitted that a jury's independence of thought might be more easily demonstrated in a normal criminal case than in a political sedition trial. A good example of this reluctance of a jury to accept judicial direction came in January 1791 when James McGhie was being tried for killing George Paterson. Paterson had attacked and killed McGhie's father in front of him and this extenuating circumstance was why the Lord Advocate, prosecuting, had put forward alternative charges of murder and culpable homicide and left it to the jury to consider the circumstances and return a verdict accordingly. McGhie's counsel argued that the pannel had not had any intention of committing murder. Lord Justice-Clerk Braxfield summing up observed:

> . . . that he considered a son, in defending the life of his
> parent, equally justifiable as if in defence of his own, and, if
> the jury should be satisfied, that the life of the pannel's father
> was in danger when the stroke was given, which he did not
> think was the case, they would no doubt return a verdict of
> not proven. If they should be of a different opinion, then they
> would return their verdict guilty; for he held, that the
> alternative in the indictment of culpable homicide, could not
> at all enter into the consideration of the jury. (27)

Which was a clear enough direction. However the jury returned their verdict:

... finding, by a great plurality of voices, the pannel guilty of culpable homicide.

Earlier in the eighteenth century Scots juries had the options of finding cases Proven or Not Proven. In many ways this was a commendably logical choice of verdicts calling for a jury's decision on the strength of the case and the evidence presented rather than the search for absolute truth implied by the verdict of Guilty or Not Guilty. Matters changed in 1728 when an earlier Robert Dundas, defending Carnegie of Finhaven on the charge of murdering the Earl of Strathmore, persuaded the court to allow the jury to return to a long-disused verdict of Not Guilty.

Criminal cases, once commenced, generally continued without respite in order to protect the jurors from the danger of outside interference. This could lead to a somewhat arduous form of public service. In the case of Deacon Brodie the trial commenced at 9am on Wednesday 27th August, the Lord-Justice Clerk commenced his summing-up at 5am the next morning, the jury retired just before 6am and came back with their verdict at 1pm.

However although the jury and the public galleries may have lacked for refreshment the bench did not. Lord Cockburn's splendid description of the important place that strong drink played in the operation of the Court of Session is coloured by his distaste for what he saw as eighteenth century coarseness and barbarism – but it remains a characteristically vivid piece of descriptive writing, well worth quoting at some length:

> At Edinburgh, the old judges had a practice at which even their barbaric age used to shake its head. They always had wine and biscuits on the bench, when the business was clearly to be protracted beyond the usual dinner hour. The modern judges – those I mean who were made after 1800, never gave in to this; but with those of the preceding generation, some of whom lasted several years after 1800, it was quite common.
>
> Black bottles of strong port were set down beside them on the bench, with glasses, caraffes of water, tumblers, and biscuits; and this without the slightest attempt at concealment. The refreshment was generally allowed to stand

untouched, and as if despised, for a short time, during which their Lordships seemed to be intent only on their notes. But in a little, some water was poured into the tumbler, and sipped quietly as if merely to sustain nature. Then a few drops of wine were ventured upon, but only with the water, till at last patience could endure no longer, and a full bumper of the pure black element was tossed over; after which the thing went on regularly, and there was a comfortable munching and quaffing, to the great envy of the parched throats in the gallery. The strong-headed stood it tolerably well, but it told, plainly enough on the feeble. Not that the ermine was absolutely intoxicated, but it was certainly sometimes affected. (28)

In the absence of a written criminal code the Justiciary Court depended on specific statute and the previous practice of the criminal courts. In a similar fashion to the *nobile officium* referred to above in the context of the Court of Session the Justiciary Court had at its disposal the doctrine of "native vigour" – the power Lord Cockburn so distrusted and criticised, the power to:

> . . . create new crimes and apply to them any punishment short of death that it chose. (29)

A power the more dangerous, in Cockburn's view, because of the lack of any appeal, other than to Royal clemency, from the verdicts of the Court of Justiciary.

More positively it should be said that the criminal justice system had a considerable degree of flexibility and adaptability. In 1747 one Robert Spence was tried for murder and his defence that he was "furious" or insane was accepted. In the light of his insanity he was sentenced to life imprisonment in the Tolbooth or until bail was given by his friends for his being kept secure for life. This acceptance of the defence of insanity antedates by nearly fifty years the better known case of Kinloch, presided over by Braxfield, which is often held to be the first example of the acceptance of a diminished responsibility plea. Kinloch like Spence was to be confined by his friends for life with a substantial bail forfeited if he was found at liberty. The Court of Justiciary had considerable discretion, as Lord Braxfield explained in a report to Henry Dundas:

Great part of the criminal law of Scotland, even in capital
cases, is founded in usage not in Statute, and where the
punishment of any crime, not capital, is not ascertained by
special statute, the High Court of Justiciary have, by the
common law of Scotland, power to punish every such crime
by what is termed an arbitrary punishment.

In the law of Scotland an arbitrary punishment signifies
such punishment less than death as upon due consideration of
the nature and circumstances of the case, shall in the discretion
of the Court appear to be adequate to the offence.(30)

When Lord Braxfield was given the additional appointment of
Commissioner of Justiciary in February 1780 the ever-active James
Boswell published an anonymous pamphlet. In it he complained about
the lack of dignity caused by the circuit judges no longer going on
circuit with the former degree of state and skimping on their
entertainment of local gentlemen. Each judge on the Southern and
Western Circuits got an allowance of £150 for expenses, and on the
Northern Circuit a £180 allowance, reflecting the longer distances and
greater expense, was paid. Boswell noted that there had been
parliamentary comment on corruption in the Scottish civil establishment and observed that it would be unfortunate:

... if the least countenance were given to such a reproach, by
even a suspicion that any of the money which is allowed by
the public for maintaining the dignity of criminal justice in
the circuits is pocketed by the judges. (31)

This, it must be said, is not an accusation that was ever to be levelled
against Lord Braxfield. Alexander Young, while exonerating Braxfield,
echoes Boswell's accusations of judicial penny-pinching and illicit
profiting from the entertainment allowance:

Although contrary to the practice of most of the Judges of the
Court of Justiciary who had an allowance from Government
for entertaining the Gentlemen and Juries at their Circuits,
and were generally (in particular Lord Kames) accused of
doing it in the most shabby manner, Lord Braxfield always
gave them as much wine of every kind as they thought
proper till they cried Amen... (32)

Boswell also condemned the irregular practice of judges sitting alone:

> His Majesty's subjects are by law entitled to have the opinion
> of two Judges upon the Circuit, in questions concerning their
> life, liberties or properties, unless when one of the Judges has
> not it in his power to attend, either by reason of indisposition,
> or of such an avocation as can be bona fide pronounced to be
> necessary. (33)

He also observed that criminal trials were in some regards better conducted in England. In Scotland he felt that greater credence was given by judges to the prosecution case than to defence evidence. All this might, he felt, be explained by:

> ... there being a better spirit of office, more propriety of
> behaviour, and a more civilised mildness of manners on the
> south of the Tweed, but may perhaps be chiefly ascribed to
> the custom of prisoners being allowed counsel in Scotland
> during the whole course of the trial.

This, Boswell felt, meant that defence counsel acted with such 'warmth and eagerness' as to encourage judges to add their weight to the other, to the prosecution side. This interesting viewpoint from an experienced practitioner before the Scottish courts does suggest that the behaviour complained of in Braxfield's famous cases was not altogether untypical of his judicial brethren. Boswell's comments, it should be recollected, were written on Braxfield's appointment to the Justiciary bench, and therefore not in response to any action he had taken in that environment.

Boswell concluded, 'The office of one of the Judges of the High Court of Justiciary, is indeed an arduous trust.' And he went on in his most sententious manner:

> But when honest and honourable intentions are joined with
> knowledge and abilities, the faithful execution of it may be of
> the greatest benefit to society, may teach men to "fear God
> and honour the King", to be sensible of the excellence of
> subordination; and by not hurting others, to enjoy peace and
> quietness themselves.

Indeed the Justiciary Court was an 'arduous trust' – quite apart from the duties in the High Court in Edinburgh, and the civil cases which constituted the Court of Session work, the Commissioners of Justiciary and the Justice-Clerk had a lengthy circuit to perform, albeit leisurely and in some comfort, twice a year. When the Treasury enquired into the costs of the Scottish Courts in 1799 (some forms of Government behaviour seem to be timeless) Lord Eskgrove responded on behalf of the High Court of Justiciary, Braxfield, the Lord Justice-Clerk being seriously ill at the time. Eskgrove noted:

> . . . the Circuits which take place twice in the year to very distant
> parts of Scotland. In the course of them many long and
> important trials occur and the time which they require occupies
> a great part of the Vacations of the Court of Session. (34)

Almost by definition the judges undertaking this work were not young men. When, in 1780, Braxfield received his justiciary gown the average age of his brethren on the High Court was over sixty three and at fifty-seven he was the second youngest man on the bench. The great veteran of the Justiciary bench was Henry Home, Lord Kames, who continued to carry out a full circuit programme until 1782, the year of his death, when he was eighty-six years of age.

Even the leisurely stages of a circuit progress, with frequent stops and overnight entertainment at the homes of country gentlemen or the inns in assize towns, must, in the difficult travelling conditions of eighteenth century Scotland, have been something of a burden for the older members, like Kames. However, for evidence that the vigour and lively spirits of a Kames could survive this ordeal, and for a glimpse into the domestic manners of the older members of the Court of Session, we can again turn to James Boswell, who notes in his diary for September 1780 that Lord Braxfield stayed at Auchinleck House in Ayrshire on his way to the Southern Circuit and was joined by Kames, who was Braxfield's partner that year on the Southern Circuit, and his wife and son for dinner. Boswell, normally no mean *bon viveur* himself, was in one of his consciously restrained moods and noted, somewhat disapprovingly, the behaviour of his elders and seniors in the law:

Was a little too lively, but soon checked my vivacity. I drank one glass of Madeira and one of claret. Was somewhat uneasy even by taking so much, and felt the company disturbed the calmness of Auchinleck. Lord Kames raved and Lord Braxfield roared – both bawdy. (35)

CHAPTER 4

McQueen the Man
1722–1799

" . . . his faults and foibles bore some proportion
to his bright and useful endowments . . ."

Robert McQueen, the future Lord Braxfield, was born on 4th May 1722, the son of John McQueen of Braxfield and his wife Helen Hamilton. John McQueen, who was a lawyer in the burgh of Lanark, had married Helen, the daughter of a minor Lanarkshire landowner, John Hamilton of Gilkerscleugh, in July 1719 and Robert was the first-born of their seven children. John's precise date of birth cannot be established from the Parish Registers but, to judge from obituary notices published at the time of his death in November 1771 which reported him to have died in his 85th year, he must have been born around 1687.

The McQueen family had been settled in southern Lanarkshire for some time. John's father, Robert, was employed as a gardener on the estate of Charles Douglas, Earl of Selkirk at Crawford. This Robert, from the evidence of the Register of Testaments, died at Castlemains of Crawford in 1748. The gardener's son John, showing promise, was apparently given help and encouragement by the Earl and trained in the law with a view to his becoming the Crawford estate's "baron-baillie" or man of business. By 1710 John had, according to some accounts, bought the small property of Braxfield, near Lanark. However there does not appear to be good evidence for the purchase at this date. In the minutes of the Justices of the Peace for Lanarkshire for August

1716 there is an entry which shows John McQueen entering on his duties as the law-agent for the barony of Crawford and Crawfordjohn, and also qualifying as a law agent in the local courts:

> John McQueen, writer in Lanark, compeared and qualified as baillie deputy of Crawford and Crawfordjohn, and as pror. [procurator] fiscal to the commissariot of Lanark, as pror. before the Sherriff and Town Courts of Lanark. (1)

He is described as 'John McQueen, writer in Lanark' not 'John McQueen of Braxfield, writer in Lanark'. Such distinctions were of considerable importance and it would have been most unlikely that, if McQueen had owned the estate of Braxfield at that time, he would not have been given the customary dignity of the 'of Braxfield' appellation. The first relevant entry in the Register of Sasines for Lanarkshire comes in 1719 when he appears as 'John McQueen of Braxfield, writer, of Lanark' and on 21st February 1720 he was to receive a charter under the Great Seal of Scotland of the lands of Braxfield. It is difficult to see why it should have taken ten years to get the charter if he had purchased Braxfield as early as 1710. It is also fair to point out that if he had been able to buy the property by 1710 he would have to have had a very quick rise to prosperity to be able to purchase Braxfield by the age of twenty three. A purchase seven or eight years later seems much more probable, and ties in nicely with his marriage in 1719.

In any event John McQueen developed a successful and prosperous legal career. Certainly the property he owned reflects this – between 1719 and 1778 there are twenty separate references to him in the Lanarkshire Register of Sasines, the land register of the county. At a later stage in his career he was appointed as a Sheriff-substitute for the Upper Ward of Lanarkshire, an appointment which reflected both his social status and his professional standing.

His son Robert was sent to the local grammar school in Lanark. As the obituarist in the *Scots Magazine* noted:

> The grammar school in Lanark was then in considerable repute. . . In this period classical literature was held to be the chief requisite in all the learned professions. . . Mr McQueen was endowed by nature with a retentive, as well as comprehensive memory, the chief requisites for acquiring the knowledge of a dead language: he, therefore was clearly

84

noticed by his master, and marked by him as worthy of the highest rank among his contemporaries, being frequently at the top, or, as it is termed, *dux*, of the school. (2)

Young Robert was not the only contender for fame in the ranks of the Lanark Grammar School. General William Roy (1726–90), the founder of the Ordnance Survey, was a slightly younger contemporary. Robert would be followed to Lanark Grammar school by his younger brothers, John, baptised 1724, James, baptised 1729 and Charles. James might also have taken up the law – he may well be the James McQueen, writer in Edinburgh, who handled the purchase of the Hardington estate for Robert McQueen in 1769–1770. Two sisters, Elizabeth and Helen born in 1730 and 1734 completed the family of six. Robert McQueen was described earlier as the eldest of seven children, however one brother, Charles, baptised in 1732, must have died in infancy because in 1735 another christening of a Charles McQueen is recorded.

Lanark, although the county town, was already overtaken in size and importance by other Lanarkshire centres such as Glasgow and Hamilton. In the eighteenth century it was a busy market town serving the surrounding agricultural districts. Although towards the end of Robert McQueen's life the textile mills of New Lanark were to be, in part, built on a piece of the Braxfield estate there was little evidence of industrialisation in the Lanark of his youth. The family home at Braxfield overlooked the picturesque Falls of Clyde and was surrounded by farmland where the young McQueen delighted in traditional country pursuits such as searching for birds' nests. The burgh school the McQueen boys attended could trace its origins back to 1183 and the town's links with national history were equally ancient. It was in Lanark in 1297 that William Wallace is said to have first taken up arms against the English occupation forces and killed Hazelrig, the English sheriff of Lanark. In the religious wars of the seventeenth century the Covenanters had set out from Lanark to meet their fate at the Battle of Rullion Green in 1666.

Robert's father, it is suggested by some writers, intended that his eldest son be trained to succeed him in his Lanark legal practice. However young Robert McQueen's legal education went beyond that which would have been required for a country practitioner and the *Scots Magazine* obituary speaks of his attendance at University being with a view to his 'being bred to the profession of a Writer to the Signet'.

In any event in 1737 he was sent to Edinburgh to study at the University. The University he knew was not, of course, the harmonious classical masterpiece of the Old Quad. This work by Robert Adam, completed by William Playfair, dates from 1789 and replaced a much older, and by McQueen's time rather ruinous, set of buildings on the same site which had housed the "Townis College" from its foundation by James VI in 1582.

McQueen's matriculation in the class of John Stevenson in April 1737, just a few days short of his fifteenth birthday, does not imply any special precocity or genius. Fourteen or fifteen was at that time a perfectly normal age to commence higher education in Scotland, as Dr Johnson's acerbic comment about Scottish students going to university as boys and leaving before they are men reminds us. Robert presumably followed a normal course of study for three or four years, but there is no record of his graduation. His class at the University included such future luminaries of the Scottish scene as Alexander "Jupiter" Carlyle, later minister of Inveresk, whose autobiography provides such a lively and valuable insight into Scottish life in the eighteenth century; and William Robertson, later Principal of Edinburgh University and the historian of Europe whose work was so highly praised by Voltaire. (3) They were under the supervision of John Stevenson, whom Carlyle describes thus:

> . . . I went to the Logic class, taught by Mr John Stevenson,
> who, though he had not pretensions to superiority in point of
> learning and genius, yet was the most popular of all the
> Professors on account of his civility and even kindness to his
> students, and at the same time most useful . . . (4)

Other contemporaries included future advocates, clergymen and academics. One of these fellow students is reported by James Ramsay of Ochtertyre as saying:

> They would have fought for Robbie Macqueen, whose
> honesty and good nature made him a general favourite. (5)

We next have evidence of McQueen around 1740 when the *Scots Magazine* says he became apprenticed to an Edinburgh Writer to the Signet, Thomas Goldie. This would seem to be a confirmation of the reported parental plan for the young McQueen to enter the Society of Writers to the Signet. Such a career was, as we have seen, a considerable move up from a country solicitor's practice and McQueen was fortunate in being apprenticed to one of the more distinguished members of the Society of Writers to the Signet, Goldie holding the appointment of Writer to the Privy Seal and also acting as agent for the Duke of Queensberry. Thomas Goldie died in 1741 and there seems to be no record of the arrangements that would then require to have been made for the rest of McQueen's apprenticeship.

There is no evidence in the archives of the Society that McQueen ever became a member and it would seem that at some point in his apprenticeship that he decided instead to follow a career as an advocate. His obituary describes the origins of this change of direction:

> By superintending the management of processes before the supreme court, towards the end of his apprenticeship, Mr McQueen's mind began to develope. In preparing the information for counsel, he had an opportunity of trying his own strength. Becoming conscious of his own powers, and of his knowledge in his profession, Mr McQueen soon bent his mind on the bar; he resolved to enter advocate and try his fortune as a pleader before the supreme courts of his country. (6)

This path from a Writer's chambers to an Advocate's gown was not too unusual a one in those days. McQueen's senior colleague on the Bench, Henry Home, Lord Kames, was just one prominent figure who had taken a similar course.

Many years later Braxfield would talk to James Boswell about the course of his legal education and the formative influences on his development as a lawyer. Boswell asked him how he had attained such a great knowledge of the law and diligently recorded in his diaries the Judge's observations:

> He said he had a good foundation of Civil Law. He did not attend a Scotch Law professor. He put on the gown before candidates for being advocates were being examined on that law. . . He read Lord Stair's *Institutions* three times. He said

there was sometimes a perplexity in his style. But that made
him think all the more attentively, and he found the meaning
always solid.

. . . But he said he had learnt law chiefly by thinking. The
rudiments, to be sure, must be had from books, but he had
acquired his knowledge by considering points himself. He
regretted as I did that the Civil Law was gone into disuse so
much, as it was from thence that the great principles of reason
and sound sense were to be drawn; and he said that it was
true, what I observed that it was the great glory of our law to
proceed on principles and be more of a system than the law in
England. As to decisions, he said one should not learn law by
reading them, but after studying a point should then see what
the decisions have been upon it. (7)

The decision to change the course of his career having been made,
McQueen then had to satisfy the requirements of the examinators of
the Faculty of Advocates. The culminating step in this process was for
the aspirant advocate to publish and sustain a thesis on some topic
from one of the classical law texts. McQueen's choice was a title from
the 11th book of the Pandects. The Pandects are a collection of excerpts
from the works of classical jurists omitted from the main body of law
codified by the Emperor Justinian in the sixth century. The thesis
McQueen prepared was on the somewhat recondite topic of the burial
of the dead and the erection of monuments. His Latin thesis was
published by the Edinburgh printers T & T Ruddiman as *Disputatio
juridica, ad tit. ult. lib. XI Pand. De mortuo inferendo, & sepulchro aedificando*
. . . and McQueen successfully sustained this thesis in public
examination on 11th February 1744. On 14th February he was called
before a full bench of the Court of Session, presided over by Duncan
Forbes (Lord Culloden). The Book of Sederunt of the Lords of Council
and Session has a marginal note for that date: 'Robert McQueen Yngr.
of Braxfield admitted advocate' (8) and it should then go on in the
usual form:

The Lords of Council and Session having considered the
literature and qualifications of . . . and the proofs given by
him of making a publick lesson upon a title of the Civil Law
assigned to him by the Dean of Faculty Together with a report
by the said Dean and Advocate Examinator bearing that after
private and publick examination of the said Mr . . . they

found him qualified to exercise the office of an advocate and having called him in their presence they have admitted and hereby admit . . . to the office of advocate.

Unfortunately the Clerk of Session would seem to have been under some stress of business and simply left a blank space in the Book of Sederunt to allow for the later insertion of the formula and McQueen's name – a practice he was to repeat a week later for the admission of another young advocate.

He was now a few months short of his twenty second birthday and 'qualified to exercise the office of an advocate', to plead a cause before the Supreme Courts of Scotland – if anyone cared to employ him. Many young advocates found to their distress that putting on an advocate's gown did not guarantee a flow of work and a considerable time might be spent pacing up and down Parliament House waiting for work to be offered, although an apprenticeship in a prominent Writer's chambers and a father in legal practice in the country could hardly be anything other than helpful.

A full discussion of the details of McQueen's career at the bar comes in a later chapter – for the present we turn to his family and domestic life and the more personal aspects of his biography.

1744 was not, perhaps, the most propitious time to start a career at the bar – as we have already seen the Edinburgh Courts were to be shut during a large part of 1745 and 1746 due to the Jacobite rising. However, by the age of thirty one McQueen seems to have established himself well enough to be able to marry, in June 1753, Mary Agnew, the daughter of Major Agnew of Bishop Auckland. (9) Mary Agnew was three and a half years younger than McQueen, if as seems most probable, she was the Mary Agnew, daughter of James Agnew, who was baptised at St Martin's in the Fields, London on 28th November 1725. It was undoubtedly what the eighteenth century would have described as a good match. Mary's father, James, was a Major in Kerr's Dragoons and, despite the Bishop Auckland address was the son of Sir James Agnew of Lochnaw, Bt., the 11th Hereditary Sheriff of Galloway. The Agnews were a well-established gentry family from Galloway, although Major Agnew's military duties obviously entailed travel and residence in England. Although Major Agnew was doubtless happy to see his daughter married to a promising young advocate it is equally true that the Crawford gardener's grandson had married into the upper echelons of society. Two of Mary Agnew's brothers became Generals and a third was a Captain in the Royal Navy.

There is evidence of a continuing friendly relationship between Robert McQueen and his Agnew in-laws, which is of some interest in view of the frequent suggestions that McQueen's coarseness made him *persona non grata* in polite society. In 1789 the then head of the Agnew line, Sir Stair Agnew, Bt., Mary's cousin, was concerned about the marriage settlement of his daughter Isabella and approached Braxfield and Braxfield's son in law, William Honyman for advice. Braxfield's reply, written while he was at Stirling on the Autumn Justiciary Circuit, displays obvious affection, warmth and family concern and after making some suggestions as to the settlement concluded:

> Nothing further occurs to me & now permit me to wish you and your daughter much joy and happiness in the intended marriage. She is an amiable young woman & possessed of the sweetest temper and disposition which bids fair for making it a happy marriage. Indeed she is so much possessed of my good opinion that if it should prove otherways (which God forbid) I should pronounce it not the fault of her. But as I have always heard a very good character of Mr Hawthorn so there is no reason to be apprehensive of any such event. Mrs McQueen who is with me here desires to join with me in love & best wishes to you & the bride & family. Dear Sir Your most obdt. humble servant
>
> Robt. McQueen (10)

Robert and Mary McQueen were to have four children. It is a reflection on the somewhat ineffective eighteenth century record keeping that, even in the case of a prominent lawyer like McQueen the birth dates of all four of his children are, at best, only approximately known. The first born, Mary was born before 1760, the second, tactfully christened Robert Dundas after the former Lord Advocate and current Lord President of the Court of Session, was born in either 1760 or 1761, the third Katherine or Catherine, is recorded in the Lanark parish registers as being christened at an unspecified date in 1762. The fourth child, John, was probably born by 1769 as he had married by 1789.

Robert Dundas McQueen followed his father in a legal career, and after completing his professional education in Holland was admitted to the Faculty of Advocates in 1782. In the best eighteenth century style and with disregard for accusations of family influence he was appointed Chief Clerk of Justiciary in May 1795, having before this held other appointments in the courts and having regularly accompanied his father on circuit. Robert Dundas McQueen again demonstrates the upward mobility of the McQueen's – he made an even better marriage than his father. In February 1796 he married Lady Lilias Montgomery, the daughter of the 11th Earl of Eglinton.

The McQueen daughters were described by Alexander Young as "both handsome women, the eldest clever, and the second eminently beautiful". (11) The clever one, Mary, in 1777 married a young advocate newly admitted to the Faculty, William Honyman of Graemsay. Honyman, the son of an Orcadian landowner, would seem to have become a protégé and friend of McQueen's as well as his son-in-law and it seems not improbable that this connection helped win him office as Sheriff Depute of Lanark in 1786 and promotion to the Court of Session bench in 1797, just twenty years after his admission to the Faculty of Advocates, a significant reduction on the average time taken to gain a Judge's gown. Honyman would also gain swift promotion to the Justiciary bench, being one of the two appointees made to fill the gaps caused by his father-in-law's and Lord Swinton's deaths. In 1804 Honyman was created a baronet. The Honymans owned a country house, Smyllum, on the outskirts of Lanark, near to the McQueen home at Braxfield and William Honyman acted for McQueen in a number of personal capacities, for example serving as his proxy at meetings of the Heritors of Lanark Parish.

There are sadly few of Robert McQueen's personal letters which survive. One that does and that very clearly and attractively shows the man behind the Senator of the College of Justice and Commissioner of Justiciary, is addressed to Mary Honyman at her townhouse in Windmill Street, Edinburgh. McQueen is writing from his snow-bound country house at Hardington in Lanarkshire on 15th April 1782.

> My Dear Mary
>
> I was extremely sorry to hear by Baby's letter that you had got a fresh cold. I am afraid that you are in too great a haste to be well, but I was glad to hear that my dear little Peter had got better – tell him that his horse is in great good health. We have had nothing but snow since we came here which is very disagreeable. But I am more concerned on account of Mr Honyman than myself as it will make his Journey very

disagreeable & also greatly retard it so that I am afraid I will
not see him before I set out for Jedburgh which I do tomorrow
& will be in Jedburgh on Thursday morning. I intend to be at
Traquair on Tuesday evening to dine there on Wednesday and
go to Muirhouse in the evening & to Jedburgh on Thursday
morning which is the first day of Circuit being the 18th. Mr
Honyman knows the days of the Circuit. The 1st of the Circuit
at Dumfries is Thursday the 25th of April altho' Mr Honyman
is not in time to go alongst with me from this yet I hope he
will come to me as soon as he can. If he can be at Jedburgh
before I leave it let him come directly there from Edinburgh. If
he cannot be in time to meet me at Jedburgh let him come
directly to Dumfries & in that case his best road is by
Hardington – let him come there the first night & he can
easily go the next day to Dumfries. William who I must take
alongst with me from this will bring back Mr Honyman's
horses. It will be a great disappointment to me if Mr
Honyman does not come. My love to my dear little Peter and
Bob. My best Complts. to your two young Ladys (sic).
Wishing you all happiness I ever am with great sincerity

    My dear Mary

    Your most affectionate father

    Robt McQueen

    (ps) Your mother as well as myself will be much obliged to
you if you could find out a good man servant in place of Mr
Francis (?) & if he can shave & dress ty (sic) wigs it will be
most agreeable. (12)

'Baby' it seems fair to assume was the family name for the younger
daughter Catherine as the Honyman children would surely be too
young to be corresponding with their grandfather at this date. McQueen
is about to set out on the Spring riding of the Southern Circuit to
Jedburgh, Dumfries and Ayr, an unpleasant duty in the unseasonable
snow of mid-April. His partner on this Circuit was the veteran Lord
Kames but Honyman was evidently expected to accompany the Judges
on their journey, though whether as companion, court official, or
advocate is not clear.

    However what is very clear is McQueen's evident affection for
Mary, his grandchildren and his concern for William Honyman's
difficult journey. The McQueen shown in this letter seems something
of a worrier and a fusser rather than the tyrant of the Bench. There are

also indications that McQueen was suffering one of his periodic bouts of the "servant problem" – thus the postscript appeal for Mary to look out for a good man servant able to shave and dress wigs. McQueen evidently felt that his daughter in the thick of things in Edinburgh was more likely to come on such a treasure than he was in the snows of Lanarkshire or riding the Southern Circuit.

Catherine McQueen, the 'baby' of Braxfield's letter, married a Highland chieftain, John MacDonald of Clanranald in March 1784. Catherine, it will be recalled, was described as 'eminently beautiful' and John Mowbray, an Edinburgh Writer to the Signet, in a letter to Alexander Young recalled that he had once travelled the Northern Circuit with Braxfield and Lord Stonefield and:

> . . . had the good fortune of dancing thirteen successive country dances with his fair daughter, then Miss Catherine McQueen, a very beautiful young lady and a first rate dancer. (13)

Unfortunately Mowbray's recollection would seem to be a little at fault, John Campbell, Lord Stonefield, only became a Justiciary Court judge in 1787, by which time Catherine was Mrs MacDonald of Clanranald. It seems possible that Mowbray recollected Campbell being on the Northern Circuit perhaps as an Advocate Depute and from the perspective of 1838, when he wrote his letter to Young, understandably confused the circumstances. However we can perhaps more confidently rely on his very first hand evidence of Catherine's beauty and social talents.

Sadly, the MacDonald marriage was to end in divorce. In 1790 John MacDonald instituted divorce proceedings on the grounds of infidelity against 'Catherine McQueen, second lawful daughter of Robert McQueen of Braxfield, Lord Justice Clerk for Scotland'. (14) Captain William Payne, of the 1st Dragoons, was named as co-respondent. The MacDonalds had had four children, two of whom died in infancy. Catherine did not defend the divorce action, which alleged that she had, in the uncompromising language of the documents in the case:

> . . . at many different times given herself up to Unseemly, Indecent, Obscene, Venereal and Adulterous practices,

fellowship and company with the said Captain William Payne and to having Carnal, Whorish and Adulterous Conversation with him.

These acts had taken place at Ballencrieff, the MacDonalds' country house near Aberlady in East Lothian, in the autumn and winter of 1790 while John MacDonald was absent in the north. Captain Payne, who was stationed a couple of miles away at Haddington, had been a regular visitor to the MacDonalds. Evidence taken from the domestic staff told of Payne and Catherine kissing, but a letter from Catherine to her husband, dated 7th December 1790, confessing to adultery, and which was identified by the family solicitor as being in her hand, put matters beyond doubt:

> . . . I must with pain and contrition acknowledge the justice
> and truth of your suspicion against me of my criminal
> intercourse with Captain Payne. . .

while going on to reassure MacDonald: '. . . I never injured your honour as my husband with any man other than him. . .' and ending with a plea: 'Take care of my poor children for their own sake as they deserve it'. Divorce proceedings started immediately after Catherine's letter and the process was completed in May 1791.

The second McQueen son, John, for a time followed a career in the Army, becoming a Captain in the 13th Foot. John married twice, firstly to an Irishwoman, Anne Macann, by whom he had a son, Robert, and by his second wife, Margaret Wilson, he had four children. A career as a junior officer in the Army was not, in the eighteenth century, in itself a recipe for financial security. Promotion came by purchase of commissions and officers were expected to have private means and not look to live on their salaries. John's father was clearly worried about his younger son's future and took the very eighteenth century course of seeking to obtain an official post for him. Inevitably the Dundas connection came to the fore and in December 1798, near the end of his life, the elderly and ill Braxfield wrote to Henry Dundas. Dundas at this time was Treasurer of the Navy, Secretary of State for War and President of the Board of Control for India – but more relevantly to Braxfield's concerns was still the Government's Scottish manager and controller of Scottish patronage. The Duke of Portland the letter refers to was the Home Secretary of the day – he had in fact taken over the post from Henry Dundas in 1794.

> My dear Sir,
>   Tho' I have not the least doubt that you will in due time attend to the subject of my application to the Duke of Portland on behalf of my son John, and to which his Grace returned me the very polite answer I put into your hands, at your desire, in order to enable you to follow out what you was so good as to say seemed to be most reasonable and proper to be done; yet I hope you will forgive my anxiety in reminding you of it.
>
>   My age and state of health for sometime, have naturally increased my desire to see my second son John (at present unprovided, and having a large family) secured in something that he can rely upon, and as you thought that there lay no objection to his being appointed to the survivancy of Sir Robert Anstruther's Commission of Clerk to the Bills, it will be a most essential favour to me if you can accomplish it. – Tho' I am indebted to his Majesty and to the Duke of Portland for the handsome manner he expressed himself on the subject to me, yet it is upon your friendship and knowledge of me that I rely; and it will be a lasting proof of it to me, if I have the satisfaction of seeing my Son secured in the Reversion of that office – I have the honor to be
>
> My dear Sir
> Your mo. obed. & faithful
> humble servt.
> Robt. McQueen
> Edinr. 9th Dec. 1798 (15)

The letter is signed Robt. McQueen, in a somewhat shaky hand, but was written by another hand. The post of Clerk to the Bills, the reversion of which he sought for John on the death or resignation of the present incumbent, was a senior post in the administration of the Court of Session and would have provided a satisfactorily comfortable niche for John McQueen. McQueen's request was not acted upon. In May 1799 as McQueen lay gravely ill Robert Dundas, the Lord Advocate, wrote to his uncle, Henry Dundas, saying that he proposed to call on the Lord Justice-Clerk:

I shall in consequence of a note from him, see him Saturday morning. When I called last week, he was so unwell that Mrs Macqueen dissuaded me from going up to him. He will be expecting an answer about the Proposal about the Clerk of the Bills for Jack. (16)

John, or Jack as he would seem to have been known socially, was to be disappointed. When Sir Robert Anstruther gave up the post of Clerk it went, in 1806, to his son Robert. Leaving aside any consideration of John McQueen's fitness for the post, it is possible to feel that the Lord Justice-Clerk's influence and political clout was waning with his life. It had been five months since he had written seeking the promise of the reversion of the post on Anstruther's death and no answer had been given. As an experienced player of the political game McQueen would have known that his influence would cease with his death and that if anything was to be done for the unprovided-for Jack then it had to be done while he was still living.

In 1791 Robert McQueen suffered the loss of his wife of thirty eight years, Mary, who died on 6th October at their country home, Hardington in the south of Lanarkshire. The *Scots Magazine* was later to write:

Lord Justice Clerk was an affectionate husband, and a tender parent; he had a warmness of temper and benevolence of heart, which made him highly susceptible of domestic attachment. As a companion and a friend he was peculiarly beloved by such as stood in those relations to him. (17)

This close to contemporary opinion is worth bearing in mind when some of the more colourful Braxfield stories are told or some of the more patronising assumptions are made. For example, W Forbes Gray observes:

What kind of a domestic life Braxfield led it is impossible to say, but from what is known of his public character and habits, it is permissible to assume that the family circle would not be the brighter for his presence. (18)

Lack of evidence did not appear to restrict Gray's ability to sneer or speculate, even though one of Gray's other writings on Braxfield, an article in the *Scotsman* of 2nd April 1921, provides some useful insight into Braxfield's social milieu and social acceptability. When his Edinburgh home in George Square was being renovated in the early part of the twentieth century a number of visiting cards and dinner invitations from the Braxfield era were found, including calling cards from Lady Duncan, the wife of Admiral Duncan, (later to win fame as the victor of the Battle of Camperdown), invitations to dinner with the Lord Advocate and so forth. These confirm, if confirmation is required, that McQueen was, despite suggestions of his grossness of behaviour and boorishness, perfectly acceptable in polite society.

Gray manages, on the basis of an invitation card, which from internal evidence must date from 1788, addressed to Captain & Mrs McQueen, to theorise that Braxfield had held the rank of Captain in a volunteer unit – ignoring both the existence of McQueen's soldier son, Captain John McQueen, and the extreme improbability of sending a formal dinner invitation to the Lord Justice-Clerk and not using either the title of his appointment or his judicial title. Gray in fact notes that another invitation from the same source, Sir James Colquhoun, one of the Principal Clerks of Session, was addressed to the Lord Justice-Clerk, which makes his overly-imaginative leap to a military career for Robert McQueen all the more peculiar.

After Mary's death in 1791, McQueen waited for fifteen months, and re-married. His second bride was Elizabeth Ord, the daughter of the late Chief Baron Ord, who had been the head of the Scottish Exchequer Court. With the pardonable urgency of a man who has passed his seventieth birthday McQueen is supposed to have proposed to Miss Ord in his own characteristic fashion:

> Lizzy, I am looking out for a wife, and I thought you just the person that would suit me. Let me have your answer, off or on, the morn, and nae mair aboot it. (19)

Contemporary sources speak of Lord Braxfield as being a great friend to dispatch in legal affairs and it would seem that he put the same admirable principle to work in his personal relationships. Miss Ord's acceptance of this less than romantic proposal might have been influenced by the fact that she was hardly in the first bloom of youth herself. Elizabeth Ord may, however, have proved to be a match for him. One of Lord Cockburn's stories about Lord Braxfield has the butler coming to him and resigning his post. When asked why he wished to quit, the butler said that he could no longer stand Mrs McQueen's continual scolding. The judge responded:

> Lord! ye've little to complain o'; ye may be thankfu' ye're no married to her. (20)

For all his possible problems with his second wife McQueen delighted in good company, especially the company of women, in good drink, in music and song. According to James Ramsay of Ochtertyre, a contemporary with some personal knowledge of the man, one of his favourite remarks was "what a glorious thing it is to speak nonsense" a free translation of Horace's "*Dulce est desipere in loco.*" (21) Ramsay also observes that:

> A man of his vigorous comprehensive mind, warm affections, and communicative disposition, could not fail to be a pleasing and interesting companion when the conversation took a proper turn. If his wit and humour would have revolted Lord Chesterfield as coarse and at times unseemly for his station, yet in his highest glee he was always pleasant and good-natured, most desirous to oblige and inform. As a proof of his social powers there was a number of people warmly attached to his person, who praised the qualities of his heart no less than his head.

McQueen's 'highest glee' could, at times, be overwhelming. Even the usually lively and convivial James Boswell tells how, in February 1776 he had spent the evening at the home of a fellow advocate, David Moncrieffe:

> I went at night to Moncrieffe's, it being the last meeting of his club for the session. Played at cards ill, and lost. Was overpowered at supper with Macqueen's noise. (22)

Alexander Young, from the basis of a long and close acquaintance with McQueen, gives another sidelight on an aspect of his character:

> Lord Braxfield was particularly fond of, and took great

delight in, old Scotch Music, both words and song and for
providing some amusement to his Lordship in that line it was
the practice, both of his son in law, Sir William Honyman, and
myself, when he dined with us, to invite persons eminent for
their skill and execution of Scotch Music, from whose
performances Lord Braxfield derived great pleasure. (23)

Young relates how, although McQueen appreciated the singing of
plaintive songs such as *Lochaber no more*, his real delight was in the
lighter works of the Scottish folk tradition:

But Lord Braxfield was still more partial to another eminent
professor of Scottish Music, Mr James Balfour, Accountant in
Edinburgh, whose songs of "Muirland Willie", "Fye, let us a'
to the Wedding" and "My Joe Janet" so much pleased Lord
Braxfield, that he never was satisfied till he had hear them
sung twice or thrice over.

That this keen musical interest was not just confined to the family and
domestic circle is confirmed by McQueen's membership, from 1775, of
the very fashionable Edinburgh Musical Society, which met in St
Cecilia's Hall in the Cowgate.

Even the sympathetic Young can make out no great case for
McQueen as an enthusiast for English literature:

In general literature it appeared to me that he was somewhat
deficient and I remember well that Shackleton's
Characteristics, the works of Sir William Temple and some of
Swift's Prose Works were the only English Authors which he
said he had read out and out and dipped into other than once.

However he does assert that McQueen was:

. . . a very good scholar and particularly conversant with the Latin
Classics, of which, as I was then pretty much master of the Latin
Language myself, I thought I could form a correct judgement.

Which is all more than just a little different from Cockburn's dismissive
summation of him as:

Illiterate and without any taste for refined enjoyment,
strength of understanding, which gave him power without
cultivation, only encouraged him to a more contemptuous
disdain of all natures less coarse than his own. (24)

One of McQueen's great recreational pastimes was whist. Young tells
of his enthusiasm for the game:

He was passionately fond of Whist, at which he generally
amused himself at his leisure hours on the Circuit in so much
that he had a small table in his Travelling Coach, with a
drawer containing two or three packs of cards, and as the
Judges and their retinue did not travel very fast, Lord
Braxfield in a long stage usually got over several rubbers with
his Son Dundas, and the Deputy Advocate, one or other of
them playing the dead man. On one occasion when I was the
substitute of Mr George Muir, Principal Clerk of Justiciary, I
was pressed into this service as a fourth hand, but I was then
so bad a player, that Lord Braxfield lost all patience with me,
and on our arrival at Langholm from Annan, I was
transferred to the Carriage of Lord Hailes . . . (25)

Other accounts confirm McQueen's lack of patience with poor card
players – one lady, partnering him, who played the wrong card was
sworn at by McQueen, who on being remonstrated with for his
ungentlemanly conduct explained that he thought it was his wife he
had been speaking to. The tensions of domestic whist or bridge are not
unknown even in our own day.

In the 1830s Charles Hope, Lord Granton, the then Lord President
of the Court of Session, was angered by the "checkmate" story, referred
to in Chapter 1, and the currency which was given to it by its inclusion
in Lockhart's *Life of Sir Walter Scott* and took steps to confirm its error:

. . . that story told of him by Lockhart I knew instantly to be
an infamous falsehood – for, with you, I am quite certain that
he never played at chess in his life. It was much too tame a
game for him. A man who loses at chess has nothing to blame
but his own bad play – whereas at whist honest Braxfield
used heartily to curse the cards & his partner & even his
adversaries.
But to make quite sure of the falsehood of the Chess Story I

ordered a search to be made in books of the Circuit Courts, &
I found that Braxfield never tried any case of forgery when at
Ayr or Dumfries – and that the only man he ever tried and
condemned for forgery was at Stirling & instead of being any
acquaintance of his, he was a miserable shopkeeper in the
Town of Falkirk. Lockhart has not done credit to himself or to
Sir Walter by his life of him – for there are many stories in it
equally false, tho' not as malignant.

I have many many queer anecdotes of Braxfield, which
come across my memory at times, which, if I could recollect
them all at once, would make a splendid *Ana*. (26)

It is worth observing that Hope, although over forty years younger
than McQueen, was admitted to the Faculty of Advocates in 1784 and
as an Advocate Depute from 1786 would have ample first hand
knowledge of the Lord Justice-Clerk's manners and ways. His more
sympathetic approach to McQueen's character contrasts with the still-
younger Cockburn's and deserves consideration for its useful
foundation in personal experience and the all-important daily contact
in the courts.

Another lawyer, James Boswell, records in his diary McQueen's
less than detached approach to the game of whist:

Dined and drank tea at Mr David Erskine's with Lord Braxfield,
the Solicitor, Harry Erskine, Maclaurin, and several more. . .
I sat by and saw whist played and I betted against the Solicitor.
Lord Braxfield, exultingly pleased that the Solicitor and
Maclaurin, against whom he played, were losing. . . (27)

Naturally enough card games tended to have their alcoholic
accompaniments and McQueen was, like a great many of his
contemporaries, a famous drinker. His drinking habits however never
seem to have interfered with his duties. According to an Irish friend of
McQueen's, a Mr Patrick of Dublin, whom Alexander Young met while
on holiday, McQueen was both a heavy drinker and good judge of
wine, two qualities which were and are not always found in
combination. He could certainly be irritated when the supply did not
live up to his expectations. The story is told that on one of his Circuit

journeys he was invited to dinner with Lord Douglas at Bothwell and found to his displeasure that short measure was the order of the day in that only port was being served. He enquired if: '. . . there was nae claret i' the castle.' His host replied that there was, but that his butler had advised him that it was not good. McQueen replied shortly, 'Let's pree't' – that is test it. A bottle was produced and found to be excellent as expected – and duly enjoyed by all except the parsimonious host.

Braxfield had a strong head – and Alexander Young, while confessing to a hangover himself, claims that he only saw Braxfield the one time the worse for drink:

> The only time I ever saw Lord Braxfield take more wine than was suitable for a Judge was in the House of the Celebrated John Bushby at Tinwald Downs during the time of the Assize at Dumfries at that period when the Judges remained eight days in each of the Circuit Towns.
>
> On this occasion the two Judges Hailes and Braxfield with the King's Advocate Mr Colquhoun of Killermount and many others were invited to dine at Tinwald Downs on the last Saturday of the Circuit and the invitation was generally accepted but declined by Lord Hailes. A very jovial meeting took place, where amongst other *bons vivants* there was present Mr John MacMurdo, factor for the Duke of Queensberry (Old Q) and a great companion and frequent Partner of Lord Braxfield in the Game of Whist. Much good wine was consumed, and great good humour prevailed with the company in general, when Lord Braxfield and Mr MacMurdo having frequently saluted each other his Lordship at last exclaimed "MacMurdo Providence surely made a mistake, when it did not make you Duke."
>
> At dinner in the "King's Arms" next day, Lord Hailes said "I am told you had all a shameful debauch at Bushby's yesterday" to which Lord Braxfield replied "In truth My Lord we did harm to nane but ourselves". (28)

A useful response which many might wish to remember and use on the morning after the night before.

Colquhoun and Young had failed to turn up for morning worship and the censorious Lord Hailes had sent to enquire the reason for their absence and both had reported that they had been unable to leave their beds. Young reports that Braxfield's comment, which nicely combines cynicism with a belief in the value of religious observance, was:

> . . . at all rates I should have come to the Kirk for though many a scoundrel came there regularly few honest men staid away.

McQueen's appetite for drink was far from unique. It was an age of heavy drinking when, as we have seen, the very judges on the bench did not think shame to sustain their judicial deliberations with deep draughts of port wine and when a meal with only one wine to it was seen as short measure. One of McQueen's junior colleagues on the Court of Session bench, George Fergusson, Lord Hermand, took a commitment to drink far beyond even McQueen's enthusiastic appetite. He was trying a case of homicide and burst out in amazement:

> We are told that there was no malice, and that the prisoner must have been in liquor. In liquor! Why he was drunk! And yet he murdered the very man who had been drinking with him! . . . Good God, my Laards, if he will do this when he is drunk, what will he not do when he's sober? (29)

While Lord Hermand was perhaps exceptional in his passion for drink and Cockburn notes that: 'Common-place topers think drinking a pleasure, but with Hermand it was a virtue', (30) it is nonetheless true that heavy drinking was the rule of the age rather than the exception.

McQueen's drinking and coarseness of language have been seen as incompatible with the possession of a sincerely held religious belief. James Ramsay, somewhat judgmentally, noted that McQueen was, in his own judgement a sincere Christian, being thoroughly persuaded of the truths of that religion:

> . . . though it did not always produce suitable fruits or make him set a watch on his lips; and therefore, when he transgressed its precepts, he sinned against conviction. (31)

The most famously blasphemous comment associated with McQueen ('muckle he made o' that, he was hanget') has already been discussed and there seems good reason to believe, with Roughead, that it was an invention – even if its currency and widespread acceptance might indeed suggest that it was very much in the style of Braxfield.

It would be good to have more reliable evidence about McQueen's character and what Ramsay calls the qualities of his head and his heart, so comprehensively denigrated by Cockburn and those who have over-readily followed his line. However what contemporary evidence there is available deserves to be examined and considered carefully. For example a letter he wrote in September 1795 to a friend, Charles Gordon of Braid in Edinburgh, who had evidently suffered a bereavement, suggests both a warmly sympathetic response to loss and a practical desire to help, by offering to have the Gordons visit him at Braxfield. It is also written by one who, at the most grudging estimate, must be on this evidence considered both familiar with the conventions of religion and comfortable with these conventions:

> My Dear Sir
>
> I returned from my Circuit yesternight when I found your letter here. I can with truth say that none can wish you & your family better than I do & therefore I would be unfeeling indeed if I did not participate of your distress. It is a severe stroke indeed & I pity you & Mrs Gordon much. The true philosophy is a perfect resignation to the Will of heaven. We receive good at the hands of God & shall we not receive evil also. However I know it is much easier to read that than to practise but I must beg of you not to indulge grief & melancholy too much. Consider your life is valuable to many especially to your own family endeavour therefore to amuse yourself & what occurs to me as the most natural & easy is a jaunt to you & Mrs Gordon. I know that change of place etc has a good effect in such circumstances and if you can spare me few days here I shall endeavour to make everything as comfortable to you as in my power. May God Almighty grant you and Mrs Gordon a proper degree of Christian fortitude under so severe a dispensation of his providence. My best wishes attend you & her & all the family & I am with much regard
>
> My Dear Sir
> Your most faithfull humble servant
> Robert McQueen Braxfield 15th September 1795. (32)

As against this image of the concerned and kindly McQueen praying for the blessings of Christian fortitude to be given to Gordon must be placed James Ramsay's strictures on his foul language and taste for profanity:

> It was mortifying to hear an aged judge, revered for talents and usefulness, swearing without provocation. . . What was no less indecent, he took pleasure in relating obscene or profane stories in a way that scandalised persons the least strict in their notions or practice. (33)

Ramsay after noting his taste for cards and drink goes on to say:

> Yet of wine no man stood less in need; for so exuberant were his spirits, that even in his sober hours he might be said to be in a state little short of inebriety.

He also makes a further interesting point:

> Yet, when in company with persons of a sedate serious turn, he could, when very merry, refrain from these topics which he knew were offensive to their ears.

This last observation does tend to suggest that McQueen's exuberance, his swearing and his pleasure in scandalising those that his younger contemporary Robert Burns characterised as the 'unco guid', might have been something of a deliberate performance. If McQueen could, on what he saw as suitable occasions and with suitable company, refrain from topics 'offensive to their ears', even when merry, then he was not lacking in some capacity for discrimination or in an awareness of the likely sensitivities of his audience. That he chose not to exercise such discrimination on all occasions may by some be considered to be a matter for regret. It may equally well indicate an independent minded spirit unwilling to be trammelled by the narrowing conventions of a changing age. Nor was he alone in that age in his taste for hard drinking, bawdry, and rough humour. While the elderly Lord Justice-Clerk was, perhaps, scandalising the polite drawing rooms of George Square and the refined *salons* of Queen Street, Robert Burns and the lawyers and *literati* of the Crochallan Fencibles were gathering in Dawney Douglas's howff in the Royal Mile, drinking their fill and collecting the bawdy verse and song that was to be published as *The Merry Muses of Caledonia*.

Quite how scandalised the drawing rooms and *salons* were is, of course, difficult to say. The 'unco guid' – and here we must undoubtedly include the, then very young, but irredeemably priggish and Whiggish Henry Cockburn – doubtless felt that they had to be scandalised. Some – such as James Ramsay – could take a more balanced view. His balanced judgement on McQueen was that: '. . . his faults and foibles bore some proportion to his bright and useful endowments.' (34) Others, such as the friendly Alexander Young, clearly had some difficulty recognising the man they knew in much of the later portraiture:

> I humbly think that therefore unless I was totally unqualified
> to form a correct judgement of character, or had a very undue
> partiality and affection for him I must have known whether
> or not he merited that odium and reproach which of late
> years has been cast on his conduct as a Gentleman and his
> proceedings as a Judge. (35)

It is also, of course, possible to believe that many people in Edinburgh society relished the coarse old Judge and passed on the latest Braxfieldisms, perhaps improving them, or even inventing them, as they went the rounds. It is equally possible to believe that the coarse old Judge was very well aware of the impact of his speech and behaviour and to some extent was playing to the gallery and that much of his coarseness and broad Scots was, in part, a stand for an older world against the mim-moued, perjink, Anglicising trends of the Select Society and their followers.

It is also clear from the letters quoted in this chapter that if McQueen spoke broad Scots he wrote a pretty standard English – the only very obvious exception being the use of 'alongst' in his letter to Mary Honyman. However he would hardly be the first Scot to be bi-lingual – Burns's use of Scots and English in his poetry demonstrates the tendency perfectly.

McQueen's childhood upbringing at Braxfield, by the picturesque Falls of Clyde near Lanark, had left him with an evident affection for the family property. In the 1770s, while his father still lived and after he had bought property at Hardington, Robert McQueen was formally referred to in documents as "Robert McQueen of Hardington". However on his father's death he assumed the territorial designation "of Braxfield" and, of course, five years later, in 1776, he would adopt Braxfield for his judicial title. John Ramsay of Ochtertyre wrote of the estate of Braxfield that it was: 'a property more romantically situated than considerable' (36) and of Robert McQueen that:

> In his prime and decline he spent every hour he could command at his country seat, which he loved the more that he had gathered birds' nests there in his boyish years, and made great addition to and decorations upon it. He took much delight in farming upon a great scale, without embarrassing his affairs, like many of his contemporaries. (37)

McQueen was in fact a substantial landowner and also an improving laird in the best eighteenth century tradition. Braxfield, although it had come to him from his father and had its sentimental attractions, was not the most significant part of the large sweep of property McQueen owned in Lanarkshire and Peeblesshire. His main country residence was the estate of Hardington in the south Lanarkshire parish of Wiston and Roberton, purchased in 1769, when James McQueen, writer in Edinburgh (possibly his younger brother), acted as procurator and attorney for Robert in the formalities of buying the estate. (38) In the 1771 Valuation Roll for the County of Lanark Hardington was assessed at an annual valuation of £574.0.0 – the patrimonial inheritance of Mains of Braxfield and Delves in Lanark Parish in contrast was assessed at a mere £58.12.4. The parish minister wrote in the 1790s:

> The present Lord Justice Clerk is the only considerable heritor. He has a seat in the parish, round which his Lordship has made great improvements in farming, planting, and inclosing. There are no inclosures or growing timber worth mentioning in the rest of the parish. (39)

Wiston was a fairly remote, and it would seem, somewhat backward parish. Even as late as the writing of the Old Statistical Account the minister could report that:

> . . . about the village of Wistoun, the tenants of the croft lands

have not their possessions separately divided, but intermingled with one another is small spots here and there, or run-rig.

Ten miles away to the north east, across the County boundary in Peeblesshire, lay the village and parish of Broughton, of which McQueen became the sole proprietor. The estate of Broughton had long been owned by the Murray family, the last Murray proprietor being Sir John Murray, the Secretary to Prince Charles Edward Stuart during the '45 and who became notorious for saving his skin by turning King's Evidence after the failure of the rising. After the Murrays lost their fortune the estate was owned by James Dickson and was then exposed for public sale in August 1774. The Scottish Record Office, has, in the Register of Deeds the *Articles and Conditions of Roup of Lands of Broughton* which narrates the process by which McQueen purchased the property. (40) The asking, or upset, price was set at £14,000 and the sale started with the turning of an hour glass. Robert McQueen bid £14,000, but was outbid by one John Mossman who bid £14,100. McQueen responded with a bid of £14,200 and: 'being the last and highest bidder at the outrunning of the sand glass' acquired most of the 4660 acres of the parish of Broughton. It is a reflection on McQueen's success at the Bar that he was able to purchase Broughton – the sum paid would require to be multiplied by perhaps 100 to arrive at a late twentieth century equivalent. In 1779 his status as a major landowner, a tenant in chief of the Crown, was recognised by the grant of a charter under the Great Seal of Scotland for the lands of Broughton. His father had, as we have seen, received a similar Charter for Braxfield in 1720. In 1783 McQueen completed his ownership of the parish by the purchase of the small property of Burnetland.

There are other scattered and tantalising pieces of evidence of McQueen's financial activities and growing prosperity. In December 1766 he was able to lend the sum of £1000 to David Thompson and Patrick Heron. There was a problem about the repayment of this debt and McQueen was obliged to raise letters of horning, at that time the way of enforcing payment of debt. However by August 1774 the debt had been paid, and David Rae, advocate, (the future Lord Eskgrove) acting as McQueen's procurator was able to have recorded the discharge and exoneration of Thompson and Heron. (41)

Apart from his inheritance from John McQueen of the house and lands of Braxfield and some other properties around Lanark, McQueen built up an extensive estate, purchasing land in Lanark from the Town Council whenever opportunity presented itself. In November 1788 McQueen carried out the normal procedure of ensuring that the family property would be kept intact after his death by entailing the land, that is placing it in permanent trusteeship with liferent possession to the eldest male heir, whom failing the second son, daughters and so forth. As the opening sentence of the Deed of Taillie put it:

> I Robert McQueen of Braxfield, Esquire, one of the Senators of the College of Justice, for the better preserving and continuing the succession of the land and estate aftermentioned in my name and family do therefore hereby give grant and dispone heritably and irredeemably to myself in liferent and to Robert Dundas McQueen my eldest son and the heirs whatsoever of his body in feu whom failing to my other heirs of Taillie and provision aftermentioned . . . (42)

This lengthy document lists twenty-eight separate properties or parcels of land in Broughton, Peeblesshire; and in the Carluke, Carnwath, Roberton, and Lanark parishes of Lanarkshire. These ranged from the simply designated, though extensive and high-status, Barony of Broughton to more curiously named properties whose names go back far into the complex feudal past of Scottish landholding – 'the nine merkland of Fallside' or 'half the twenty shilling land of Auchengray'. Some properties were of even less size and significance such as 'The acre in the Burgh of Lanark formerly belonging to Alex. Lockhart'. His ownership of property around Lanark brought him into contact with David Dale, the founder of the New Lanark cotton mills and the Register of Sasines for Lanarkshire show McQueen feuing parts of the lands of Braxfield and Bankhead to Dale.

One of the specific conditions laid down in the deed of entail was an obligation on the heirs of taillie to:

> . . . use bear and constantly retain in all time after their succession the surname designation and coat-armorial of McQueen of Braxfield. . .

and a history of Peeblesshire depicts the coat of arms of McQueen of Braxfield and Broughton. The arms show three wolves heads, couped (that is decapitated), sable (that is black). However it is not clear how authoritative this is. The Highland chiefly family of McQueen of Corrybrough, from whom the Lanarkshire McQueen's are held to descend, have a similar device of three wolves on the first and fourth quarters of their coat of arms as reproduced in *Burke's Landed Gentry*. However no arms have been matriculated for McQueen of Corrybrough and no grant of arms for McQueen of Braxfield is on record at the Court of the Lord Lyon King of Arms in Edinburgh, or at the College of Heralds in London or, indeed, with the Irish heraldic authority, Ulster King of Arms. Whether McQueen failed to register arms that he had designed, or never got round to designing arms is, sadly, unclear.

With or without the benefit of a properly matriculated coat of arms the estate of McQueen of Braxfield and Broughton was a substantial one and of course carried with it a variety of local responsibilities. As a major landowner he was a heritor and thus, with his fellow landowners, had responsibility for the provision and maintenance of the parish's ecclesiastical buildings. This covered not only the Church itself, but the minister's manse, the school and the schoolmaster's house. In Lanark he occupied as a heritor a pew with ten sittings in the Parish Church, and a similar provision could be expected for the owner of Hardington at the Kirk in Wiston and Roberton. In Edinburgh he attended the Tron Kirk in the High Street.

In Broughton the proprietor's house, Broughton House, had been destroyed by fire in 1775 and there is little evidence of McQueen spending much time in that area – while there are few enough extant McQueen letters those few that have been traced are written from Hardington or Braxfield. Broughton was perhaps more of an investment than a residence. However one document relating to the Broughton estate, quoted in a local history, is an offer to lease one of the properties on the estate and is written from Rachan, a house in the area, which McQueen presumably used as his base when he needed to visit his Peeblesshire properties. For an eminent lawyer the letter has a certain simplicity and attractive informality. It is addressed to one James Wilson and opens: 'James, I hereby offer to sett to you . . .' (43)

Not included in the entailed estate was McQueen's Edinburgh home, presumably because this was intended as his widow's jointure. In the earlier years of his Edinburgh professional career McQueen had lived in a house in Covenant Close in the High Street of Edinburgh, conveniently situated just a few moments walk away from Parliament

House. However, as we have seen, in 1770 he, like Henry Dundas and Walter Scott Senr., took a feu in the new and extremely fashionable development of George Square. By 1773 building works were completed and the Edinburgh Directory of that year has him listed at his new home, 13 George Square. The house no longer stands, having been demolished to make way for one of the singularly graceless modern structures that Edinburgh University has intruded into what was a fine and harmonious group of Georgian buildings.

It was in his George Square home on 30th May 1799 that Robert McQueen died after a lengthy illness. The *Glasgow Courier* of 1st June, carried in its Edinburgh news column a brief obituary:

> Yesterday died here, the Right Honourable Robert McQueen
> of Braxfield, Lord Justice-Clerk, and one of the Senators of the
> College of Justice. His Lordship has for many years filled
> these important posts with great ability and integrity.

The *Scots Magazine* produced a brief obituary in its July issue. This noted, of his professional career at the Bar, that he had enjoyed

> . . . the first distinction as an advocate and . . . greater
> emoluments from his profession than any Scotch Counsel had
> before received. (44)

James Ramsay rounds off his portrayal of him in *Scotland and Scotsmen in the Eighteenth Century* with a note of his death. Unfortunately Ramsay did not exactly give a very clear picture or a precise medical definition of the cause of death when he wrote:

> For more than a year before his death his Lordship was not
> able to attend Parliament House, owing to a complication of
> diseases, from which he suffered very severely. (45)

The fuller biographical notice in the 1801 *Scots Magazine* is no more specific about the fatal illness:

> His constitution was good, and he enjoyed a great share of
> health till a year or so before his death. He was all his life
> accustomed to rise at an early hour, he was regular in

attendance on business as a Judge, even in winter he was in
use to be upon the bench at 9 o'clock in the morning. His
complaints encreased much during the summer and autumn
1798. He continued in town and attended the bench during
that session but in spring became worse, till a period was put
to his life upon the 30th day of May 1799, in the 78th year of
his life. In his death his country sustained the loss of an
intelligent, able, and candid judge. (46)

Of his judicial career it further commented:

His inflexible integrity and unparalleled candour gave weight
to his opinions, which, upon, abstract and difficult points of
law, were most luminous and convincing – while his
unaffected manner of expression was most happy and
energetic. His Lordship held the important office of Justice
Clerk of Scotland during the most interesting and critical
period which this country ever saw. A well tempered
integrity of conduct, and a wise and faithful application of the
law, will immortalize him in the annals of his country.

Some information on the later stages of McQueen's illness comes from
Henry Dundas. Writing, in a rather hasty looking scrawl, from his
London home at Wimbledon to the Duke of Portland on 18th May 1799
he says:

... By a letter I saw yesterday the Justice Clerk cannot hold
out long. A Fistula, a Rupture and a violent ?purgery are too
much for 77. (47)

McQueen was buried on 5th June 1799 in the family burying place, the
old kirkyard of St Kentigern's in Lanark. For some unaccountable
reason the most famous of the Braxfield McQueens has no monument
or headstone bearing his name, although a number of later members
of the family are thus recorded.

He was survived by his second wife, Elizabeth, who died in
November 1820. Robert Dundas McQueen inherited the entailed estates
but, dying childless in August 1816, was succeeded by his brother,
Captain John McQueen. John was, in turn, succeeded by his son Robert,

who had also followed in the family legal tradition and had been admitted to the Faculty of Advocates in 1810. On Robert's death in 1867 the descent passed through a collateral line and the last of the McQueen's of Braxfield, J Rainier McQueen, died in 1913. After the First World War the properties were sold and in 1921 the estate agents Knight, Frank & Rutley advertised for sale the 1218 acres of the Hardington Estate – comprising the mansion house, four farms & shooting and fishing rights, and in October of that year the *Glasgow Herald* noted the sale of the greater part of the estate.

In 1922, the bi-centenary year of Robert McQueen, Lord Braxfield's, birth the legal historian William Roughead recorded a sentimental journey he had made to Lanark:

> The house of Braxfield stands upon the pleasant slopes of a green and watered valley, shaded by immemorial trees and girt about by undulating pastures, while ever on the ear falls the murmurous song of Clyde. The mansion, four square, with a courtyard in the centre – the back said to be older than the front – is now unoccupied and fast tending to decay. With its many chambers, curious stairways, and stone-vaulted passages, it would be in the past a very paradise of childhood. (48)

William Honyman

*William Honyman was admitted to the Faculty of Advocates in 1777
and married Lord Braxfield's daughter Mary McQueen later that year.
After serving as Sheriff Depute of Lanark he was appointed to
the Court of Session Bench in 1797 as Lord Armadale.
He was created a Baronet in 1804.*

CHAPTER 5

McQueen the Lawyer
1744–1776

". . . consulted on all knotty points . . ."

When the twenty-one year old Robert McQueen appeared before James Graham of Airth, the Dean of the Faculty of Advocates, and successfully sustained his thesis in February 1744 his career as an advocate was launched. However there was no guarantee that a young advocate would be able to succeed in the competitive world of the Scottish Bar. The list of advocates admitted in 1744 was a talented one. It included, for example, another future judge, Frances Garden (Lord Gardenstone) and each year saw between six and a dozen young hopefuls enter the profession. While McQueen was to have a spectacularly successful career, eventually earning more from the exercise of his profession than any other advocate of his day, his success was not to be immediate. Indeed according to an obituary notice:

> After his admission to the bar Mr McQueen did not soon find opportunity of displaying those talents which he so eminently possessed. (1)

However at the first opportunity after his admission the Faculty of Advocates displayed a certain measure of confidence in the young McQueen. Each January at their Anniversary Meeting the members of the Faculty made appointments of office-bearers for the ensuing year.

At the Anniversary Meeting held in Edinburgh on 8th January 1745 McQueen was appointed as one of the fifteen "publick Examinators" appointed by a ballot of the members of the Faculty to conduct the entrance examinations of aspiring advocates. The panel of examinators was a cross section of the Faculty, with newly admitted advocates like McQueen and Garden and more senior members, lawyers of twenty and thirty years standing like Henry Home, Peter Wedderburn and John MacLeod – men who had been admitted to the Faculty before McQueen's birth.

One of McQueen's undoubted advantages in making his way at the Bar was a family connection with the law – not that he was unique in this, the legal world being, as we have seen, a highly dynastic one. However McQueen was soon able to take effective advantage of his father's valuable Lanarkshire connections. On 1st March 1745 the Lanark Sheriff Court Act Book records:

> At Lanark the first day of March 1745 compears Mr Robert McQueen, younger of Braxfield, who produces a commission granted by Mr George Sinclair, Advocate, Sheriff-Depute of Lanarkshire appointing him to be joint sheriff substitute along with John McQueen of Braxfield his father . . . (2)

In March 1745 the ancient system of heritable jurisdiction still prevailed and the vast majority of the Sheriffdoms of Scotland were the property of, and in the hereditary possession of, a great landowning family. In the case of Lanarkshire the Ducal house of Hamilton had held the office, although it had passed to the Earl of Selkirk in 1716. On the Earl's death in 1739, a commission under the Great Seal was drawn naming the Earl of Hyndford as Sheriff Principal.

Fortunately perhaps for the administration of justice, the noblemen who possessed these jurisdictions were not required to sit in judgement on the people of Lanarkshire. The custom had been, since the Middle Ages, for the hereditary Sheriff to appoint a legally qualified Depute to carry out the judicial functions of the post, and it was this function that the advocate George Sinclair fulfilled. However, the Sheriffdom of Lanark being a very large one, with courts sitting in Glasgow and Hamilton as well as in the burgh of Lanark, a single Sheriff was unable to overtake all the work and John McQueen of Braxfield as Sheriff Substitute was the regular judge in the Sheriff court in Lanark, which covered the Upper Ward of the County. The appointment of a Sheriff Substitute was a matter which was at the discretion of the Sheriff Depute and the Substitute's salary was paid by the Sheriff Depute. The court sat at least once a week with either John McQueen or another lawyer, John Orr, writer in Lanark, on the bench. John Orr's commission, dating from July 1744, however specified that he would only act as Sheriff Substitute in the absence of John McQueen.

Robert McQueen's commission was more much generously drawn; he and his father were to be joint and equally empowered Sheriffs Substitute, who would perform all the functions of the post and hold office during the pleasure of George Sinclair. Following the registration of his commission Robert McQueen presided at the normal sitting of the court on 1st March. On 19th March he swore the varied oaths of allegiance, abjuration, assurance and supremacy required of all office holders in eighteenth century Britain.

In the first year of his service as a Sheriff there were fifty sittings of the court. Of these his father presided at thirty two diets, Robert at seventeen and with two McQueens now available for service John Orr was called to preside at only one sitting.

This post as joint Sheriff Substitute was a useful appointment for a young advocate without, as yet, a busy Edinburgh practice. Useful in assuring him of a little income in those first difficult months at the bar, and useful in the experience it gave him of the practical administration of the law.

It is noticeable that a few years later, while McQueen would still do a number of sittings at Lanark, these now seemed to be timed to avoid the Court of Session winter term – perhaps an indication that McQueen's Edinburgh practice was more demanding and growing at a satisfactory pace. For example between 1st January and 19th March 1748 there were twenty four sittings of the Sheriff court at Lanark, fifteen of these being taken by John McQueen, three by John Orr and six by Robert McQueen, all of these last being after 4th March – the Court of Session's winter session ending in that month.

However this valuable connection with the Lanark Sheriffdom ended in April 1748. As a consequence of the coming into force of the Heritable Jurisdiction Act of 1746 George Sinclair, the Sheriff Depute who had appointed McQueen left Lanark to be appointed as Sheriff Depute of Selkirk. George Crosse, an advocate who had been admitted in 1735 and who had been Professor of Law at Glasgow University from 1746–47, was appointed to Lanark in Sinclair's place. In a commission recorded in the Sheriff Court Act Book on 8th April 1748 Crosse appointed Richard Dick, writer in Lanark, as his Sheriff Substitute for the Upper Ward. There is no evidence to suggest why Crosse preferred the service of Mr Dick to that of the McQueens but with Dick's appointment the McQueens cease to appear as the presiding officers of the Lanark court.

One odd coincidence links Richard Dick and John McQueen – they both had sons who were advocates; indeed Robert Dick was admitted advocate just a week after Robert McQueen and, similarly to McQueen's case, the formal record of his calling has never been inscribed in the Books of Sederunt. Like McQueen, Dick was appointed one of the Faculty's examinators in 1745. However Robert Dick was educated at Glasgow rather than at Edinburgh University, matriculating at Glasgow University in 1734. The precise nature of the link between the Dicks and Crosse is not known but perhaps some Glasgow contact may be imagined.

However Robert would seem to be keeping busy back in Edinburgh. The Jacobite Rising of 1745 may have made little difference to the day to day administration of justice in Lanark – but in the capital city matters were rather different as the Minute Book of the Faculty of Advocates somewhat obliquely noted:

> ... by Occasion of the Troubles in the Country, the Court of
> Session had not been held during the last Winter Session. (3)

This abandonment of the Supreme Court's winter session, the Jacobite occupation of Edinburgh and the absence of most of the members of the Faculty from the city explained why the anniversary meeting of the Faculty for 1746, normally held in the first week of January, was not able to be held until 5th June. At that delayed meeting Robert McQueen was again appointed as one of the Faculty's "publick Examinators", which suggests that his service in this role had been acceptable. The 1747 meeting brought no Faculty appointment for McQueen but in January 1748 he was one of four members appointed to serve as advocates for the poor for that year. The young men given this task, a function dating back to James I's legislation of 1424, were all admitted to the Faculty in 1743 or 1744 and the appointment as "advocate for the poor" would seem to have been something of a forcing house for young talent with McQueen and two of his colleagues (Frances Garden and David Dalrymple) going on to become Court of Session judges – the fourth member of the team being his Lanark contemporary Robert Dick. McQueen's appointment to the panel of advocates for the poor was continued in 1749 and 1750. In the latter year he was also appointed as a publick Examinator, after a three year break from this task. These appointments suggest that the young advocate McQueen was as popular and well-thought of as the student McQueen had been – who, it may be recalled, James Ramsay of Ochtertyre reports as being a general favourite with his fellow students.

The aftermath of the Jacobite Rising saw a concerted programme of repression and a range of legal measures designed to eliminate the possibility of a repetition of what had been an alarmingly close call for the British state. The banning of tartan and bagpipes for all except Government soldiers was a very public demonstration of the official determination to tame the Highlands. However more significant steps were taken – one of these was the extension of central judicial control over all Scotland by the abolition of heritable jurisdictions. One of the consequences of this we have seen in the appointment of new Sheriffs Depute, including the transfer of George Sinclair to Selkirk and the appointment of William Crosse to Lanark, and the subsequent loss of Robert McQueen's post as Sheriff Substitute. Another plank in the Government's policy was to break up the social and economic power of the Highland chiefs. The captured Jacobite leaders were tried for their part in the rising and a number were executed and had their property confiscated. Even those who escaped execution, together with those who had fled overseas, frequently suffered the forfeiture of their property and the legal complexities which inevitably surrounded the affairs of these Forfeited Estates proved to be the young McQueen's great professional opportunity.

His obituary in the *Scots Magazine* in speaking of his apprentice and student days noted:

> . . . he became a most assiduous student of the civil, as well as
> the feudal law; in both of which he acquired a knowledge and
> proficiency that gave him a readiness in practice, and
> clearness in judging, which were always conspicuous in Mr
> M'Queen, both while at the bar, as a pleader, and upon the
> bench. It may be remarked here that the Scotch law has, in a
> peculiar manner, adopted the Roman law in the regulations

respecting moveable property; and, where not already fixed, our judges have always recourse to the civil code. To become an intelligent lawyer, therefore, it is indispensably necessary, to be a good civilian. With regard to heritable property, it is chiefly regulated by the feudal law. (4)

The writer goes on to note that there were many eminent lawyers practising at the Scottish bar in the 1740s and confirmed that it proved to be no easy matter for the young McQueen to make his way. However:

Several years after the 1745, when the country became settled and quite a number of questions occurred before the Court of Session, regarding the consequences of these forfeitures. Mr McQueen's abilities pointed him out as a fit person to be employed on these law suits; and he was retained as counsel on the part of the crown, here he found a field for the full display of his knowledge and abilities as a feudal lawyer.

The anonymous writer goes on to remark that this work meant that McQueen:

... deservedly attracted the notice of practitioners, and soon came into high estimation as a profound lawyer. His employers were much pleased with his easy unaffected manners, his luminous and convincing mode of stating his opinions, and his happy and energetic method of pleading his causes.

One client who would seem to have been very satisfied with McQueen's work was Edinburgh Town Council which, in August 1758, made him a burgess and guild brother, gratis: 'by act of Council for good services'. (5)

McQueen's involvement with the work of the Faculty of Advocates also continued. He was appointed as a publick examinator again in 1751. The Faculty introduced changes in its admission procedures and separate examinators in Civil and in Scots Law were appointed. McQueen filled one of the posts for private examinator in Civil Law in 1752, 1760, 1762, 1764, 1766 and 1768 and in Scots Law in 1754, 1756, 1758 and, aged fifty-one and a very senior member of the Faculty, in

1774. (6) Advocates in eighteenth century Edinburgh did not work from offices. Many consultations and discussions were held pacing up and down within the busy environs of Parliament Hall. For more private discussions the normal manner of preparing for court was for the advocates in the case to hold a consultation with the writer concerned with the suit in either a convenient tavern or in the home of the senior advocate. James Ramsay observed that these tavern consultations, which could understandably merge into social occasions, also showed McQueen in a good light.

> Whilst they admired with reason an uncommon mixture of shrewdness and application, his social hour delighted them beyond measure; for he could be serious or frolicsome as occasion required, talking to every one in his own way, without fastidiousness or forbidding pride. (7)

The *Scots Magazine* noted that:

> . . . at these consultations, as they are called, Mr M'Queen particularly shone; abstract and difficult points seemed to vanish before him; and the openness and candour with which he gave his opinion were highly to his honour.

James Boswell's diaries, recording a consultation which he, as a young advocate, admitted in 1766, had in 1774 with the, now, very senior and eminent McQueen, confirm this quality of 'openness and candour'. Boswell's problem, concerned another McQueen, the Rev William McQueen, who had been left a legacy witnessed by one notary and two witnesses, rather than the two notaries and four witnesses which would normally have been required by the size of the deed. Boswell was unsure whether a testament, that is to say a will, was excluded from this provision but advised his client:

> . . . that I should also ask his namesake, Mr Macqueen. I did so; and Macqueen, with that excellent candour which he always has, told me he really could not tell how the matter stood. . .
> I asked him if he actually did not know so plain a thing one way or other. He declared he did not. "Well," said I, "that

flatters me very much, for I'm like to hang myself when I
cannot answer a question, and here are *you* at a loss." (8)

Less than two years later Boswell, who was not normally easily
impressed, noted:

> . . . at seven I was carried out in a chair to Macqueen's to a
> consultation. The soundness and vigour of his abilities
> humbled me. (9)

By the 1750s and 1760s Robert McQueen had become a figure of some
significance in the Scottish legal scene. In the Saltoun Papers in the
National Library of Scotland there are two certificates signed by
McQueen. The first dating from 1754 and signed by McQueen, Robert
Dalrymple, Writer to the Signet and Robert Hamilton, Professor of
Divinity at Edinburgh University testifies that: 'William Hay, writer in
Edinburgh is well affected to His Majesty, His person and govern-
ment'. (10)

A similar document from 1762 sees McQueen in even more
distinguished company:

> We Thomas Miller Esq. of Barskimming his Majesty's advocate
> and Mr Robert McQueen advocate Do hereby Certify that Henry
> Home writer in Edinburgh is a person of good character and
> well affected to his Majesty's Person & Government both in
> Church and State Given and Subscribed by us at Edinburgh the
> Nineteenth day of June 1762 years. (11)

The certificate of loyalty was almost certainly produced for Henry
Home (a namesake and presumably distant relative of the advocate
and judge Henry Home, Lord Kames) on his admission to the Society
of Writers to the Signet on 29th July 1762. By this time McQueen, at
forty years of age and with his career developing well, is evidently a
figure of sufficient stature to be coupled with the Lord Advocate, the
chief law officer of the Crown in Scotland, as a character witness.

A good deal of McQueen's success came from his service as an
Advocate Depute, that is as part of the Crown's team of prosecuting
lawyers. Prosecutions were conducted by the Lord Advocate, and his

Advocates Depute, a group comprising the Solicitor General and one or more advocates who received a commission of deputation to act in the Lord Advocate's name. The *Scots Magazine* obituary rather oddly comments that:

> It is believed Mr McQueen never enjoyed the appointment either of a sheriff, or of one of his Majesty's Depute Advocates.

While this is certainly true of an appointment as a Sheriff Depute as we have seen he did occupy a Sheriff Substitute's bench for just over three years. On the question of the Advocate Depute appointment James Ramsay of Ochtertyre notes:

> When his friend Mr Dundas became Lord Advocate, he was appointed one of his deputes, an office neither permanent nor lucrative but one admirably calculated to unfold shining and useful talents . . . (12)

The "Mr Dundas" in question was Robert Dundas of Arniston, Henry Dundas's brother, who was appointed Lord Advocate in July 1754. The appointment of an Advocate Depute was a process at the discretion of the Lord Advocate, a process somewhat analogous to the appointment of Sheriffs Substitutes by a Sheriff Depute. There are in consequence no commissions under the Great Seal for such posts as there are for a variety of other appointments, including the Lord Advocate's. Such appointments were, however, recorded in the Books of Adjournal of the High Court of Justiciary and the entry therein for 15th January 1759 confirms the point:

> This said day Compeared Mr Robert McQueen – advocate and produced a Deputation from Robert Dundas of Arniston Esqr his Majesties Advocate nominating and appointing Mr Andrew Pringle advocate his Majesties Solicitor and him Conjunctly and Severally to be his Deputes and crave the same might be read and recorded, and which was accordingly done and the Tenor whereof follows –
>
> I Robert Dundas of Arniston Esqr his Majesties Advocate considering that my necessary affairs may occasion my

absence from the Dyets of the Court of Justiciary, to the end his Majesties Service may not suffer, nor any prosecution be delayed on account of my absence, when the same may happen Have nominated constituted and appointed Mr Andrew Pringle Advocate his Majesties Solicitor and Mr Robert McQueen Advocate conjunctly and severally to be my Deputes, with power to them or either of them in my absence to Compear before the Court of Justiciary, and Insist in, raise and Carry on all Trials Complaints or prosecutions for his Majesties Interest that may be there depending, to Consent to the Deserting of Dyets or restricting of Lybells as they or either of them shall see Cause, and generally every other thing to do in relation to the Promises that I might do if personally present, Providing always that this Deputation shall be revocable when I think fit . . . (13)

The record then goes on to record the formal process of taking office:

Thereafter the said Mr Robert McQueen qualified himself as advocate depute to his Majesty King George the Second by taking and Swearing the Oaths of Alledgeance and Abjuration and subscribing the same with the Assurance and then took the Oath *de fideli*.

Andrew Pringle had been an Advocate Depute since June 1755 and in July 1755 became Solicitor General. He and McQueen served as joint Advocates Depute until Pringle was promoted to the bench and Thomas Miller took over as Solicitor General. In March 1760 a new commission deputised Miller, McQueen and Sir David Dalrymple as Advocates Depute. In June 1760 Miller became Lord Advocate, and James Montgomery and Francis Garden became joint Solicitors General. On 9th August 1760 Montgomery and Garden, together with David Dalrymple appeared before the High Court and presented commissions as Advocates Depute. McQueen was not included in this commission and his service as Advocate Depute thus ended. Curiously enough the marginal annotation in the Books of Adjournal for this entry reads "Deputation by Mr Miller in favour of Mr McQueen etc." – which is precisely what it is not – a reminder that even eighteenth century clerks could err.

However the list of those involved in the work of the public

124

prosecution service was considerably wider than just those officially deputised as Advocates Depute and both before and after McQueen's term as Advocate Depute he was one of the counsel regularly engaged on such duties.

For example in December 1754 he was retained in the prosecution of Cameron of Fassifern and Charles Steuart for forgery. This complex case required, on the Crown's side, the services of the Lord Advocate, the ex-Lord Advocate William Grant of Prestongrange, the joint Solicitors General Patrick Haldane and Alexander Horne, and three other advocates including McQueen. In the same month he was engaged along with the Advocate, the joint Solicitors General and two other advocates on prosecuting a charge of hamesucken – the offence of assaulting a person within their home.

Not all cases required quite such an extensive, or expensive, array of talent – in February 1755 an appeal was heard in the trial for murder of Nicol Brown. The Crown case was conducted by the joint Solicitors General, and John Craigie and Robert McQueen. The original trial of Nicol Brown had been another long day's work for all concerned – the report of the hearing notes that the process of the case:

> . . . employed the court till about twelve o'clock at night. The
> jury sat till between six and seven next morning. . . (14)

Later that year he and David Dalrymple assisted Solicitor General Pringle in the prosecution of Andrew Wilson for poisoning and the same team, with the help of John Craigie, in January 1756 prosecuted Hugh MacDonald on the charge of being a 'Jesuit priest or trafficking papist' – a reminder that the penal laws against Roman Catholics were still in force.

McQueen's work as Crown counsel did not just involve him in criminal cases. The *Scots Magazine* obituary spoke of his work for the Crown in the affairs of the Forfeited Estates and in October 1756 he appeared for the Crown before an ecclesiastical court – the Synod of Merse and Teviotdale – in a case concerning the disputed presentation of a minister, the Rev John Douglas, to the parish of Jedburgh. The rights of a lay patron, in this case the Duke of Breadalbane, to nominate the minister of a parish was a cause of frequent dispute and many of these cases were argued out in Presbytery, Synod or General Assembly with the assistance of leading advocates. This issue of patronage was, of course, the cause of many of the divisions within Scottish presbyterianism. George Ridpath, the minister of Stitchell, and a member of the Synod, noted in his diary:

> Wednesday October 27th – In the forenoon dyet heard parties in the Jedburgh cause, in which M'Queen was advocate for the Crown, and Sir John Stewart for the opponents of Douglas the presentee, and after a very short reasoning, referred it simpliciter to the Commission, who were empowered by the late Assembly, to judge in any question relating to this affair. Din'd at Wood's with M'Quean and a large company, entertained at the expense of Lord Braidelbine, whose minister Douglas is . . . Spent the evening again with M'Quean and his company. Gave this attendance on M'Quean on account of his commission with the Advocate. Sate too long and drank a good deal too much. (15)

McQueen's prosecution work extended through the 1750s and 1760s – but it did not engage all his time. It would indeed seem likely that he may have given up the appointment as Advocate Depute to free himself to take on other work. There was no other obvious reason why he should not have continued to hold an Advocate Depute's post and he was regularly listed in the prosecution team in cases for years after his official commission ended. However, freed from the duties of an Advocate Depute, he was also able to take on other work and in January 1761 he is listed as pleading in the High Court as a defence advocate.

Much of the work of an advocate, then and now, was in chambers rather than in court, that is, in the preparation of written opinions. The facts of a case would be presented in writing by a law agent to an advocate of standing who would submit to the agent his view of the law on the subject under consideration, the precedents that might be considered and his assessment of the likely outcome that would result if the case came to trial. A great deal of this work was increasingly to come McQueen's way. In 1766 we find McQueen and Ilay Campbell giving their opinions on a matter concerning the entailed estate of Stewart of Castlemilk and a marriage settlement (16) – the type of issue concerned with feudal law and heritable property which other evidence suggests had very much become McQueen's speciality.

In 1766 the Dean of the Faculty of Advocates, Alexander Lockhart, appointed McQueen to a vacancy on the Dean's Council, a group of nine senior members of the bar who advised the Dean and shared in the management of the affairs of the Faculty. McQueen would continue to serve on the Dean's Council, under Lockhart and his successor Henry Dundas, until his appointment to the Court of Session Bench. The high-powered nature of this Council is suggested by its composition in 1775, the last year of Lockhart's Deanship, when it comprised, Joseph Williamson, Lord Advocate James Montgomery, John Swinton (later Lord Swinton), David Rae (later Lord Eskgrove), Ilay Campbell (Later Lord Succoth), David Dalrymple (later Lord Hailes), H.M. Solicitor Henry Dundas (later Dean of the Faculty, Lord Advocate, Home Secretary, and finally Viscount Melville), and Andrew Crosbie. McQueen's inclusion in this inner group is surely evidence both of his legal abilities and of his personal and social acceptability. (17)

An opinion of 1768 on issues arising from the will of Lord Milton, a former Lord Justice-Clerk, is of some interest in that it appears to be written in McQueen's own hand rather than that of his clerk and one or two idiosyncrasies of spelling perhaps allow us some impression of McQueen's voice and colloquial style. He argues, for example, that Milton had wanted to put his three younger children on "an equale footing" and also notes that:

The question itself is attended with a good dale of difficulty and a great dale may be said upon both sides . . . (18)

Throughout this opinion he consistently spells 'deal' as 'dale'. In the quotation given above the comment that: 'a great deal may be said upon both sides' has obvious echoes of that noted English justice of the peace, Sir Roger de Coverley's, dictum: 'that much might be said on both sides' (19) – although none of the commentators on McQueen's limited reading habits have ever suggested that Addison and Steele's *Spectator* essays were among his tastes.

Although the opinion referred to above may be in McQueen's own hand most of the legal documents he signed would be written, at his dictation, by his clerk. There are two relevant documents which tell something of this side of his legal practice in the National Library of Scotland. One from 1771, is endorsed as being written by: 'William Lockhart, Clerk to Robert McQueen' (20) and the other one is from

McQueen's period on the Bench – a decree arbitral, again written by 'William Lockhart my Clerk' and signed 16th January 1784. (21) Whatever problems McQueen may have had with his domestic employees, William Lockhart seems to have coped well enough with him to have survived as his clerk for at least fifteen years.

In the 1760s McQueen was engaged as one of the counsel for the claimant in the Douglas case. This dispute over the rightful heir to the Duke of Douglas was, in William Roughead's apt phrase: 'a Brobdignagian lawsuit, which absorbed for eight years the energies of all the big-wigs of the bar'. (22) It is not surprising that McQueen was engaged in this cause – it would have been much more surprising had he not been involved, such was the scale of the case. The issue centred on the status of the claimant, Archibald James Edward Douglas. Archibald Douglas, the 3rd Marquis and 1st Duke of Douglas had died in 1761 without direct heirs and the titles became extinct. His sister, Lady Jane Douglas had, it was alleged, married secretly and in 1748 at the age of fifty given birth to twins in somewhat obscure circumstances in Paris. The Duke, during his lifetime had never recognised Jane Douglas's children as his heirs. The surviving twin, Archibald James, if legitimate, was the nephew and heir to the Duke's estate but not his titles, which could not descend in the female line. However other members of the family, with a claim to the estate if the sister's line could be proved to be invalid, claimed that the twins were French changelings.

Lawyers, not apparently including McQueen, travelled to France to take depositions and attend hearings and the case was, after five years decided, by the casting vote of Lord President, Robert Dundas of Arniston, against Archibald Douglas and in favour of the Duke of Hamilton and other potential heirs. However the case was appealed to the House of Lords in 1769, where the Court of Session decision was overturned.

The Douglas Cause was a remarkably divisive issue which stirred emotions even among those with no obvious involvement in the matter. When the House of Lords verdict was announced, an Edinburgh mob, among whom was numbered James Boswell, rioted and attacked the houses of the Court of Session judges who had earlier found for the Hamiltons. One such judge was Boswell's own father, Lord Auchinleck. Boswell had been retained in the Douglas interest and was a keen partisan of the Douglas side – a loyalty which four years later caused him some embarrassment when he visited Inveraray on his Highland jaunt with Dr Johnson and had to meet the Duchess of Argyll, who was a relative of the Hamilton family and was thought to have resented Boswell's enthusiasm in the Douglas interest. The rioting of the Edinburgh mob on 2nd March occasioned an emergency meeting of the Faculty of Advocates and Robert McQueen was appointed to a committee instructed to wait on the Lord President of the Court of Session and to assure him that the Faculty were anxious to:

> . . . support the dignity of the Court, the regular and quiet
> Administration of Justice, to protect the persons of the
> Judges, to preserve the publick peace and tranquility at
> this juncture and to bring the disturbers thereof to
> punishment. (23)

It is interesting to speculate what the Faculty's reaction would have been had the involvement of that rising young advocate, James Boswell, in the breaking of the Lord President's windows been officially known. However in the small world of legal Edinburgh rumour could not be stilled. David Dalrymple, raised to the bench as Lord Hailes in 1766, and one of those judges whose windows had been broken and door attacked, wrote in some anger to Boswell on 4th March. He had clearly heard rumours of Boswell's involvement, rumours which he had shared with Lord Auchinleck and which he sought to give Boswell an opportunity to deny:

> I am not at liberty to suppose that you had any hand in such
> things directly, and I wish that you may have an opportunity
> of letting me know that you did not countenance the mob
> when in my neighbourhood and just in the street where I
> live; I never could ask you any more particular question, for
> this reason which upon recollection will suggest itself to
> you, that had you in an unguarded hour forgot yourself and
> me, and had you acknowledged it, this would [have] been a
> circumstance for proving one of the greatest insults that has
> been committed, except those against the President. (24)

There was clearly much need for a public re-affirmation of a commitment to law and order. The Lord President had been attacked in his sedan chair on his way to Parliament House and the involvement, even if it could not be proved, of a member of the Faculty of Advocates in these scenes of riot clearly called for some bridge-building between the Faculty and the Court of Session – hence the appointment of the committee on which McQueen served.

Involvement with the Douglas Cause was not, however voluminous the paper work, long-winded the proceedings and financially rewarding the fee-income, a sole occupation. McQueen, we are told in the *Scots Magazine* was particularly fond of, and adept at, the verbal pleadings before the Lord Ordinary in the Outer House, rather than the proceedings by written memorials before the fifteen judges of the Inner House. It notes:

> . . . of these pleadings he had a very large share, he is known
> to have, repeatedly, pled from 15 to 20 causes in one day.
> When it is considered that he behove to make himself
> master, not only of the points of law involved in each
> question, but of all the facts and circumstances relating to
> them, the versatility of his mind will appear as remarkable
> as the tenaciousness of his memory.

One curious description of the legal scene and its personalities around 1771, the *Court of Session Garland*, a doggerel ballad supposed to have been written by James Boswell and a fellow-advocate John MacLaurin, does suggest that, despite McQueen's supposed preference for oral pleadings, his written pleadings were not to be despised. The case recounted in the poem is moving from an oral hearing before the Lord Ordinary in the Outer House to the fifteen judges of the Inner House:

> The Ordinary, not chosing to judge it at random,
> Did with the minutes make *avizandum;*
> And as the pleadings were vague and windy;
> His lordship ordered memorials *hinc inde.*
>
> We, setting a stout heart to a stay brae,

Took into the cause Mr David Rae.
Lord Auchinleck, however, repelled our defence,
And, over and above, decerned for expense.

However, of our cause not being ashamed,
Unto the whole lords we straightway reclaimed;
And our Petition was appointed to be seen,
Because it was drawn by Robbie Macqueen. . . (25)

Robert McQueen's industry and professional success both became famous. Boswell and some friends professed themselves astonished one evening in June 1774 to find McQueen, actually at his ease, enjoying a walk in the Meadows, the open parkland to the south of his George Square home. This sight must have been a very unusual one because Boswell later wrote in his diary:

> We met Macqueen walking, which I said was an emblem of idleness, as grass growing at the Cross of Edinburgh was an emblem of desolation. (26)

At around the same time Boswell dined with Ilay Campbell at Campbell's house near Leith. Campbell who had been admitted to the Faculty in 1759, fifteen years after McQueen and would become Lord Advocate in 1784 and, as Lord Succoth, Lord President of the Court of Session in 1789, was then arguably, as Boswell opined, "the first writing lawyer at our bar". (27) The conversation between the two advocates perhaps inevitably turned to professional gossip and in particular to McQueen's career and income and his legendary income of £1900 per annum. Ilay Campbell and Robert McQueen were by this time among the most sought-after advocates in Scotland and were often both instructed in important cases. There are, for example, in the collections of the National Library of Scotland joint opinions by Campbell and McQueen dated 1775 and 1776 on issues of trust estates and feudal law.

One interesting legal opinion of McQueen's, dating from 1775, shows McQueen taking a view which might be surprising to anyone who had only read his more reactionary pronouncements at the time of the sedition trials. McQueen had been asked to comment, by a written opinion, on a variety of legal problems posed by a solicitor acting for

Colonel James St Clair of St Clair, the laird of Dysart in Fife. St Clair was evidently in dispute with the townsfolk of Dysart over a variety of long-established rights – these included their entitlement to draw water from wells, to use local quarries, to dry the sails of their fishing vessels and to cast out their ships' ballast on a piece of land near the harbour. St Clair felt that these rights were not enshrined in any title deeds and, in consequence, he could restrict or charge for them. McQueen's professional opinion was that, for example, the right to take water from wells was:

> ... founded in Immemorial possession which in a case of this kind without any other title is sufficient. (28)

He also quoted a similar case of traditional common rights affecting the burgesses of Kelso where the Court of Session had found for the inhabitants but, on appeal to the House of Lords, this verdict had been overturned. McQueen noted however:

> But I cannot help thinking that the judgement of the Court of Session was more agreeable to the principles of the Law of Scotland.

This question of conflict between the system of law practised in Scotland and the English law which prevailed when civil appeals went to the House of Lords was a matter which exercised McQueen on a number of occasions. As one might imagine from a man with a strong personal and emotional commitment to an old-fashioned Scottishness in his speech and manners the prospect of an alien legal code interfering in matters which he felt should be governed by Scots law was not an attractive one. His opinion of 1773, with its pragmatic judgement of the realities of the situation, has already been quoted:

> ... as this question will in reality be determined by English Judges, the ideas of the Laws of England will have considerable influence on their judgement. (29)

The appellate function of the House of Lords was exercised by peers who would include a small number of Scots – the sixteen representative Scottish peers and any Scots who had received post-Union British peerages. The House did not necessarily include in its membership any Scots professionally qualified in Scots law. The modern convention whereby the appellate function of the House of Lords is discharged by the Lord Chancellor and Lords of Appeal in Ordinary only dates from the late nineteenth century. The possible difficulties that the eighteenth century House of Lords could have when dealing with Scots matters are fairly obvious – there was even indeed at times a basic problem of understanding. In the aftermath of the Porteous Riots in Edinburgh in 1736, the city's magistrates were summoned to the House of Lords to assist in their Lordship's inquiry into the disturbances. The Provost was asked by an English peer, the Duke of Newcastle, what kind of shot the town-guard, commanded by Captain Porteous, had loaded into their muskets. His reply:

> . . . juist sic as ane shutes dukes and sic like fules wi'. (30)

very nearly got him locked up for contempt. Fortunately the Duke of Argyll was in the chamber and was able to translate "dukes" and "fules" as ducks and fowl.

If communication could break down on such simple linguistic grounds then it does not take much difficulty to believe that there was even less chance of an appreciation of the differing practical and philosophical distinctions between the Scottish and English systems of law. The assumption that Scotland had been incorporated into England, rather than that the two nations had united to form a new entity, has always had a considerable degree of currency south of the Border – a point reflected on in the twentieth century by the eminent Scottish judge, Lord Cooper, in the context of Parliamentary sovereignty in his judgement in McCormack v The Lord Advocate:

> Considering that the Union legislation extinguished the Parliaments of Scotland and England and replaced them with a new Parliament, I have difficulty seeing why it should have been supposed that the new Parliament of Great Britain must inherit all the characteristics of the English Parliament but none of the Scottish Parliament, as if all that happened in 1707 was that Scottish representatives were admitted to the Parliament of England. (31)

The point that Lord Cooper made was one that could, with appropriate modifications, be applied to the legal situation in the eighteenth century. Scottish law, as we have seen, was protected by the Treaty of Union but the House of Lords did not take on board any part of Scottish law, lawyers, practice or theory when dealing with Scottish cases, thus the post-Union House of Lords inherited all the characteristics of the pre-Union English House of Lords. This contact with a second legal system presented considerable difficulties to lawyers like McQueen when they were called upon to advise clients on the law and the probable outcome of a suit. It could often be clear enough what the Scottish answer might or should be – but that answer was not always going to be the final one. James Boswell was not the first, nor would he be the last, Scottish advocate to think that qualifying at the English bar would be a sound move and place him closer to the real centre of legal and political power.

However not all the legal traffic was one way. In 1776 McQueen and Ilay Campbell were asked to provide an opinion for Joseph Banks, of Lincoln's Inn, London. Banks had been investing English mortgage funds in Scottish properties, to take advantage of higher interest rates, but was concerned about possible differences in the law on such matters as deathbed settlements, the transmission of heritable property and feudal law. (32)

McQueen's expertise in these fields also came into play when he was retained in 1773 and 1774 to provide opinions for Haldane of Gleneagles in his effort to claim the extinct Earldom of Lennox. This case, which produced voluminous memorials, copies of charters, family trees and pedigrees, hinged on the succession to the Earldom on the death of Duncan the 7th Earl in 1425. (33) It was a splendidly complicated matter, enlivened and confused by questions of irregular possession of the title in the late fifteenth century by Sir John Stewart, Lord Darnley, whose line was now extinct; the surrender of the title to James VIth, the creation of a new Lennox title, but this time a Dukedom, not an Earldom, first of all by James VI for his nearest male relative Esmé Stewart and secondly by Charles II for his natural son the Duke of Richmond; the effect of the act of attainder against James VII and II; and, of course, as ever, the differences between Scottish and English law. While McQueen and his colleague Alexander Lockhart, the Dean of the Faculty, were able to comment: '... we have seldom seen such a long pedigree so well connected and so fully proved in every link of the chain,' they were unable to win Haldane's case, even if their opinion was later endorsed by an unknown hand: 'This is most favourable to Mr Haldane's claims' and: 'By Messrs Lockhart and McQueen who were the greatest lawyers'. This annotation was later changed to the somewhat more restrained: 'By Messrs Lockhart and McQueen who were great lawyers'.

The pre-eminence of Lockhart and McQueen was attested to in a murder trial in 1769–1770, a case which attracted a great deal of public attention, in part because the victim of the alleged murder was Alexander Montgomerie, the 10th Earl of Eglinton, and in part because of the controversial and politically charged circumstances of the case. Mungo Campbell, an excise officer, had been found by the Earl in his grounds near Saltcoats armed with a gun. Campbell asserted that he was on official duty and required his weapon against a possible encounter with smugglers. The Earl, who had had previous encounters with Campbell over alleged poaching, demanded the surrender of the gun. Campbell refused, the Earl insisted, Campbell retreated from the advancing Earl, fell and his gun discharged killing the Earl.

Unusually the case was prosecuted not simply by the Crown through the Lord Advocate but by the Lord Advocate in conjunction with Archibald, the half-brother of the dead Earl, and now his successor as 11th Earl. The prosecution team was remarkably large, the Lord Advocate (James Montgomery), the Solicitor General (Henry Dundas), the Dean of the Faculty, Alexander Lockhart, McQueen, Ilay Campbell and five other advocates. The defence was in the hands of John Dalrymple, David Rae, John McLaurin, and Robert Cullen (a not inconsiderable array of talent – the three last named would in time all become Court of Session judges). McQueen's role in the proceedings seems to have been to prepare the documentation, the information for the prosecution, which the *Scots Magazine*, in its report of the case over three months' issues, noted amounted to: '45 pages large quarto' (34) David Rae, in summing up for the accused, or in the appropriate Scots law term, the pannel, felt himself obliged to make the point:

> That in place of his client's having the assistance of that able,
> experienced counsel, Mr Lockhart, who had generally, in the
> course of a long practice, been the friend of the accused, the
> whole force of his eloquence and knowledge had been
> exerted against the unhappy pannel at the bar. That he was
> likewise deprived of the aid of the best counsel in the country,

who had been retained on behalf of the prosecutor; and whose number and abilities combined against him, were formidable indeed! (35)

The Dean's presence on the prosecution side was a matter of some note and comment, and the suggestion made by David Rae would perhaps seem to imply that the best talent had been retained for the prosecution side to make them unavailable for the defence. In any event Rae's additional comment on the best counsel in the country would seem intended to describe McQueen and Ilay Campbell.

There was preliminary legal skirmishing on the court's jurisdiction – the Earl had been killed on the sands below high water mark. An appeal was made to the House of Lords on the question of jurisdiction, but was rejected. After these preliminaries the trial of Mungo Campbell, which took place on 26th February 1770 at the High Court in Edinburgh before Lord Justice-Clerk Barskimming and a full Bench, demonstrates very vividly the rigours which judges, counsel and juries had to endure in this period. The May issue of the *Scots Magazine* reprints a brief account of it under the heading "Extracts from Letters" which gives something of the flavour of a major criminal trial in McQueen's days at the bar.

Yesterday came on, before the high court of Justiciary, the trial of Mungo Campbell, so long the important subject of public attention and anxiety. The court sat down at eight o'clock in the morning, and continued examining witnesses till near twelve at night; – when Mr Lockhart charged the jury on the part of the prosecutors, till about half an hour past one. Mr Lockhart's abilities have been long known; though it has been observed, that he has always shone most on the side of a prisoner. He pleaded Mr Campbell's offence very high, charging it as a felonious and cruel murder, and bestowed many severe epithets on the prisoner. Mr Rae then charged the jury on the part of Mr Campbell. His charge lasted about three hours; and indeed a more manly, spirited, and affecting piece of eloquence, has seldom been heard in any court. He did great justice to the prisoner, and great honour to himself. The court did not rise until half past four this morning; when, according to our form, the jury were inclosed. (36)

'The jury were inclosed' – in other words they retired to consider their verdict twenty and a half hours after the commencement of the case. The eighteenth century jury did not get taken off for an overnight stay to a comfortable hotel, and the eighteenth century judges and advocates did not enjoy office hours – Robert McQueen may have earned a substantial income but one feels that he and his contemporaries earned it!

The jury, we are told:

> . . . sat together about and hour and a half; and then had their verdict written, sealed up, and deposited with their chancellor.
>
> This evening at six. the court again met. The whole six judges were present. The verdict of the jury was then read "by a great plurality of voices finding the pannel guilty of murder. Upon which Mr Campbell was sentenced to be hanged, at Edinburgh, on Wednesday the 11th of April next.
>
> The Lord Justice-Clerk addressed himself to Mr Campbell as a condemned man, with decency, and in a very pathetic manner.

In fact, Campbell was to cheat the hangman. On being taken back to prison, '. . . having received sentence of death with a composure and resolution that astonished everyone who saw him,' he managed to hang himself by using a table-napkin and a pocket handkerchief. Even in death Campbell's case presented difficulties for the authorities. The sentence of death had been pronounced in the common form:

> . . . to be hanged by the neck, by the hands of the common executioner, upon a gibbet, until he be dead; and the body thereafter to be delivered to Dr Alexander Monro, professor of anatomy in Edinburgh, to be by him publicly dissected and anatomized . . .

But the dissection was contingent upon the execution, and Campbell's suicide had prevented the execution, so arguably rendering invalid the order for dissection and anatomising. One view was that as a suicide his body should be at the disposal of the city magistrates and sent by them to Surgeon's Hall for Dr Monro's use in the education of the Edinburgh medical students. As a suicide, consecrated ground was not available for interment; in the event Mungo Campbell's body was buried near Salisbury Crags but was not allowed to rest even there:

> . . . the populace having discovered it, they dug it up, and
> some insults were committed upon it. His friends therefore
> had it carried to Leith, and having been put on board of a
> small boat, it was sunk in the frith of Forth.

Campbell's case attracted great public attention. Not only was the victim an Earl, in an age when Earls expected and received great deference, but evidence was presented to show that the Earl of Eglinton had a violent record of attacking suspected poachers, furthermore the Earl's servant was known to be hostile to Campbell. Mungo Campbell himself held unconventional religious views, had a somewhat muddy military record and was a hot-tempered and difficult character who seldom seemed to have forgotten an injury – in short he was "passionate" as the age would have described it. During the preliminary stages of the trial Lord Auchinleck disposed of the notion of passion being acceptable as an excuse for crime.

> I should be sorry if it were the law of Scotland, that passion
> will excuse a man for taking away his neighbour's life . . . for if
> passion were to be an excuse, the more boisterous a man is, the
> less danger would he run of being criminal; and a very
> irascible man would be exempted from punishment altogether,
> and might commit murder as often as he pleased. (37)

There was much popular argument about the rights of landowners, and debate about whether Campbell's action was self-defence or manslaughter. Lockhart told the court that in England the case had attracted much attention and toasts were being proposed: 'Health to the man who in defence of his property will kill a Peer.' (38) As an Ayrshire murder case the personalities were known to the Ayrshire resident James Boswell – his future wife, Margaret Montgomerie wrote to Boswell, who was in England, with an account of the killing in which she says:

He [that is Campbell] confessed that he shot my Lord, but

insists that he was in the way of his duty and therefore not
culpable. He had information of smugglers coming that way,
if one can credit his method of telling the story. But surely the
law was open to him; if my Lord did an unwarrantable thing,
he therefore ought to have sought his redress in that way. (39)

In a later letter Margaret, who as a Montgomerie looked upon the Earl
as the chief of her clan or name, suggests that Boswell may be
approached to act as Campbell's counsel, an offer which if made was
certainly not accepted. Robert McQueen was later to become related to
the Eglinton family. His son Robert Dundas married the daughter of
the 11th Earl, the joint prosecutor in the Mungo Campbell case.

The Eglinton murder was just one of many significant cases which
McQueen was involved in. As his obviously well-informed obituarist
remarks in the *Scots Magazine:*

It would be endless to enumerate the important and
remarkable causes in which Mr M'Queen was engaged;
indeed, few occurred during his 33 years practice, in which he
was not employed on the one side or the other. (40)

He also notes that:

Mr M'Queen never declined doing his duty in any cause; he
was remarkably diligent and active. The numerous papers
which he wrote are proof of this. The Belles Lettres, and what
is generally known by the term of polite literature, did not so
much then, as now constitute a branch of education. Mr
M'Queen's stile of writing was extremely clear, distinct, and
energetic; although neither his language nor his
pronunciation were much polished.

Reading such of McQueen's opinions as survive in public collections
would tend to confirm the obituarist's opinion. The style is forceful,
but not dogmatic. For example in the opinion previously cited relating
to Lord Milton's will he clearly and carefully expounds his view of the
matter but concludes that he would not be surprised if judges took
another view. A 1762 opinion from the Barcaldine Muniments and
printed by the Stair Society attracts the following note from the editor:

The style – trenchant and unencumbered by references to
precedent – gives a foretaste of the forthright delivery which
characterised McQueen's pronouncements from the Bench. (41)

What will perhaps seem to many readers to be a fair summation of
McQueen's career at the Bar and his talents as an advocate is given by
his contemporary James Ramsay of Ochtertyre:

> ... the best lawyers were fond of having Mr Macqueen for an
> adjunct in business, his frankness and honesty, which scorned
> artifice or duplicity, joined to better qualities, recommended
> him strongly to the more sensible practitioners who prefer
> substance to show. (42)

Ramsay is speaking of writers or solicitors who had to choose which
advocates to engage on behalf of their lay clients. He goes on:

> ... And what was of the greatest consequence to a practising
> lawyer, he became as great a favourite of the judges as of the
> agents. It was obvious to everybody that his papers and
> pleadings made a deep impression on the Court from his
> keeping close to the matter at issue, without any rhetorical
> flourishes or digressions.

Ramsay indeed suggests that some more rhetoric would, in some
situations, have been useful to him:

> The truth was Mr Mcqueen undervalued rhetoric too much,
> trusting chiefly to the strength of his intellect and skill in
> supporting unadorned facts by principles. This was probably
> the reason why he was so little employed for the subject in
> the Courts of Judiciary and Exchequer.

Ramsay is making the point that, for example, a criminal defence lawyer
must be able to sway the emotions of a jury as well as deal with the
evidence and issues on an intellectual level. Ramsay reflects however
that:

> His sound sense and sound law, urged with a boldness and

an energy peculiar to himself, more than compensated for his want of the eloquence of the schools.

He also notes that:

> On Pitfour being made a judge, [James Ferguson was appointed to the Court of Session Bench as Lord Pitfour in 1764] he was succeeded by this gentleman [McQueen] as the chamber counsel, to be consulted on all knotty points,

and many of the legal opinions which have been referred to above reflect this role of McQueen as the specialist adviser, rather than McQueen as the courtroom pleader. In the former role Ramsay suggests that some critics found fault in his rashness and points out that:

> . . . the impetuosity of his temper, and the liveliness of his fancy might doubtless have warped his sound judgement, and hindered him from weighing deliberately all that can be said on both sides of the question.

Ramsay however concludes that this was a charge more easily made than proved. His informed summation of McQueen's career as an advocate was:

> When called to the bench, he was one of the most popular characters at the bar; and what was rare, indeed, seemed to have no enemies. Being in the receipt of prodigious fees, his promotion prevented him from making a very large fortune. It was said to be contrary to his own inclination. He could not, however, resist the importunities of the Ministers of State of those times . . .

Ilay Campbell

Ilay Campbell was perhaps McQueen's chief rival at the Scottish Bar.
After serving as Lord Advocate he became Lord President
of the Court of Session in 1789. He was created a Baronet
on retiring from the Bench in 1808.

CHAPTER 6

Braxfield the Judge
1776–1788

*". . . a person of Loyalty, Learning, Knowledge
and experience of the Laws . . ."*

The connection between McQueen and the all-important Dundas dynasty was one of considerable importance to both sides. The *Scots Magazine* put it thus:

> Mr M'Queen had contracted an intimacy with Mr Dundas, afterwards Lord President of the Court of Session, and his brother, the Right Hon. Henry Dundas, at a very early period of life. (1)

Robert Dundas had become Lord President of the Court of Session in 1760 – his half-brother Henry was appointed Lord Advocate in 1775. Both were anxious to have McQueen on the bench, but as the *Scots Magazine* also suggested, he seems to have been reluctant to give up the rewards of his lucrative career at the Bar for the much poorer salary of a Court of Session judge '. . . Mr M'Queen for some time resisted their importunities. . .'

Contradicting this view there is evidence that in 1775 Henry Dundas had tried, seemingly at McQueen's own wish, to get him appointed to the vacancy created by the death of Lord Strichen. On applying to Lord Mansfield for his support and writing to Mansfield that McQueen wished to 'retire to the bench', (2) Dundas found that Mansfield had a preference for Alexander Lockhart, the Dean of Faculty, who was duly appointed. Lord Mansfield's involvement in this matter is an apt demonstration of the eighteenth century's capacity to blur the boundaries between the executive and the judicial spheres of activity. William Murray, Lord Mansfield, was a younger son of the Scottish Viscount Stormont who, educated chiefly in England and trained at the English bar, had enjoyed a successful legal and political career which he crowned in 1756 by becoming Lord Chief Justice of the King's Bench and Baron Mansfield. However his judicial functions did not prevent his continuing to operate at the highest political level and the Dictionary of National Biography observes:

> Though not in Lord North's cabinet, it is probable that he was in confidence of ministers, and privy to most of their measures. (3)

More significantly in the complex world of eighteenth century politics he was, in cabinet or out of cabinet, Lord Chief Justice or not, a major power broker and influence broker. Even the fairly modest appointment of a Court of Session judge was a piece in some fairly involved games of political chess and exchanges of favours. Mansfield, as a Scot close to Government, had a particularly significant part to play in Scottish politics, even if he was somewhat removed from any regular Scottish contact. A similarly influential role, in which personality seemed to play as large a role as any official position, was exercised by Lord Loughborough, the Lord Chancellor from 1793–1801. Despite his very English title and office, Loughborough was a Scot, Alexander Wedderburn, who had qualified as an Advocate in Edinburgh before moving south to the English Bar and a politico-legal career in England. After McQueen's death Loughborough was to be consulted by the Lord Advocate on the possible options for promotions to the Court of Session Bench.

If indeed McQueen was disappointed by his failure to get Strichen's seat then he had not long to wait. In 1776, just a year after Henry Dundas became Lord Advocate, George Brown, Lord Coalston died. Coalston had served as a Senator of the College of Justice since 1756 and as a criminal judge, a Commissioner of Justiciary, since 1764.

On Friday 22nd November 1776 James Boswell went into the Court of Session to find Parliament House in a state of considerable excitement:

> The news came that Lord Coalston's vacant gown was offered to Mr Macqueen, and he could not refuse it. This made a great stir amongst us at the bar. Sandy Gordon said a day or two ago, 'Take care of yourself, Macqueen, I hear there's a press-gang going about for able-bodied judges. I said Ilay Campbell would cut off his thumbs rather than be pressed up to the bench. I spoke to Macqueen today of his promotion, and he said it was cursedly hard. (I think that, or 'a damned hardship,' was his expression.) It was giving him at the most, with a double gown, £900 a year, and his practice as a lawyer brought him near £2,000 a year. It was indeed an honour to have such an office given him without solicitation. But as Falstaff liked no such grinning honour as that of a dead warrior, Macqueen liked not honour which took so much money from him. But if he should refuse it, he could not expect to have it afterwards. (4)

This apparent conflict between the notion of McQueen reluctant to leave the high earnings of the bar and Dundas's report of McQueen wishing to "retire to the bench" may be reconciled by either accepting either that Dundas was being less than truthful to Mansfield and hoped to bounce McQueen, by way of a *fait accompli*, into accepting office; or that McQueen was being less than frank with Boswell and his colleagues in the Faculty and was simply putting on an act of being coerced into accepting judicial office in order to sustain the view that he had got the appointment "without solicitation". It is also perfectly possible to believe that any earlier offers of judicial preferment had been rejected by him in favour of building up the family fortune and the McQueen estate but that by 1775 and having reached the age of fifty three he was willing to contemplate a judicial post and was well enough provided for financially to be able to countenance the drop in income. In any event, it should be noted that even after going to the Court of Session Braxfield was still able to find the money to invest in property, his final acquisition of land in Broughton not coming until 1783.

Of course many of his contemporaries in the Faculty of Advocates had already found their way on to the judicial bench. Francis Garden and David Dalrymple, his fellow "advocates for the poor" back in 1748 had been appointed to the Court of Session in 1764 and 1766 respectively. In one sense, Braxfield, with over thirty two years service as an advocate could be seen as having been somewhat slower than average in gaining promotion. Of the judicial appointments made during McQueen's professional career the average time from admission to the Faculty to appointment to the Bench was around twenty seven years. McQueen's talents were recognised, his legal knowledge respected, a judicial appointment could certainly have been anticipated in the 1760s and when it came it seemed perfectly appropriate; Boswell, later in the diary passage quoted from above, writes of: 'Macqueen's promotion from merit. . .'

It seems perfectly reasonable to conclude that, with one friend, Robert Dundas, at the head of the Scottish judiciary, and another friend, Henry Dundas, H.M. Advocate, the chief law officer in Scotland and a significant governmental figure, the pressure on McQueen, in the mid 1770s, to accept a judicial post became too great to resist, and this certainly would square with Boswell's remark about the offer of the post '. . . and he could not refuse it.' Additional persuasive powers were applied, according to the obituarist in the *Scots Magazine*, by the Home Secretary, the Earl of Suffolk. This latter point is slightly confused in that there was not an office of Home Secretary in existence in 1776. The Cabinet minister with ultimate responsibility for Scottish affairs would have been the Secretary of State for the Northern Department – who in late 1776 was Henry, Earl of Suffolk & Berkshire and he, with a large portfolio of responsibilities and little obvious reason for a detailed knowledge of the Scottish scene would undoubtedly have taken the advice of the Lord Advocate on a matter of this nature.

It would have been possible, if somewhat unusual, for McQueen to have been appointed to fill both of Coalston's posts, a procedure which Boswell clearly thought was possible from his reference to the "double gown". There were indeed cases of newly appointed Judges going straight on to the Justiciary Bench – but this only happened in seven out of the twenty seven Court of Session appointments made in McQueen's professional lifetime, and there was often a special circumstance involved; two of these appointments were, for example, promotions from the post of Lord Advocate. It was normal for Lord Advocates, political appointees at the mercy of a change of government, to take the opportunity of a senior judicial vacancy, such as the Justice-Clerk's or Lord President's post, to have themselves appointed. Such offices were of course appointments for life. Thus Robert Dundas had gone directly from being Lord Advocate to fill the most senior judicial post as Lord President on the death of Robert Craigie, Lord Glendoick. In the event the claims of Francis Garden, Lord Gardenstone, to Coalston's Justiciary gown were felt to be stronger and he was given the additional appointment to the High Court of Justiciary; while Robert McQueen, aged fifty four, was appointed a Senator of the College of Justice and assumed the judicial title of Lord Braxfield. McQueen's father, John, had died five years previously and Robert had since then been formally known as Robert McQueen of Braxfield, rather than Robert McQueen of Hardington, the style he had used since his purchase of the Hardington estate in 1769.

A week before McQueen's promotion took effect Boswell records:

> Friday 6th December. Dined at Mr Ilay Campbell's with a company to take leave of Mr Macqueen before he went to the bench. Baron Maule kept us all merry with his forcible humour and variety of anecdotes. I drank largely. Then went to Moncreiffe's, played at whist, and lost. Macqueen was here too, and much noisy, coarse jocularity went round. I drank largely again, went home between one and two, gorged but not drunk. (5)

To add to the general good feeling Lord Mansfield, who had apparently blocked his promotion a year earlier, and himself had by this time been advanced in the peerage from a Baron to an Earl, a reflection of his political significance, was to speak highly of McQueen's 'disinterested conduct' in accepting a judicial post. The Court of Session met on 10th December and recorded in the Book of Sederunt:

> This day the Lord President presented to the Court His Majesty's letter Directed to the Lord President and the rest of the Senators nominating and appointing Robert McQueen, Esq. to be one of the Ordinary Lords in place of the Lord Coalston deceased which was read and ordered to be recorded in the Books of Sederunt and he to enter on his trials by going to the Outer House with the Lord Ordinary. (6)

The King 's letter had said:

Right trusty and Well-beloved, We greet you well understanding that there is a place of one of the Ordinary Lords of our Session now vacant by the death of George Brown Esq. and it being requisite that a person of Loyalty, Learning, Knowledge and experience of the Laws should be preferred thereto, To the end that in default of the Ordinary number of the Senators of the College of Justice in that part of our Kingdom of Great Britain called Scotland there be no hindrance of the administration of Justice; and we being well informed of the Loyalty, Literature and good qualifications of our Trusty and Well Beloved Robert McQueen, Esq. and of his abilities and willingness to serve us in that place, Therefore we have thought good to nominate him unto you. Requiring you effectually to try and thereafter to admit and receive him to the ordinary place, accepting him as one of your number. And we do verily ordain him to have and enjoy all privileges thereunto belonging, with vote amongst you, and to be participant of your salaries, taking his oath as use is and as you will do unto us acceptable service. . .

In accordance with the Court's rules he went through the probationary process of sitting beside a Lord Ordinary in the Outer House and reporting a case to the assembled bench of the Inner House. On 13th September the Court met again and:

The Lords having this day considered that Robert MacQueen Esq. of Braxfield had undergone the trial appointed by Act of Sederunt for cognoscing the qualifications of persons nominated by His Majesty for supplying the vacant places in the Session, in so far as the said Robert McQueen, Esq. after sitting three days in the Outer House with the Ordinary and reporting in the presence of the Lords the causes taken to avisandum by the Ordinary during that time And this day after hearing a Cause in the Inner House Resumed the debate and gave his opinion on the several points thereof. And the Lords being satisfied therewith and of the proof there given of his qualifications, And he having subscribed the oath of Allegiance and abjuration and subscribed the same with his assurance and given his oath de fideli and to maintain the privileges of the house, the Lords have admitted and hereby admit the said Robert MacQueen Esq. in place of the late Lord Coalston conform to His Majesty's Letter recorded the tenth currt. To be possessed and enjoyed by him with all the honours, dignities, profits and casualties thereto belonging suchlike and as freely as any of the Lords do possess or have possessed and enjoyed the like place.

Braxfield was to spend four years as a judge in the Court of Session before the opportunity of further advancement came his way with an appointment to the High Court of Justiciary. His work in these four years, although traceable in the records of the Court such as the Outer House Rolls, is perhaps inevitably somewhat more anonymous and obscure than the better reported work of a criminal judge on circuit or in Edinburgh, let alone the high-profile role he was to assume as Lord Justice-Clerk.

That Lord Braxfield was not inhibited by his elevation is suggested by one anecdote from the Court of Session. One of Braxfield's judicial brethren had advanced a view on the law relating to a case under consideration and Braxfield asked him from where he drew this legal opinion.

'From Stair,' replied the Judge. 'Na, na,' quoth Braxfield, 'that canna be, for there's nae noansense to be fund in Stair!' (7)

It will be recollected that Braxfield had told James Boswell of his great regard for Lord Stair's *Institutions of the Laws of Scotland* and his respect for this key work of seventeenth century legal scholarship was well known.

James Ramsay's evidence of Braxfield's performance as a judge is worth considering. However, due to Ramsay's absences from Edinburgh it is, as he admits, drawn less from first hand experience than his memories of McQueen as an advocate. Nonetheless his informed and contemporary judgement has to have some weight:

In the Court of Session he fully justified the sanguine expectations of his friends and admirers. His ambition to excel was happily seconded by great learning, quick apprehension, and a perfect knowledge of business. What wonder, then, that in all nice questions of feudal law, and in perplexed causes, he should, after the death of some great judges, be listened to as an oracle, who often struck light out of darkness. He was not only acute and expeditious in giving judgement, but candid to a great degree; for if he had laboured under any misapprehension, he would upon reconsidering the case, all at once give up his former judgment, and assign good reasons for it. In short, he was devoid of that obstinacy which is often the concomitant of great talents. (8)

This analysis: '. . . great learning, quick apprehension, and a perfect knowledge of business' is, it is worth recalling, being made of the same Braxfield, so attacked by critics from Henry Cockburn in the nineteenth century to W. D. Lyell in the twentieth century. Sheriff Substitute Lyell wrote:

> . . . it is narrated that by his comprehensive grasp of principle and erudite knowledge of the Institutional writers and the civil law, he attained eminence among his brethren of the bench, and earned the entire confidence of the bar and the country. All this is tradition, and nothing more. (9)

Surely not. There is, and Ramsay is just one part of it, ample evidence to suggest that the statement Lyell makes, just to knock down, is in fact a pretty fair summary of Lord Braxfield's judicial career. Even Cockburn, no friend to Braxfield, does have to admit that:

> . . . within the range of the Feudal and the Civil branches, and in every matter depending on natural ability and practical sense, he was very great. . . (10)

It must always be kept in mind though, that Braxfield was nearly three years into his judicial career when Henry Cockburn was born – so Cockburn's evidence is inevitably second hand. The view of the avowedly sympathetic, but genuinely contemporary, Alexander Young tends to support Ramsay and was that:

> . . . as a Judge in the Civil Court, I never till lately heard a public opinion uttered concerning him except in praise. He was a great friend to dispatch in business, and there never was insinuated any complaint of undue favour displayed by him in the whole course of his judicial career, which is more than I can say of some very eminent Judges who sat on the Bench at the same time as him. (11)

In February 1780, Alexander Boswell, Lord Auchinleck, resigned his Justiciary appointment although retaining his seat on the Court of Session. The Court of Session at the start of 1780 was made up of the following members:

Judicial Title	Family Name	Appointed to Court of Session	Commissioner of Justiciary
Lord President Arniston,			
Lord Justice-Clerk	Dundas	June 1760	–
Barskimming (later Glenlee)	Miller	June 1766	–
Kames	Home	Feb 1752	Yes
Auchinleck	Boswell	Feb 1754	Retired
Elliock	Veitch	March 1761	–
Barjarg (later Alva)	Erskine	June 1761	–
Stonefield	Campbell	June 1762	–
Gardenstone	Garden	July 1764	Yes
Kennet	Bruce	July 1764	Yes
Hailes	Dalrymple	March 1766	Yes
Monboddo	Burnett	Feb 1767	–
Covington	Lockhart	March 1775	–
Ankerville	Ross	Feb 1776	–
Braxfield	McQueen	Dec 1776	Yes
Westhall	Dalrymple	July 1777	–

The vacancy on the Justiciary Bench was filled by the promotion of Braxfield. Braxfield had moved ahead of a number of more senior colleagues; there were, as the table indicates, six judges more senior in terms of Court of Session service who might have been thought to have a better claim to the vacant Justiciary gown. James Boswell's activity in support of one of these putative claimants, Lord Covington, was noted in Chapter 3.

Of course not all Braxfield's senior colleagues would have wished for the vacant Justiciary appointment. Some presumably felt themselves to be now too old for the peripatetic life of a Commissioner of Justiciary on circuit, or would not relish the additional workload of weekly High Court diets in Edinburgh. James Burnett, Lord Monboddo, had previously refused promotion to the High Court Bench as the additional duties and the increased time commitment would have interfered with his intellectual activities and his regular visits to London to mix in literary and philosophical circles there. Monboddo was also a keen agriculturalist, an interest he shared with his judicial colleague, Lord Kames. While Braxfield was an improving laird and the owner of ever-widening acres it does seem probable that much more of his interest and commitment was centred in the law than was the case with some of his colleagues. Boswell was of this opinion and noted in his diary in 1777: '. . . Macqueen dealt in nothing but law.' (12) Kames's enthusiasm for agricultural improvement and his wide range of literary, legal and philosophical writings, Monboddo's interest in anthropology, or even Lord Gardenstone's touching attachment to pigs, finds no parallel in the *curriculum vitae* of Lord Braxfield.

Quite what Braxfield's critics would have made of him had he followed Lord Gardenstone down the path of pig fancying is difficult to say. Dean Ramsay's portrait of Gardenstone gives something of the flavour of this leading light of the Scots judiciary:

> . . . he indulged in the love of pigs and the love of snuff. He took a young pig as a pet, and it became quite tame, and followed him about like a dog. At first the animal shared his bed, but when, growing up to advanced swinehood, it became unfit for such companionship, he had it to sleep in his room, in which he made a comfortable couch for it of his own clothes. His snuff he kept not in a box, but in a leathern waist-pocket made for the purpose. He took it in enormous quantities, and used to say that if he had a dozen noses he would feed them all. (13)

The same writer reminds us of the qualities of James Burnett, Lord Monboddo, and his views on anthropology:

> His speculations regarding the origins of the human race have, in times past, excited much interest and amusement. His theory was that man emerged from a wild and savage condition, much resembling that of apes; that man had then a tail like other animals, but which by progressive civilisation and the constant habit of sitting had become obsolete . . .

to say nothing of his opinions on transport:

> His mode of travelling was on horseback. He scorned carriages, on the grounds of its being unmanly to "sit in a box drawn by brutes." (14)

Other sources suggest that Monboddo, a keen classicist, felt that as the carriage or stagecoach was not known to the ancients he would not wish to encourage such an unwarranted innovation. Even into extreme old age he made the arduous journey of his annual visit to London on horseback.

As ever a vacancy produced a flurry of lobbying and gossip but Lord Advocate Henry Dundas, repelling Boswell's pro-Covington scheme, had Braxfield promoted and his appointment was announced on 26th February 1780. Quite apart from the honour of the position the office brought in an additional £200 per year of salary – which must have been some consolation for giving up his earnings at the bar.

For reasons which seem difficult to fathom James Boswell now felt it appropriate to issue, anonymously, a pamphlet entitled *Letter to Robert Macqueen, Lord Braxfield, on his promotion to be one of the Judges of the High Court of Justiciary*. This remarkable effusion was written, hurriedly, in late April and sent to the press on 28th April and was published on 8th May. If a little pompously, the *Letter* starts off politely enough:

> It is not the intention of this letter to pay your Lordship compliments on your promotion to a seat in the Supreme Criminal Court of Scotland. These you may have from other quarters. But when a man of such eminence for knowledge of the Law, and of such distinguished vigour of mind, is appointed one of the Lords of Justiciary, it is deemed a very fit opportunity for publickly submitting some considerations upon the duty of that important office with which your Lordship is now entrusted. (15)

Boswell goes on to expatiate on the need for a judge to be solemn and religious and to assert that an irreligious man who accepts office as a criminal judge is an impostor. Interestingly in view of various comments on McQueen's religious views and irreligious practices Boswell goes on to say:

> This remark will be approved of by your Lordship. For, with an impetuosity of animal spirits, and higher passions than ordinary, you are steady in your belief in the great doctrines of our holy religion. This is well known to those who know

> you best. It is honourable to yourself, and comfortable to them; honourable that a man of your superior abilities has the candour to submit his mind to the evidence of what we cannot fully comprehend; comfortable that such a man unites the weight of his opinion to confirm the hopes, without which the life of every thinking being, who is not dull indeed, must be very dreary . . .

Having given Braxfield a clean bill of health on religious orthodoxy he goes on to pray that:

> Far from the Bench of the High Court of Justiciary be the vulgar familiar phrase; but farther still be that "foolish jesting" which is so incompatible with the solemn business of the Court, and would be so offensive in any of its Judges.

It is far from clear what Boswell was aiming at here. Braxfield had not yet, apart from his youthful service as Sheriff Substitute at Lanark, had an opportunity to perform as a judge in the criminal courts, although, of course, Boswell could in theory have had doubts about his character or fitness for this role. However there does not seem to be any trace of such doubts recorded in his private diary writings of the period. His record of his conversation with Braxfield about the judge's legal education and formation, which took place just five months later, and which was quoted in Chapter 4, carries no suggestion of any suspicion of Braxfield's fitness for office. Indeed Boswell in his diary for 21st April 1780 notes that he had contemplated this publication for some time and: '. . . wished to publish before he began his first circuit.' (16)

The editors of the Boswell diaries suggest that the real target for Boswell's strictures on judicial indecorum might be Lord Kames. This may be so, and it would hardly be untypical of Boswell for him not to realise that linking his pamphlet to Braxfield's promotion was more or less bound to make many people, particularly those who heard of the publication rather than read it, assume it to be an attack on Braxfield.

Boswell quickly moves on from his concerns about the need for judicial solemnity and religious orthodoxy to a discussion of the inappropriateness of Judges passing opinions on matters of fact, as opposed to points of law, in their charges to the jury. He also, as was noted in Chapter 3, spent much space condemning the reduced magnificence of judicial circuits and the skimping on entertainment allowances.

This bizarre publication naturally attracted considerable attention and Boswell must have figured very prominently on any knowledge-able reader's shortlist of possible authors. A few days after publication Boswell called in at the Justiciary Office because he:

> ... wished to hear what the clerks said of the pamphlet. I was
> mentioned as one of the authors or persons supposed to be
> the writer. I denied it, as a man is entitled to do, as to deny his
> being at home, because denying is the only mode of
> concealing what a man has a right to conceal. Mr Crosbie, Mr
> Hugo Arnot, and the Hon. Henry Erskine were also
> mentioned. The author was allowed to be well-informed. (17)

A day or so later he was walking with Principal Robertson who said:

> ... he had read the *Letter to Lord Braxfield*, and that it would
> do good, for it would show the judges they are not above
> censure. (18)

Boswell's plan to publish his pamphlet before Braxfield could go on his first circuit does tend to confirm the view that Braxfield was his pretext, not his target, and, had he succeeded in getting it out in time, this timing would have tended to make his intention a little clearer. However this plan was, like so many of his good intentions, doomed to failure. The Spring Circuit was coming to an end as the pamphlet appeared.

Braxfield's first judiciary circuit, carried out in April 1780, saw him accompanying Lord Hailes on the Western Circuit. Hailes was four years younger than Braxfield, and had, as David Dalrymple, been McQueen's colleague as "advocate for the poor" back in 1748. The Western Circuit took the two judges and their retinue of clerks, advocates depute, court officers and defence advocates to Stirling, Glasgow and Inveraray.

Braxfield's next recorded contact with Boswell does not show any evidence that the Judge had taken much offence, or notice, of the advocate's publication. Boswell and Ilay Campbell had been appointed as arbiters on a disputed question of an entail. Boswell's diary entry displays no embarrassment at the contact, rather a genuine appreciation of Braxfield's abilities, an appreciation which may be taken as all the more sincere in that it was intended for no eyes other than his own:

> I wished to consult Lord Braxfield. Mr Campbell said Lord B. would determine him. My Lord was so good as to go to Mr Campbell's with me when he came out of Court, and was clear against his opinion. But struck out a new point quite clear which had not occurred either to parties or to us Arbiters. (19)

In the Autumn the allocation of duties for the circuit, "on the hay", as the Autumn circuit was known (the Spring circuit being described as "on the grass") took Braxfield and Lord Kames on the Southern Circuit. Braxfield and Kames stayed with their colleague Lord Auchinleck at Auchinleck House in Ayrshire on their way to the first diet of the circuit at Ayr on 6th September. The other ports of call on the Southern Circuit were Dumfries, where Kames and Braxfield sat from 14th September and, Jedburgh where they sat from 20th September. The Ayr diet saw the trial of Matthew Hay, a tenant farmer at Dundonald for the murder of William Wilson and his wife. Hay had poisoned the Wilson family's cooking pot of sowens (a type of porridge made from oatmeal husks) in an attempt to kill the daughter of the family in order to conceal the fact that she was pregnant with Hay's child. This case was the occasion for the "checkmate" remark attributed to Braxfield, but in fact made by his colleague Kames.

Braxfield is depicted by Boswell in March 1781 in what is the perhaps somewhat unfamiliar guise of peacemaker. Boswell and Lord President Dundas had quarrelled in Court over some comments Dundas had made about the independence of the: 'gentlemen of Ayrshire'. The context for this argument was one of the regular tussles over the eligibility of voters at elections which had ended up in the Court of Session. Boswell was determined to write to Dundas in protest at this slur on the electors of his native county of Ayrshire, but a friend persuaded him to get Braxfield to act as an intermediary and deliver his letter to the Lord President. This was duly done and on Friday 9th March he records:

> . . . I went to the Robing Room, and Lord Braxfield told me

the President desired him to say that he did not mean to say anything against the gentlemen of Ayrshire or any one of them; that he only meant to say they were not independent of party. (20)

Boswell could hardly argue with this and noted:

This was pretty well. The President came up and we shook hands, but he said nothing.

Braxfield's Justiciary duties on circuit in the Spring and Autumn and week by week in Edinburgh during the court sessions were in addition to his on-going commitment to the civil cases being dealt with in the Court of Session. A disconsolate Boswell noted on 3rd July 1781 that he had:

Lost two causes: one before Lord Braxfield and one before the Lords. I was quite clear I was in the right in both, and was really hurt to find justice so ill-administrated. (21)

Boswell's failures were cases in the Outer House, before Braxfield sitting as a Lord Ordinary, and a hearing before the full Bench in the Inner House. Braxfield himself would seem to have had his moments when even what Boswell had described as his 'impetuosity of animal spirits, and higher passions than ordinary' apparently failed him. On 9th August 1781 Braxfield and Boswell met in the Meadows and the Judge remarked: 'It's a cursed business, ours' to which the equally disenchanted Boswell replied: 'You labour hard and get no thanks.' (22)

That Autumn Braxfield was sent on the Western Circuit and sat alone at the Glasgow and Inveraray sessions. This absence of the second Judge on Circuits was one of the abuses that Boswell had drawn attention to in his *Letter to Robert Macqueen* – Braxfield was to be joined for the Stirling diet by Robert Bruce, Lord Kennet.

In 1782 Braxfield accompanied the veteran Henry Home, Lord Kames on the Southern Circuit in the spring and on the Northern Circuit to Aberdeen, Inverness and Perth in the autumn. It was this Spring Circuit, evidently carried out in unseasonably inclement weather, which was the occasion for his letter to his daughter Mary Honyman quoted in Chapter 4. Lord Kames died on 27th December 1782, aged 86, just three months after completing his last Justiciary circuit. His famous valedictory remark: 'fare ye a' weel ye bitches' to the Court of Session as it rose for the Christmas vacation that year was entirely in character for this remarkable member of the judiciary. Apart from his agricultural and intellectual activities Kames had published many significant legal works, including important collections of decisions and a major work on equity and had also been something of a legal innovator.

1782 was marked by an exceptional number of changes in the composition of the Court of Session. Apart from the loss of Kames the year had seen the death of Alexander Boswell, Lord Auchinleck and Alexander Lockhart, Lord Covington. Auchinleck's seat was taken by David Rae, Lord Eskgrove and Covington's place went to John Swinton, Lord Swinton. The Court of Session and Justiciary seats held by Lord Kames were filled by the appointment of Alexander Murray, who took as his judicial title Lord Henderland. Murray's accelerated promotion, getting on to the Justiciary Bench in one step, was undoubtedly influenced by his political connections. He had been Solicitor General since 1775 and was a Member of Parliament for Peeblesshire. His promotion to the College of Justice resulted in Ilay Campbell briefly becoming Solicitor General, a political appointment which he lost on the Coalition Ministry of Portland, North and Fox coming to power. However on Pitt gaining power in December 1783 Ilay Campbell's rise continued with his appointment as Lord Advocate.

The 1780s saw Braxfield's elder son, Robert Dundas McQueen, admitted to the Faculty of Advocates on 17th December 1782, his second daughter Catherine married to Clanranald in 1784 and his purchase of the remaining part of the parish of Broughton completed in 1783, while his son-in-law William Honyman took a further step up in his career with his appointment as Sheriff Depute of Lanarkshire in 1786.

Apart from the formal work of the courts Braxfield was asked to act as arbiter in a number of cases. In 1783 he was asked to rule on a Sinclair family dispute involving William Sinclair, Earl of Caithness, John Sinclair of Ulbster (the originator of the Statistical Account) and John Sinclair of Freswick – a problem whose origins lay in an agreement signed by the Earl's grandfather in 1696. (23) His previous connection, as an advocate, with the family of Fletcher of Saltoun presumably led to Braxfield being chosen as sole arbiter to settle claims over property in the Canongate of Edinburgh arising out of the death of the late Lord Milton's widow, Elizabeth Kinloch. (23) The case was presented to

Braxfield for his adjudication by James Boswell and Andrew Crosbie and again one must note that if Boswell's opinion of Braxfield was as critical as one might imagine, judging by a casual reading of his *Letter to Robert Macqueen*, then he seemed to go out of his way to seek his views and take his opinion. Nor should it be thought that Boswell was a lightweight figure – his being instructed alongside major figures like Ilay Campbell and Crosbie does suggest that he was seen as being an advocate of some merit; indeed on McQueen's promotion to the Bench in 1776 Boswell had been instructed in a number of cases which had previously been in McQueen's hands. It is surely a reasonable indication of the younger man's standing that he could be seen as an acceptable substitute for McQueen.

A case in the High Court of Justiciary in Edinburgh in March 1785 gives some idea of the judicial climate of the age. A young man, Archibald Stewart, had been arrested for multiple offences of shopbreaking and housebreaking and one Charles Gordon for reset, that is receiving the stolen goods. The court and the prosecutor, the Solicitor General, Robert Dundas (the son of the Lord President – the Dundas dynasty continued) were both alarmed to hear it alleged that a witness in the case, Duncan Fraser an accomplice in one of the crimes, had been flogged until he gave evidence and the same treatment had been threatened to Stewart. However the case continued, and as usual once the jury were chosen the process went on to the bitter end, in this case 12 midnight. Stewart was found guilty of theft and Gordon of reset. Gordon's good character and Stewart's youth (he was only fifteen) were noted but the sentence pronounced by Lord Justice-Clerk Glenlee was that Stewart should be executed and Gordon whipped through the streets of Edinburgh on 30th March and then banished to the plantations for seven years, with five years of this sentence to be spent as an indentured labourer. The accusations of flogging witnesses to induce confessions and a flow of evidence were subsequently strenuously denied in a letter to the *Caledonian Mercury* by Archibald Cockburn, the Sheriff of Edinburgh, whose officers had been alleged to have carried out the flogging. While admitting that:

> . . . from the great number of boys in this place that commit crimes, and are not objects of public trial and punishment, it has been in use, after repeated transgressions, sometimes to order them a private chastisement, and dismiss them. Stewart and Fraser had repeatedly been before me as thieves and

pickpockets, and were both banished from the county in
February 1784. After which they were again taken up for
house breaking; and Fraser, was on that occasion, ordered a
private chastisement, and then dismissed.

Cockburn indignantly denied that any interrogation took place during
these chastisements and, with some justice regretted that he had not
been in court during the examination of the witnesses and that:

> ... the counsel of either side did not send for me after it was
> concluded, as it would have afforded me an opportunity of
> giving immediately the explanation I have now done. . . (25)

In July 1786 the trial of James Graham on a charge of fraud took place
at the High Court in Edinburgh. Graham entered a plea of guilty and
the only question before the Bench was the appropriate sentence. The
stereotypical view of Braxfield as the draconian "hanging judge" is
somewhat dented by the report which shows that Lord Hailes proposed
a sentence of fourteen years transportation with seven years bonded
service while Braxfield successfully moved for a sentence of seven years
transportation with five years labour.

The contentious issue of the reduction of the size of the Court of
Session to fund increased salaries for the remaining judges was settled
in 1786 by an Act of Parliament which raised the salaries for the Senators
of the College of Justice to a more appropriate level.

Post	Old Salary	New Salary
Lord President	£1211.11.0	£2000
Lord Justice-Clerk	£1111.11.0	£1600
Lords Commissioners of Justiciary	£811.11.0	£1300
Lords of Session	£611.11.0	£1000

(26)

The somewhat odd figures for the old salaries were based on a basic
traditional salary funded from the old, pre-Union, customs. The sum
of £1666.13.4 was available from this source for division among the
"fifteen" – making approximately £111.11.0 a head. To this was added
a modern augmentation of £1100 for the President, £1000 for the Justice-

Clerk and £500 for each of the other members as well as additional payments of £200 each to the other Justiciary Court members – bringing the salaries up to the levels shown. It is interesting to note from the same period, 1761, that the salary for the Lord Justice-General, by this time a sinecure, was £2000 and the head of the separate Court of Exchequer, the Chief Baron, enjoyed the same salary.

This increase in 1786, substantial as it was, still hardly made the Court of Session an attractive proposition for a high-earning advocate. It will be recalled that twelve years before McQueen had been earning £1900 a year and Ilay Campbell £1600 a year. To come from an income of that level to the £1000 of a Court of Session judge's salary was a significant drop in income and it may not been entirely surprising if some of the Commissioners of Justiciary, who had an expense allowance granted to them for the expenses of their circuit journeys attempted to make economies, even if such parsimonious behaviour attracted critical comment from Boswell and others. Whatever the financial loss for a high-earning advocate there was a certain moral pressure on men like Braxfield who had made a good fortune at the bar to assume their civic duty. Others, somewhat less successful in advocacy, doubtless found the assured comfortable income and prestige of a Court of Session place attractive enough and were more easily persuaded to go on to the Bench.

On 13th December 1787 Robert Dundas, Lord President Arniston died aged seventy four. The appointment of a successor as Lord President was, as always, as much a political as a legal decision. Henry Dundas could undoubtedly have had the post for the asking. As his biographer Michael Fry suggests, the honour to the house of Arniston of providing a third Lord President would have been great. Such an appointment must have had its attractions for a man who never lost touch with his Scottish roots and valued family sentiment. (27) However "Harry the Ninth", as James Boswell had aptly christened him, was operating on a rather wider, British scale, in 1787. He was a Member of Parliament, Treasurer of the Navy, a Commissioner of the Board of Control for India, and, as Boswell's jest suggests, uncrowned King of Scotland. He also enjoyed the profitable sinecure of Keeper of the Signet for Scotland. On the occasion of a later vacancy in the Lord Presidency he explained to the Home Secretary, Lord Grenville, his views on the matter:

There are many circumstances both public and private which

prevent me from entertaining any wish respecting the President's chair. It was certainly for many years the ultimate object of my ambition, and I would not speak true if I was not to admit that I see it pass by me, both on occasion of the former and present vacancy, with considerable regret. It is a situation of great respect, and if the duties of it are ably and conscientiously discharged, it is a situation of great dignity and utility to the public service. (28)

Henry Dundas was at this time forty five years old and perhaps was able to entertain ideas of filling the Lord President's chair at a later stage.

If one distinguished ex-Lord Advocate was not going to fill the President's chair there was much precedent in favour of the promotion of the current wearer of the Lord Advocate's gown, Ilay Campbell. The problem was, from Dundas's viewpoint, that Campbell was only fifty three and thus might well reign as Lord President for two or three decades, which would eliminate the possibility of Henry Dundas ever occupying the post. In passing it might be noted that service on the Court of Session seemed to be a recipe for longevity – in an age of generally low life-expectancy a remarkable number of the Senators of the College of Justice comfortably exceeded the three score years and ten: Bankton 75, Braxfield 77, Covington 82, Eskgrove 80, Hermand 84, Kames 86, Monboddo 85, Succoth 89 are just some of the examples. An older, stop-gap candidate would seem a prudent appointment.

In the event the seventy one year old Thomas Miller, Lord Glenlee, the Lord Justice-Clerk was promoted to the Presidency. Miller was a friend and political ally of Dundas, so his appointment fitted nicely enough into the game of politics. Glenlee would receive the additional honour of a Baronetcy in 1789.

If Henry Dundas did in fact make such a cold-blooded actuarial calculation then he was proved right. Lord President Glenlee died in September 1789, but at that time, as we have seen, Dundas was still unable or unwilling to extricate himself from the task of running the country to run the Scottish judiciary. Bowing to the inevitable, Ilay Campbell was allowed the usual Lord Advocate's perquisite and was made Lord President, taking as his judicial title Lord Succoth. The calculation proved to be sound – Lord Succoth lived until 1823, although he retired from the Court in 1808. Henry Dundas died in 1811.

Glenlee's promotion of course left a vacancy for Lord Justice-Clerk, the head of the Scottish criminal judiciary. One possible appointment might well have been Ilay Campbell; after all Thomas Miller had gone from Lord Advocate to Justice-Clerk. The five remaining Lord Commissioners of Justiciary from whom the post might be expected to be filled were:

Judicial Title	Family Name	Appointed to JusticiaryBench
Lord Hailes	Dalrymple	1766
Lord Braxfield	McQueen	1780
Lord Henderland	Murray	1783
Lord Eskgrove	Rae	1785
Lord Stonefield	Campbell	1787

To nobody's great surprise Braxfield was appointed. James Boswell, experimenting with a career at the English bar, was in Whitehaven when he read the news of the promotions in the *Gazette*. The three appointments – Glenlee to Lord President, Braxfield to Justice-Clerk and John MacLaurin to the bench as Lord Dreghorn only provoked the following diary entry:

> The changes produced an agitation not unpleasant, but I felt somewhat uneasy to think that had I steadily remained at the Scotch bar I might have had the judge's place. (29)

Boswell's feeling seems to be that MacLaurin, his friend and co-author of the *Court of Session Garland,* was not much senior to him and that he might now have been a contender for judicial office had he applied himself. This is somewhat overstating matters. MacLaurin was in fact nine years senior in Faculty membership and, perhaps more importantly, had never been in a mob that stoned the Lord President's house. Braxfield's promotion, on the other hand, was clearly viewed by Boswell as unremarkable.

Robert McQueen at the age of sixty five was now an officer of state, established in the second most senior post in the Scottish judiciary – in the words of the *Scots Magazine*, 'Thus did this able lawyer and acute Judge, solely by his own merit, attain one of the highest and most important stations in the country.' (30)

KAY·DEL·SULP· 1788   105

MR BRODIE

Kay responded to the Deacon Brodie case by producing two etchings.
The other shows Brodie's first meeting with his co-accused, George Smith,
but this picture underlines the Deacon's respectability.
The playing cards on the table suggest Brodie's love of gambling.

CHAPTER 7

Lord Justice-Clerk
1788–1799

" . . . chief among the inquisitors
of capital crimes . . ."

On 15th January 1788, David Dalrymple, Lord Hailes, the senior judge of the High Court of Justiciary, presiding in the absence of Lord Glenlee, newly promoted to be Lord President of the Court of Session, convened his colleagues of the Court; Lords Henderland, Eskgrove and Stonefield. The Book of Adjournal notes the circumstances:

> The which day Compeared Robert McQueen of Braxfield
> Esquire, One of the Senators of the College of Justice, and
> produced a Commission granted by His Majesty, and passed
> under the seal appointed by the Treaty of Union to be kept
> and used in Scotland in place of the Great Seal formerly kept
> there Nominating and Appointing him to be Lord Justice
> Clerk, which place is now vacant by the Resignation of the
> Right Honourable Thomas Miller of Glenlee late Lord Justice
> Clerk and now appointed Lord President of the Court of
> Session, and desired the said Commissions might be read and
> recorded, and the same being read was ordered to be
> recorded and whereof the tenor follows. (1)

The Book of Adjournal then contains the Latin text of the King's Commission – the formality of Latin an indication of the high status of

McQueen's appointment as one of the Officers of State. His commission was dated 24th December and sealed at Edinburgh on 8th January.

> After reading and recording of which Commission the said
> Robert McQueen qualified himself to His Majesty King
> George the Third, by Swearing the Oaths of alledgeance and
> abjuration and subscribing the same with the Assurance and
> having given his oath de fideli administratione officii he was
> thereupon admitted and received Lord Justice Clerk, and took
> his Seat accordingly.

Now acting under the direction of Lord Justice-Clerk Braxfield the High Court then proceeded to the admission of the replacement Lord Commissioner of Justiciary, Lord Swinton, whose Royal Commission was drawn in English. The first regular business of the Court was another stage in the long-running charge of perjury against the Rev William Leslie, Minister of St Andrews and Lhanbryde, which had first been brought back in 1786 by Alexander Cumming and Hugh Grant. Counsel for Cumming was William Honyman, the Lord Justice-Clerk's son-in-law. This case was continued for a week, until 21st January, when it was finally dismissed.

The first major case to be heard in full under Braxfield's presidency of the Justiciary Court came on 4th February 1788. Allan Macfarlane, an excise officer and Richard Firman, a soldier in the 39th Foot, were charged with murder. On 4th July 1787 when engaged in the task of attempting to seize illicit stills at Dunoon in Argyllshire a scuffle had ensued on the shore there. Duncan Fergusson, a ferryman in Dunoon, had got into a boat, Macfarlane had ordered Firman and the other soldiers accompanying him to fire and Firman had levelled his musket, fired and killed Fergusson. Charles Hope, counsel for the pannels argued that the reference to a scuffle indicated that there was no premeditation and that in any case the accused were employed in the lawful execution of their duty, had been attacked and were in danger of their lives.

Hope claimed that Fergusson was the ringleader of the mob and was attempting to take away the boat, which represented the excise party's only means of escape from the angry crowd. The Lord Advocate, Ilay Campbell, accepted much of what Hope had said, deprecated the resistance so often shown by the populace to the officers of the excise, but said that he:

> ... considered it as his duty, when the life of a fellow-subject was taken away, to make every necessary inquiry into the fact; and when he had done so, to bring the matter to fair and open trial. Though the pannels were, in this case, indicted for murder; yet he did not mean to carry it so far as to insist for a capital punishment, being conscious that the pannels had been unlawfully attacked in the execution of their duty; but whether to such an extent as to justify firing upon their assailants, was a matter worthy of serious consideration. (2)

The Lord Advocate after reviewing the law on culpable homicide and self-defence restricted the charge to culpable homicide. After the witnesses were examined the Crown dropped all charges against the soldier Firman, who, it was considered, had acted under the direction of the excise officer. Counsel summed up and: 'the Lord Justice-Clerk summed up the evidence with great impartiality'. The jury returned a unanimous verdict of not guilty, thus ending the new Lord Justice-Clerk's first case.

One curiosity about this case was that one participant in the trial was to become considerably more famous than any of the counsel, or even the presiding judge. One of the fifteen respectable Edinburgh citizens who had been empanelled as the jury was a certain 'wright in Edinburgh' named William Brodie. This was the soon to be notorious Deacon Brodie, who would return to the High Court in just over six months to stand trial for breaking into the Edinburgh Excise Office in March, just a month after he had performed his civic duty in the case of H.M. Advocate v Macfarlane and Firman, and, who in this appearance would come face to face with Lord Braxfield and the Bench in a quite different way.

A trial at the High Court on 10th March 1788 shows Braxfield in a rather poor light, at any rate by our modern expectations of judicial conduct. John Stewart, a journeyman weaver in Glasgow, was charged with involvement in riots in the city in September 1787 and with having attacked John Anderson, one of the Glasgow town officers who was assisting the city magistrates in dispersing the riotous mob. Stewart's defence was that, while he was admittedly in the mob he had been drawn there by curiosity and, that far from maltreating Anderson, the officer had: 'knocked the pannel down, and used him in a most cruel manner.' (3) The jury found, 'by a great majority', Stewart to be not guilty. Stewart was dismissed from the bar but not before Lord Braxfield took the opportunity to address a few improving words to him:

> ... informing him of the great danger which attended the
> mingling with a mob upon any pretence whatever ...

which was perhaps fair enough comment, in that Stewart had admitted that he had been drawn to the disturbance by 'idle curiosity'. However the Justice-Clerk went on to say that:

> ... though he had now been acquitted by a verdict of his
> country, yet it was not an unanimous one; and, if ever he
> should be again arraigned for a like crime, the verdict of
> another jury might strike very deep against him.

The Scottish third verdict of "not proven" has sometimes been popularly held to mean "you did it, we couldn't prove it but don't do it again" but Braxfield's view that the verdict of not guilty by a majority of the votes of the jury, was in some sense conditional or less effectual than a unanimous verdict certainly goes against the spirit of Scottish law; a legal code which allows a simple majority verdict rather than demanding unanimity or a weighted majority.

In April the Lord Justice-Clerk, with the newest member of the Court, Lord Swinton, set off on the Western Circuit to administer the King's justice in Stirling, Inveraray (but in the Argyllshire town found that there was no criminal business to be transacted) and Glasgow.

The trial at the High Court of Justiciary in Edinburgh on 27th August 1788 of William Brodie and George Smith certainly qualifies as a notable one – less for the crime with which the pannels were charged – housebreaking and stealing £16 – than for the fall from grace of Brodie and the shock that so respectable a citizen could have led a double life. This division between the Deacon's day-time existence as a pillar of society and douce citizen and his night-time exploits as housebreaker and thief fascinated contemporaries, so much so that three full accounts of the trial (to say nothing of pirated versions and edited accounts in the press) appeared in 1788.

A century later the Brodie case was to fascinate Robert Louis

Stevenson and indeed gives us RLS's second point of contact with Braxfield. Just as he used the figure of Braxfield to inform and shape his portrayal of *Weir of Hermiston* so he made use of the Deacon Brodie story, directly, in the play *Deacon Brodie, or the Double Life* which he wrote with his friend W E Henley and, indirectly, in his gripping study of duality *Strange Case of Dr Jekyll and Mr Hyde*. Nor does this end the Deacon's literary progeny – Muriel Spark's Edinburgh schoolmistress Miss Jean Brodie is hardly accidentally named. She too, in her own way, rejected and stood outside society and represented a subversive threat to the conventions of the Edinburgh of her day.

William Brodie was forty six years of age. He was the grandson of Ludovick Brodie, an Edinburgh Writer to the Signet, and son of Francis Brodie, a prosperous wright and cabinetmaker in Edinburgh. Both Francis Brodie and William Brodie were to serve as Deacons of the Incorporation of Wrights and in this capacity sat on the City Council. When Francis Brodie died in 1782 William inherited extensive properties and the huge sum of £10,000 cash. (4) Unfortunately the Deacon was a passionate and apparently compulsive gambler and had heavy expenses, which included maintaining two mistresses.

Temptation came his way from the nature of his work – he was extensively employed as a locksmith and built up a large collection of duplicate keys to the properties of his unsuspecting clients. A spate of house and shop breakings in Edinburgh over a long period of time was undoubtedly attributable to Brodie, even though the sole charge brought against him was breaking in to the Excise Office on the night of 5th March. This might have been Brodie's masterstroke – but he failed to find £600 lying in a secret drawer in the cashier's desk. Smith and Andrew Ainslie, his accomplices, were arrested for their involvement in an earlier crime. Brodie, fearing that they would implicate him, after a bold but fruitless attempt to visit them in the Edinburgh Tolbooth to establish their intentions, fled the country. He was eventually tracked down to the Netherlands, arrested and brought back to stand trial along with Smith.

Ainslie had, in the meantime, agreed to turn King's evidence. Another accomplice, John Brown, had given information to the Procurator Fiscal two days after the robbery and would, if his evidence could legally be allowed to be heard, be a key prosecution witness. Unfortunately for the prosecution, Brown was a convicted felon who had been sentenced by the Middlesex Quarter Sessions to transportation for theft. In the view of the Scots law of the time such a criminal was considered infamous and inadmissible as a witness. To get round this problem the Scottish Law Officers had procured a Royal pardon for Brown:

> . . . under the Great Seal of England, dated 28th July last,
> which, by the law of England, renders the witness habile and
> testable. (5)

The course of the trial has been well recorded by William Roughead, and more recently by John S Gibson. (6) Much of the interest comes in the remarkable clashes between the Lord Justice-Clerk and one of the defence counsel, John Clerk of Eldin. Clerk, he who years later was famously to advise the Lord Chancellor that manners had two n's, was at this time a recently qualified advocate on his first major case. Clerk and Robert Hamilton were defending George Smith while Henry Erskine, then the Dean of Faculty; Alexander Wight and Charles Hay were engaged for William Brodie. The prosecution team was the Lord Advocate Ilay Campbell, Solicitor General Robert Dundas and two Advocates Depute William Tait and James Wolfe Murray.

The trial opened with some indication of a new efficiency being driven by the Lord Justice-Clerk. Some witnesses had failed to turn up on time and the Lord Advocate asked that the laggards be fined. However investigations revealed that no specific time had been given on their citations and:

> The Lord Justice-Clerk, to prevent similar delays, gave
> directions that in time coming the citations given to jurymen
> and witnesses should bear a specified hour at which their
> attendance is to be required. (7)

Before proceedings started Brodie's defence objected to the vague description of some of the items of evidence – a watch and a trunk. After some debate the Bench pronounced their interlocutor repelling the objection at which point Clerk started upon his running battle with Braxfield.

> Mr John Clerk – My Lord Justice-Clerk, before the
> interlocutor is written out, I beg leave to make one

objection in behalf of the pannel, George Smith.

The Lord Justice-Clerk – What! After the Court have delivered
their opinions, it is not decent in you to propose to say
anything, and I apprehend the prisoners are in no danger
of suffering anything by you not being allowed to suffer
the defects of the Dean of Faculty.

Mr John Clerk – My Lord, the Dean of Faculty has no
authority to plead for my client. (8)

Clerk should have presented his objections before the Court had
deliberated, but he shows few signs of allowing his lack of experience
and junior status to interfere with his natural truculence. It must be
remembered in reading these clashes between Braxfield and Clerk that
both men would be speaking in a broad Scots accent, a feature which
was edited out of the three contemporary versions on which Roughead
based his account. John S Gibson's modern account entertainingly
restores something of the pith and attack of the original language.

The next round in Braxfield v Clerk came when George Smith's
wife was examined as a prosecution witness. Clerk objected that a wife's
evidence could not be heard against her husband. Lord Advocate
Campbell argued that he had no such intention but that she was
nonetheless an unexceptionable witness against Brodie. Clerk,
responding, pointed out that Brodie and Smith were charged with the
same crime and that any evidence pointing to Brodie's guilt was bound
to affect Smith. Ilay Campbell sought to clarify matters by specifying
the limited questions he proposed to put to her and the Bench gave
their views, which were unanimously in favour of the admissibility of
the witness. Braxfield concluding said:

> . . . nor will I suffer one single question to be put to her or her
> to say a single word from which his [Smith's] guilt can be
> inferred; and the jury are not to give any attention
> whatever to it, if it should happen that anything should
> drop to the prejudice of her husband.

Mr John Clerk – My Lord Justice Clerk . . .

The Lord Justice-Clerk – What! Mr Clerk, would you insist on
being heard after the court have delivered their opinions?
It is most indecent to attempt it.

Mr John Clerk – I was heard, my Lord, on the general point of

the admissibility of this witness, but not on the special
objections which I have to put to the questions which my
Lord Advocate proposes to put, and on which the Court
have not delivered any opinion.

The Lord Justice-Clerk – Mr Clerk, this is really intolerable.

The Dean of Faculty – My Lord, although as counsel for Mr
Brodie I am not entitled to be heard on this subject, I find
myself called upon to interfere as Dean of Faculty. It is
perhaps not strictly in order for Mr Clerk to insist on being
heard after your Lordships have delivered your opinions,
but some indulgence ought to be shown to a young
gentleman. (9)

The "young gentleman" was not, in fact, all that young. He was thirty
one, had qualified as a Writer to the Signet and had practised as an
accountant before turning to the Bar and being admitted to the Faculty
of Advocates in December 1785. Nevertheless the Dean's plea for
indulgence for his junior member clearly had its effect, and Mr Clerk
was allowed to make his specific objection, but was overruled.

Andrew Ainslie, who had turned King's evidence, was examined,
despite the Dean's objections to him as having only given evidence as
a result of a bargain made for his life with the Sheriff of Edinburgh:

... and it was not till then he was prevailed upon to say that
Mr Brodie had any concern in this crime. No man could
withstand such a temptation, and it is impossible that the
Court can receive the testimony of a witness in such
circumstances. (10)

After some wrangling, in which the institutional status of the writings
of Sir George MacKenzie, the great seventeenth century Lord Advocate
and legal authority became questioned, the Dean's objections were
repelled. However not all the defence's objections met with such a fate.
Part of the evidence was a promissory note from the Glasgow Arms
Bank – this had been described as a bank note and Erskine argued that
such a description could only properly be applied to the notes of a
bank instituted by Royal Charter. The Court found in his favour and
the note was not allowed to be introduced in evidence.

John Brown's evidence then came to be called and Henry Erskine, in a long speech, argued that though the King's pardon might excuse Brown the penalties of his crime it could not render him a creditable witness. In a phrase which might well have influenced the Robert Burns of:

> A prince can mak a belted knight,
> A marquis, duke, and a' that,
>
> But an honest man's aboon his might,
> Gude faith he mauna fa' that!

Erskine argued:

> My Lords, I have heard it said that the King could make a
> peer, but that he could not make a gentleman; I am sure that
> he cannot make a rogue an honest man. This pardon,
> therefore, at the utmost can only avert the punishment which
> follows from the sentence. It cannot remove the guilt of this
> man, though it may save his life. (11)

This matter caused some concern to the Bench. Hailes was clearly for repelling the Dean's objection; Eskgrove would not have countenanced hearing Brown if his sentence had been from a Scottish court but felt that the principle of *comitas* or courtesy to the rulings of other jurisdictions and the understanding that in English law a pardon rendered the recipient a fit and proper witness meant he had to allow Brown's testimony. Stonefield tersely repelled the Dean's argument and Swinton aligned himself with Eskgrove's view. The Justice-Clerk argued that if Ainslie had been eligible to give evidence so was Brown and pronounced the Court's interlocutor:

> . . . they repel the objections stated and allow the witness to be
> examined, reserving the credibility of his evidence to the jury.
>
> (12)

Brown's evidence was heard and did much to convict Brodie and Smith. The court then received the written depositions which concluded the Crown case.

The Dean, in presenting the case for Brodie, attempted to establish an alibi for his client by leading evidence from Brodie's mistress, Jean Watt, that he had spent the night of the robbery with her, coming to her house in Libberton's Wynd around eight, and, complaining of a sore throat, had retired to bed with her around ten and that Brodie had left the next morning at nine. The defence evidence being concluded a few minutes after one o'clock of the morning of the 28th August the Lord Advocate addressed the jury. Ilay Campbell's speech takes over eight pages of Roughead's book.

Next John Clerk rose to speak for Smith. A couple of minutes into his address, just as he had made the, admittedly, rather tiresomely mock-modest remark:

> But, I, as his most inexperienced and imperfect counsel, will
> try and do the best I can for the poor man (13)

he was interrupted by a tetchy Braxfield.

> Lord Justice-Clerk – Be short and concise, sir, at this time of
> the morning.

When Clerk came to the evidence of Ainslie and Brown he declared that he thought that a great deal of improper evidence had been admitted for the Crown. This remark was not well received:

> Lord Justice-Clerk – Do you say that, sir, after the judgement
> which the Court has pronounced? That sir, is a most improper
> observation to address at the outset to the jury. (14)

Which it undoubtedly was. In Clerk's defence it must be recollected that there was no appeal from this court – so the modern possibility of an appeal on the grounds of improper procedure or misdirection of the jury did not exist. Clerk's conception of his duty to his client perhaps forced him to place his view of the situation before the jury – but their Lordships were not happy:

> Lord Stonefield – It is a positive reflection on the Court.
> Lord Hailes – It is a flat accusation that we have admitted
> improper evidence.

Lord Eskgrove – I never heard the like of this from any young
counsel at the beginning of his career at the bar.

Lord Justice-Clerk – With these admonitions, go on, sir; proceed.

The irrepressible Clerk did, referring to Ainslie and Brown as 'two
corbies or infernal scoundrels' he not only again attacked the admission
of their evidence, but raised the stakes.

Lord Justice-Clerk – Mr Clerk, please restrict your reflections.
The Court have admitted the witness [Brown].

Mr Clerk – Yes, my Lords, I know that very well, but your
Lordships should not have admitted him, and of that the
jury will now judge.

Lord Justice-Clerk – This is most indecent behaviour. You
cannot be allowed to speak to the admissibility; to the
credibility you may.

After some more exchanges Clerk went even further:

Mr Clerk – But, my Lords, the jury are to judge of the law as
well as the facts.

This was a fairly unorthodox view – admittedly it was the grounds on
which an earlier Robert Dundas had secured the acquittal of his client
from the charge of murdering the Earl of Strathmore back in 1728 – but
the normal doctrine was expounded by Braxfield:

Lord Justice-Clerk – Sir, I tell you that the jury have nothing
to do with the law, but to take it *simpliciter* from me.

Which clear and unequivocal ruling might have been thought enough
for even the boldest junior advocate, but:

Mr Clerk – That I deny.
[Consternation in court]
Lord Hailes – Sir, will you deny the authority of this High Court?

175

> Mr Clerk – Gentlemen of the jury, notwithstanding of this
> interruption, I beg to tell you, with all confidence and all
> respect, that you are the judges of the law as well as of the
> facts. You are the judges of the whole case.
>
> Lord Justice-Clerk – You are talking nonsense.
>
> Mr Clerk – My Lord, you had better not snub me in this way. I
> never mean to talk nonsense.
>
> Lord Justice-Clerk – Proceed – gang on, sir.

Which is a fairly remarkable exchange. Not many counsel survive
describing a judicial intervention as 'this interruption'. Not the least
remarkable feature is the degree of tolerance Braxfield extends to Clerk,
who was indeed 'talking nonsense' – or at least legal nonsense. Clerk
continues to argue that the Royal pardon was ineffective in rendering
Brown an honest man whose evidence the Court could give credence
to. Ilay Campbell intervenes and addresses Clerk:

> Lord Advocate – Sir, permit me to say, after this interruption,
> that the prerogative of mercy is the brightest jewel in His
> Majesty's Crown.
>
> Mr Clerk – I hope his Majesty's Crown will never be
> contaminated by any villains around it.

This was indeed strong stuff. Clerk was a Whig; the Law Officers who
had procured the Royal pardon in order to strengthen their case were
Tories; the law and politics were always interwoven but this was
bringing party politics into the High Court in a most overt and unusual
way. Braxfield asked the Lord Advocate if he wished Clerk's words
noted down – that is taken official note of for possible action. Campbell
declined this, suggesting that his: 'young friend will soon cool in his
effervescence for his client'. Clerk however continued to insist that the
jury were judges of law as well as fact, being warned from the Bench
on each occasion but refusing to change his line. Eventually he said
that he stood there:

> . . . as an independent Scottish advocate, and I tell you, a jury
> of my countrymen, that you are the judges of the law as well
> as of the facts.

This was, even for Clerk, an overtly political point, designed to distinguish him from what he considered the Dundas placemen who were the Law Officers and, indeed the friend of Dundas who was presiding on the Bench. A further judicial warning ensued and matters came to a head. Now, far from the Bench rebuking the advocate, the advocate, in a quite remarkable fashion decided that it was his duty to rebuke the Bench:

> Mr Clerk – This has been too often repeated. I have met with no politeness from this Court. You have interrupted me, you have snubbed me rather too often, my Lord, in the line of my defence. I maintain that the jury are judges of the law as well as of the facts; and I am positively resolved that I will proceed no further unless I am allowed to speak in my own way.

Braxfield ignored this gross impertinence, took him at his word and called upon the Dean to address the jury on behalf of Brodie. The Dean shook his head, implicitly declining to be party to any improper limitation on a colleague's right to defend his client. The Lord Justice-Clerk was about to launch into his charge to the jury when:

> Mr Clerk [starting to his feet and shaking his fist at the bench] – Hang my client if ye daur, my Lord, without hearing me in his defence!

This outburst, not surprisingly produced an unparalleled sensation in Court – the judges retired to their robing room for a consultation. Their return surely must presage an eruption from Braxfield and action for contempt against Clerk – after all was this court not presided over by a tyrant and bully? Their Lordships returned and, remarkably, the Lord Justice-Clerk simply invited Mr Clerk to continue with his speech, which he did, after a preliminary recapitulation of his objections as to Brown and Ainslie's admissibility. The record of the trial does not disclose what happened during the Bench's consultation but one might speculate that the Dean of Faculty took advantage of the recess to give a word of advice to his junior colleague. At all events the remainder of

Clerk's address, which was fairly brief and quite proper and unexceptionable passed off without further clashes. At three in the morning he sat down.

Henry Erskine then addressed the jury, on behalf of Brodie, for an hour and a half. Lord Braxfield then charged the jury. After observing:

> Mr Brodie's father, whom I knew, was a very respectable man, and that the son of such a man – himself, too, educated to a respectable profession and who had long lived with reputation in it – should be arraigned at this bar for a crime so detestable, is what must affect us all, gentlemen, with sensations of horror. (15)

He went on to re-assert the admissibility of Ainslie and Brown's evidence and reminded the jury that each had been, in open court, reminded that they ran no risk from telling the truth, that their being cited as witnesses secured them from all punishment save that for perjury. As there was no suggestion made of a corrupt bargain being made with the prosecution he suggested:

> . . . you cannot suppose, gentlemen, that they would be guilty of perjury without any advantage to themselves, and merely to swear away the lives of these prisoners at the bar.

He surveyed the evidence and the course of events concluding:

> . . . I can have no doubt in my own mind that Mr Brodie was present at the breaking into the Excise Office; and as to the other man, Smith, as I have already said, there can be still less doubt as to him. If you are of the same opinion, gentlemen, you will return a verdict against both the prisoners; but if you are of a different opinion, and do not consider the evidence against Brodie sufficiently strong, you will separate the one from the other, and bring in a verdict accordingly. (16)

At 6 am on Thursday morning, twenty-one hours after the Court had convened, the jury were enclosed and ordered to return at 1 pm.

When they did so they returned a unanimous verdict of guilty against both pannels. Before sentence could be pronounced Wight,

Henry Erskine's junior, moved an objection on the grounds that the charge had spoken of: 'the house in which the General Excise Office for Scotland was then kept', whereas there were two connected adjacent houses, or more precisely a house and an outbuilding used for that purpose. Much debate ensued on what was at best a fairly thin point, and one which should, in any case, have been raised earlier. Perhaps the most telling argument against Wight's motion was put by Lord Swinton. Arguing that the defence motion struck at the roots of the Scottish jury trial he said:

> . . . the libel is first of all to be read; the party accused is then at liberty to state his defences to the form of indictment, and to the competency or relevance of the charge; and it is the province of the judges to determine the law. . . The indictment and judgements upon it are then remitted to the knowledge of an assize. It then goes out of the hands of the judges, and the province of the jury commences, which is to try the truth of the facts, and to apply the law, that is, the judgment of the Court, to the facts, by returning such verdict as they think fit. (17)

He went on to argue that the defence motion was:

> . . . a suggestion to the judges to look back into the proof, which is the whole province and privilege of the jury. . . Is it not paving a way to make verdicts of no use, but our usurping a right to judge of the proof, independent of the verdict?

Braxfield concurring, the Bench repelled the plea offered in arrest of judgement. Braxfield, having asked his brethren for their views on sentence and having had a statement that the offences were capital pronounced sentence of death after observing that:

> You have had a long and fair trial, conducted on the part of the public prosecutor with the utmost candour and humanity, and you have been assisted with able counsel, who have exerted the greatest ability and fidelity in your defence. (18)

Brodie wrote to Henry Dundas on 10th September seeking his influence to procure a remission of the death sentence to one of transportation. There were few grounds for such remission – and perhaps less probability of Dundas seeking them in view of the political dimension which Mr Clerk had introduced into the trial. Smith and Brodie were hung on 1st October from the Tolbooth gibbet that Brodie, in his respectable persona as a master tradesmen, had designed for the city council just two years before.

The Brodie trial, quite apart from its inherent interest, and its intriguing literary offspring, shows Braxfield on the bench in a remarkably clear and full way, largely thanks to the contemporary accounts which give more of the picture than is the case for most trials, where the somewhat formal record of the Books of Adjournal must be relied upon. The Brodie case was in fact the first Scottish criminal trial to be fully reported in shorthand. William Roughead commented on Braxfield's behaviour in the Brodie case:

> . . . the thing that strikes the professional reader [Roughead
> was a Writer to the Signet] is the amazing mildness of Lord
> Braxfield in the face of John Clerk's intolerably rude and
> violent demeanour to the Bench. (19)

The bullying of counsel was one of Cockburn's main charges against Braxfield; the other was of sending people to the gallows with a jest. In the Brodie case one might argue that Clerk did the bullying rather than Braxfield and on the second count there is certainly nothing to justify such a charge. Rather he addressed Brodie with what seems to be genuine sympathy and feeling, Smith being dismissed with short shrift, but no discourtesy or mockery:

> I wish I could be of any use to you in your melancholy
> situation. To one of you it is altogether needless for me to
> offer any advice. To you, William Brodie, from your education
> and habits of life, cannot but know everything suited to your
> present situation which I could suggest to you. It is much to
> be lamented that those vices, which are called gentlemanly
> vices, are so favourably looked upon in the present age. They
> have been the source of your ruin; and whatever may be
> thought of them, they are such as assuredly lead to ruin. I
> hope you will improve the short time which you now have to
> live by reflecting upon your past conduct, and endeavouring

to procure, by a sincere repentance, forgiveness for your
many crimes. God always listens to those who seek Him with
sincerity. (20)

As Lord Justice-Clerk and thus one of the officers of state, Braxfield
was appointed in September 1788 as a Commissioner and Trustee for
Fisheries, Manufactures and Improvements. This body, established in
1727 to administer the moneys made available following the Treaty of
Union for the encouragement of linen weaving and the fishing industry
and other manufactures and improvements.

In addition to his Justiciary duties Braxfield, of course, continued
as one of the members of the Court of Session, taking his full part in
the work of that body. Private life and public life ran alongside each
other, his son John's first child, named Robert after the child's famous
grandfather in the traditional Scottish pattern of naming, was born in
1789 and he was consulted about the marriage settlement of his wife's
Agnew relations' daughter.

The September 1789 Justiciary Circuit took him and Lord
Stonefield to Stirling and Inveraray, in which evidently law-abiding
centres there were no criminal cases awaiting their Lordships, and then
to Glasgow. The cases at the Glasgow diet were a representative cross-
section of High Court cases and their disposal was equally typical.
There was one case of murder, to which the accused failed to answer
and was outlawed; four cases of theft, one of which was punished by
banishment, one by fourteen years transportation, one was deserted
by the Crown and one was found not proven; and one case of forgery
punished by fourteen years transportation.

Shortly after returning from the Autumn Circuit Braxfield would
learn of the death, on 27th September, of Lord President Glenlee. This,
as we have already seen, was Henry Dundas's second chance to come
back to Scotland and settle down as Lord President, but the time was
never right for this and the rather dour figure of the Lord Advocate,
Ilay Campbell, was appointed as Lord President Succoth. Cockburn
would describe Campbell thus:

His speaking, always admirable in matter, was the reverse of
attractive. He could only be severely argumentative, and the
painfulness of this was increased by the minuteness of his

elaboration, and the dryness of his manner. His voice was low
and dull, his face sedate and hard. Even when heaving
internally with strong passion, externally he was like a knot
of wood. (21)

Robert Dundas of Arniston was promoted from Solicitor General to
Lord Advocate and Robert Blair filled the vacancy for Solicitor General.

1790 and 1791 were, in professional terms, less spectacular years
for Braxfield, years with a full schedule of cases but none of them of
either great notoriety or deep political significance. They were, however,
years marked by personal tragedy. At the end of 1790 and through
1791 he had to witness the scandal of his daughter Catherine's divorce
– although there is no evidence that he ever reacted publicly to this,
however great the feeling of shame and distress might have been.
Stevenson's description of his fictional Lord Hermiston going "up the
great, bare staircase of his duty, uncheered and undepressed" comes
irresistibly to mind. On October 6th 1791 his wife Mary died at their
country home at Hardington.

The next year, 1792, was marked by an increasing volume of reform
agitation in the country and the example of the revolution in France
was increasingly held up as an example of what might be aspired to in
Britain. The formation of bodies such as the London Corresponding
Society (founded by Thomas Hardy, a native of Falkirk) and the Society
of the Friends of the People produced two new active organisations –
one, the Corresponding Society aimed at a popular audience with a
low subscription and a programme of drastic reform; the other, a more
elitist body with a less radical reform programme. Scotland saw a spate
of outbreaks of popular demonstrations against Henry Dundas and
the governing class – "King Henry's" effigy was burned in villages
and towns from Peebles to Aberdeen. This agitation arose from both
general reform enthusiasm – a mood heightened by the circulation of
Tom Paine's *Rights of Man* – and from local grievances such as enclosures
and road tolls.

The Justiciary Bench saw considerable changes in 1792. Sir David
Dalrymple, Lord Hailes, the longest serving Commissioner of Justiciary
died and was replaced by William Nairne, Lord Dunsinnan, promoted
from the Court of Session. Dunsinnan was one of the judges whom
Cockburn characterised as being:

... personally, mild, respectable men and as judges perfectly
honest. Henderland and Dunsinnan had done nothing to
distinguish themselves. (22)

Lord Stonefield resigned his Justiciary seat and was replaced by the
promotion from the Bar of Alexander Abercromby. Lord Abercromby,
Cockburn records, abhorred Braxfield and, whether by accident or
design, they do not appear to have ever had to undertake a Justiciary
Circuit together so there may have been some basis for this statement.
The Circuit experience threw the judges into prolonged and close
proximity and any personal distaste or animosity would be more
difficult to handle there than in the larger milieu of the High Court or
the Court of Session.

In the midst of all this change and political agitation came a
pleasant compliment to Braxfield. The son of his friend and George
Square neighbour, Walter Scott, Writer to the Signet, another Walter,
had decided to become an advocate and dedicated his thesis, on the
topic of the disposal of the bodies of condemned criminals, *De
Cadaveribus Damnatorum,* to the Justice-Clerk. Young Walter's eloquent
Latin dedication showed some signs of the literary talent which would
raise him to a fame far beyond the bounds of Parliament House. The
text's dedication read:

VIRO NOBILI ROBERTO MACQUEEN DE BRAXFIELD, INTER
QUAESITORES DE REBUS CAPITALIBUS PRIMARIO, INTER
JUDICES DE REBUS CIVILIBUS, SENATORI DIGNISSIMO,
PERITO HAUD MINUS QUAM FIDELI JURIS INTERPRETI;
ADEOQUE, IN UTROQUE MUNERE FUNGENDO, SCELERA
SIVE DEBITA SEVERITATE PUNIENDO, SIVE SUUM CUIQUE
TRIBUENDO ET TUENDO, PRUDENTIA PARITER ATQUE
JUSTITIA, INSIGNI; HASCE THESES JURIDICAS, SUMMA CUM
OBSERVANTIA, SACRAS ESSE VOLUIT GUALTERUS SCOTT.

Which may be translated as:

To the noble man, Robert MacQueen of Braxfield, chief
among the inquisitors of capital crimes, and among the
judges of civil suits, a senator most worthy, as an interpreter
of the law no less skilled than sure; and what is more,
outstanding in the performance of each office, whether in

183

punishing crimes with due severity, or rendering and securing to each man his own, with wisdom and equally with justice; Walter Scott, with the utmost respect has wished these juridical theses to be dedicated.

In July 1792 the Society of the Friends of the People spread to Scotland and within a few months the growth of this body and similar associations began to give serious cause for concern to the administration in Scotland. On 3rd October 1792 the Glasgow Associated Friends of the Constitution and of the People was formed. This body had a most respectable group of office-bearers – Lt Colonel Dalrymple of Fordell, President; Thomas Muir, younger, of Huntershill, advocate, was the Vice President and George Crawford, Writer, was elected as Secretary. Soon they had encouraged the formation of associations across west central Scotland. The programme of reform adopted by these bodies was modest – equal representation of the people in parliament and shorter parliaments. Members, who subscribed 3d a quarter, had to pledge their allegiance to a British constitution comprising King, House of Lords and House of Commons and had to promise to suppress riot, sedition and disorder. Such a pledge and such a restrained scheme of reform might have been thought to present little threat to the established order – however the real danger in the eyes of Dundas and his supporters was the involvement of the populace at large. One correspondent of Henry Dundas's put the point well:

> The success of the French Democrats has had a most mischievous effect here. Did it go not further than give occasion for triumph to those who entertain the same sentiments here, there would be little harm, for they are very few in number, and but two or three of them possessed of any considerable influence or respectability. But it has led them to think of forming societies for reformation in which the lower classes of people are invited to enter, and however insignificant these leaders may be in themselves, when backed with the mob they become formidable. (23)

It was exactly this involvement of the unenfranchised working classes which was to strike Braxfield and his fellow judges as so dangerous and so mischievous in the series of sedition trials which were to occupy the Courts and the public attention during 1793 and 1794 and which did so much to blacken Braxfield's reputation. The first of these trials was of three journeymen printers, John Morton, James Anderson and Malcolm Craig for:

> ... uttering seditious speeches, tending to create a spirit of disloyalty and disaffection to the sovereign, and to the established government. (24)

It took place in the High Court in January 1793, just five days after Braxfield had married Elizabeth Ord. The Lord Justice-Clerk's sense of duty clearly did not permit him to enjoy an extended honeymoon as he was on the Bench for this case. The accused had gone into a canteen in Edinburgh Castle and in the presence of some soldiers drunk a toast: 'George the Third and last and damnation to all crowned heads', and had, it was alleged, attempted to seduce the troops from their duty and allegiance. Cockburn notes:

> They were unanimously convicted. And there seems to be no ground for questioning the propriety of this verdict. (25)

The problem, for Cockburn, comes with the decision on sentence. It is interesting in view of his strictures elsewhere on Braxfield's severity and on the practice of transportation that it was Lord Henderland who in outlining the possible means of disposing of the case raised the question of this form of sentence:

> We can only choose one of three punishments – either transportation to Botany Bay; – banishment, for sedition, to England, is out of the question ... (26)

Banishment furth of Scotland was, as we have seen, a routine enough punishment, but Henderland's reasonable point was that it was inappropriate, for a political offence, to send the offender to another part of the same country, whatever might be the merits of so doing for a common criminal. He continued to list the options:

> ... corporal punishment by whipping and imprisonment, or imprisonment alone. Were the panels aged and inveterate offenders ... I should have had no scruple to deprive them of

the enjoyment of this happy Constitution against which they had offended, and obliged them, by hard labour in an infant colony, to repair in some measure the injury they had done here.

However Henderland concluded that, as the accused were young, industrious and of peaceful character they should, despite his reservations about the conditions, physical and moral, in the Edinburgh Tolbooth, serve a term of imprisonment. They were sentenced to nine months. Cockburn argues that there was no Statute fixing transportation as the punishment, or a possible punishment for sedition and that Henderland had simply declared the legality of transportation as punishment and by so doing settled the state of the judicial mind. This point would arise again in the following months.

The issue of transportation, as a reality rather than as a possibility, arose in the next major sedition trial, that of Thomas Muir. Something of the events of Muir's involvement in the radical movement, his journey to France and his return to stand trial were narrated in Chapter 2. A closer examination of the trial, and in particular Braxfield's role, is now relevant.

The *Scots Magazine* devoted over fourteen pages to the case in its September and October 1793 issues. The case opened on Friday 30th August. The *Scots Magazine* reported the charge thus:

> ... that the said Thomas Muir, in November last, at the societies for reform in Kirkintilloch and Campsie (which he had been the chief means of instituting), did address and harangue the said meeting, seditiously endeavouring to represent the government of this country as oppressive and tyrannical, and the legislative body of the state as venal and corrupt, particularly by instituting a comparison between the pretended existing government of France and the constitution of Great Britain, with respect to the expences necessary for carrying on the functions of government; and endeavouring to represent it as useless, cumbersome and expensive. (27)

The *Scots Magazine* then gave two pages of extracts from some of the allegedly seditious pamphlets which Muir was accused of circulating.

Muir had been offered the services of Henry Erskine, the leading Whig advocate. Erskine, who clearly knew his man, stipulated that he would only defend Muir if Muir placed the direction of the defence entirely in his hands. This Muir refused to do. Erskine, reasonably enough, declined to continue and Muir, an advocate by profession although recently struck-off the roll when he was outlawed for his failure to appear at an earlier diet of the High Court, defended himself.

The jury was empanelled, despite Muir's objections that all of them were members of a constitutionalist body – the Goldsmith's Hall association – which had previously voted to exclude him and other members of the Friends of the People on grounds of their being enemies to the constitution. His very proper argument was that by so doing they had prejudged the issue and could not form a fair and unbiased jury. One juror, a naval officer, sought to be excused from the jury on the grounds that he was a servant of the King and was unsure of the propriety of his sitting on a case of this nature. This moral qualm was overridden from the Bench and the objections to the packed nature of the jury were equally swiftly dealt with, the Lord Justice-Clerk observing that if Muir's objection were to be considered, juries in this type of case could not include anyone who had taken an oath of allegiance to the King. Which might be true, but the coincidence of the whole jury of fifteen being members of one political association does seem to be remarkably high and it will be remembered that the selection of jurors from the county lists was a matter in which the presiding judge had a significant part to play.

The Crown case was not entirely satisfactory – the first two witnesses, when cross examined by Muir agreed that he had always argued for peaceful means. The second of these, Robert Weddell, a Kirkintilloch weaver, and vice-president of the local reform society, declared that Muir had always:

> ... recommended peace, order, and constitutional measures,
> and to guard against immoral characters being members, as
> they would ruin the cause ...

The next Crown witness was the Rev James Lapslie, minister of Campsie. The egregious Mr Lapslie was to receive a government pension for his services in securing evidence against Muir. Muir objected to his evidence as he claimed that Lapslie had been present when the witnesses were being interviewed – at their precognitions – and had:

... gone up and down the country, taking notes, and putting
questions to the witnesses ...

The Lord Advocate on this being proved agreed to abandon Mr
Lapslie's evidence. Amongst the evidence which was admitted was
that of Ann Fisher, a servant in Muir's father's home. Cockburn
suggests, quite convincingly, that her evidence, which gave exact details
of books and pamphlets Muir was said to have circulated and details
of his political views, was fabricated:

> Whether she was doing more than reciting a prepared part, I
> do not know; but it has never fallen to my lot to be
> acquainted with any *servant maid* who, untutored, could have
> given such learned evidence. (28)

Among the defence witnesses was William Skirving, himself later to
stand trial for sedition, who testified that Muir had gone to Paris at the
instigation of the Society of the Friends of the People: '. . . to see if he
could have any influence to prevent the execution of the King.' (29) A
long list of defence witnesses testified to Muir's peaceable policies and
his lack of opposition to the established order of King and Parliament.
    The Lord Advocate's address to the jury got swiftly to the centre
of the Crown case. Describing Muir he said:

> He is a man, who, under the pretext of a reform, as I shall
> afterwards shew you, has been sowing mischief and sedition;
> he appears before you, after being a fugitive from his
> country . . . (30)

This last point was at least arguable. Muir's trip to France was probably
naive in its expectation that he could prevent Louis XVI's execution,
unwise in a period of heightened international tension and certainly
injudicious in its timing when he knew his court hearing was due.
However he had eventually returned of his own volition to stand trial.
But Robert Dundas went on, not disdaining hyperbole:

> This country has seen many instances of pernicious effects of
> seditious writings and conduct; but I am persuaded a wider

range of diabolical mischief will appear in this man, than ever was seen in England, or any where else.

And coming perhaps to what might be thought the real issue:

Who could believe that a man of liberal education, an Advocate at this bar, could be found among villagers, and manufacturers, poor and ignorant, for the purpose of sowing sedition and discontent?

Muir summed up in his own defence, speaking for over two hours – one point he made was that, as he was accused of speaking sedition in public, it seemed strange to have to bring the evidence of a family servant (Anne Fisher) to incriminate him. He concluded:

I feel myself supported by the consciousness of the rectitude of my intentions. I may be confined within the walls of a prison; I may even have to mount the scaffold; but never can I be deprived, or be ashamed of, the records of my past life.

Braxfield, in his summing-up, apart from his eulogy on the British constitution which has already been quoted, spent some time on ground which the Lord Advocate had previously tilled:

There was a spirit of sedition and revolt going abroad [in the winter of 1792/93], which rendered every good subject seriously uneasy. And I leave it for you to judge, whether it was perfectly innocent or not in Mr Muir, at such a time, going about among ignorant country people, and among the lower classes of the people, making them leave off their work, and inducing them to believe that a reform was absolutely necessary to preserve their safety and their liberty, which till then they never suspected to be in danger.

The court rose at half past one in the morning of August 31st and at noon the jury returned a unanimous verdict of guilty to all the charges. Cockburn observes:

. . . even if lawful, transportation was certainly not necessary. The punishment was discretionary. Yet, exercising a

discretion, the court sentenced a person in the rank of a
gentleman, convicted of a first offence, and this offence
sedition, to transportation for fourteen years. (31)

Cockburn, it will be noted, is not quite such an advanced liberal as to
be able to overlook Muir's professional and social status, but adduces
the fact that he was 'in the rank of a gentleman' as an additional
argument against his transportation. Cockburn's view of what is
expected by, for and of a gentleman is not totally different from that
expressed by Dundas and Braxfield. If they thought that it was an
additional offence for a gentleman to stir up political activism among
the lower orders, Cockburn evidently thought that a sentence of
transportation passed against a gentleman was a harsher punishment
that a similar sentence passed against a member of the proletariat. The
concept of equality before the law clearly still had some way to go,
even in the mid-nineteenth century Court of Session of Lord Cockburn's
era.

Cockburn suggests that the jury were surprised at the severity of
the punishment and that they had thought that the offence would have
been punished by a short period of imprisonment. Muir's own
comments were:

> I do not mean to trouble the court with any observations on
> my sentence. By some it may be thought lenient, by others
> severe. It is a matter of little consequence; for had I been
> condemned to be led out to the scaffold, I should have
> possessed the same calm serenity of mind I feel at this
> moment. I am conscious of the purity of my intentions; and
> that I have acted and suffered in a great, a good, and a
> glorious cause, which sooner or later will prevail, and
> ultimately save this country. (32)

Unusually, the proceedings in the High Court of Justiciary became the
subject of much comment in Parliament – but it will be easier to consider
these matters after narrating the course of the next sedition trial.

This was heard on circuit at Perth, before Lords Eskgrove and
Abercromby, in September 1793. The accused was an English Unitarian
clergyman, Thomas Fyshe Palmer, and the charges were that he had
written and circulated seditious writings. Cockburn argues that Palmer
was no more than an accessory to the composition of the seditious

writings and had advised against their production but had been outvoted and saw to the task of printing and distributing them for his reform society. In any event he was found guilty and, after some debate, sentenced to seven years transportation. It is worth reiterating that this case was tried on circuit, without the presence of the Lord Justice-Clerk. No one need attempt to defend the severity of the sentence – but the recollection that such a sentence could be given by judges other than a bench presided over by Braxfield does serve to contextualise Braxfield's approach and style.

The reports of the Muir and Palmer trials caused great interest and Lord Lauderdale and two Members of Parliament – Charles Grey and Richard Brinsley Sheridan – wrote to the Home Secretary, Henry Dundas, arguing that the Muir and Palmer sentences were illegal as the provision in Scots Law for banishment did not imply transportation. Dundas wrote to the Lord Justice-Clerk on 18th December 1793:

> A representation having been delivered to me stating
> objections to the legality of the sentence of transportation
> pronounced against Mr Muir & Mr Palmer and referring
> particularly to the Scottish Statute of 1703 I think it right to
> transmit to Your Lordship so much of the said representation
> as relates to that question and to desire that you will, in
> consultation with the Lords of His Majesty's court of
> Justiciary, report to me, whether, from what is there stated, or
> on any other grounds, you see cause to doubt the legality of
> the said sentence. (33)

Braxfield speedily replied in a letter dated from Edinburgh on 27th December:

> I have the honour of yours with the representations for
> Thomas Muir and Fyshe Palmer which I immediately laid
> before the whole Judges of the Court of Justiciary for their
> opinion. In writing to you, it would surely have been
> unnecessary to say much as you are as well acquainted with
> the criminal law of Scotland as any of us. But it occurred to us
> that others who had not the same opportunity of being
> acquainted with the law of Scotland might wish to be
> satisfied. We have therefore given our opinion at considerable
> length in a report signed by me by the appointment of the
> other Judges which I hereby transmit to you & from a perusal

thereof I apprehend it must be obvious that transportation was known in Scotland prior to the Act of 1703, at the date of it, & down to this present time.

2do./ That in the language of the law of Scotland banishment is the generic term for denoting the punishment & that transportation was not considered as a punishment separate & distinct from banishment, but as one of the modes of carrying the sentence of banishment into execution & which was adopted when the heinousness of the offence rendered it proper & that of consequence the Court of Justiciary have full powers to transport even for the precise same crime that is the object of the Statute of 1703.

But 3to/ the cases of Muir and Palmer have nothing to do with the Statute of 1703 for the crime of which they were convicted viz. that of Sedition for the very purpose of overturning our Constitution and Government is in its nexus different from that of Leasing Making which altho' it may have a tendency to promote sedition yet in our law is considered as a verbal injury. Upon the whole I am perfectly clear that the Court have full powers to transport for the crime of Sedition, so I am equally clear that in this case the punishment is not greater than their conduct merited & that any mitigation by the interposition of the Royal mercy would in the present confusion be a most inexpedient measure. In the course of two or three weeks there will be no less than five different trials before the Court of Justiciary for the crime of Sedition.

> I have the honour to be with much regard
> Sir
> Your most obedient humble servant
> Robert McQueen. (34)

With this letter went a formal sixteen page report by the judges of the Court of Justiciary which argued that if there was a power to transport in general then it must apply in a specific case such as sedition. The Act of 1703 was discussed, this had introduced the crime of Leasing-Making as a lesser, non-capital, offence to avoid the necessity to use the capital offence of treason. The Court reviewed the precedent of cases between 1687 and 1754 and reviewed the distinction, which was touched upon in Braxfield's letter, between Leasing-Making and Sedition. They concluded:

Upon the whole then we must report it as our opinion – 1mo. That the Court of Justiciary are not restrained by the Act of 1703 from punishing the crime of Leasing-Making by Transportation. 2do. That the crime of which Mr Muir and Mr Palmer were convicted was not Leasing-Making but Sedition which by the common law of Scotland may be punished with Transportation. (35)

Dundas, like the shrewd politician he was, took soundings on the matter from the Scots-born Lord Chancellor, Alexander Wedderburn, Lord Loughborough, who wrote reassuringly:

My Dear Sir

I had a full confidence that the Court of Justiciary would have pronounced no judgement that was not perfectly legal as well as properly applied to the Crime. The reasons given in support of it are drawn up in a very masterly manner & fully refute the groundless objections suggested agt. the proceedings.

Yours ever
L. (36)

Dundas responded to Lauderdale, Grey and Sheridan with the not totally unexpected news that the High Court of Justiciary was quite confident of the propriety and justice of its own recent actions, though doubtless as a canny politician, he would not have passed on Braxfield's additional and unsought views on the political inexpediency of exercising the Royal prerogative of mercy in these cases. Matters did not, however, rest here.

Lauderdale was not satisfied and on 15th April 1794 raised the question in the House of Lords. James Maitland, 8th Earl of Lauderdale, qualified as an advocate in 1780 and in 1790 was elected as one of the sixteen Scottish representative peers to sit in the House of Lords. Lauderdale was at this time on the extreme wing of the Whig party and was a strong opponent of the war with Revolutionary France. His first point was that the act under which Muir and Palmer had been indicted was the 1703 statute against Leasing-Making which was punishable only by fine, imprisonment or banishment, the latter penalty he claimed to be quite distinct from transportation. This point, of course was flatly contradicted by the Court's report which insisted that Muir and Palmer had been charged with sedition, not Leasing-Making. He then went on to raise other objections including the over-ruling of Muir's challenge to the jurors as having, as members of the Goldsmith's Hall association, prejudged the issue. Lauderdale spoke for three and a half hours. Lord Mansfield, the former David Murray, Viscount Stormont, who had succeeded his uncle the Lord Chief Justice as 2nd Earl of Mansfield in 1793, defended the Court of Justiciary. As Mansfield had been occupying the sinecure post of Lord Justice-General since 1778 this attitude may be seen as unsurprising. He commented:

> I have not the pleasure of personal acquaintance with the
> Lord Justice-Clerk, but I have long heard the loud voice of
> fame, that speaks of him as a man of pure and spotless
> integrity, of great talents, and of a transcendent knowledge of
> the laws of his country. (37)

Mansfield had been abroad in the Diplomatic Service for much of his career and had later been a Cabinet Minister – posts which had prevented him seeing anything of the Court which he nominally headed. Mansfield also reminded their Lordships:

> . . . as you have no right of revision, you must take the verdict
> to be perfectly correct. You must consider Mr Muir as
> convicted of all the crimes libelled; since, of those crimes, the
> jury have found him guilty. You must hold the proof to have
> been sufficient; since it was satisfactory to the jury who tried
> the cause. The only question, therefore, that does or can arise,
> is simply this: Was the punishment, inflicted upon those
> crimes, such as is warranted by the usage and principles of
> the law of Scotland? (38)

He concluded, which much citation from Roman law and the writings of Sir George MacKenzie, that it was and he was followed in this line by two other Scottish peers – Lord Kinnoul and Lord Chancellor Loughborough who moved:

> That it is the opinion of this House that there are no grounds
> for an interference with the criminal laws as established in the

united kingdoms, and which have been exercised with justice for the protection of our property, our liberty, and our lives.

(39)

The British Convention of the Delegates of the People Associated to Obtain Universal Suffrage and Annual Parliaments provided the next group of, according to one's taste, political martyrs or seditious troublemakers. William Skirving came to trial in Edinburgh in January 1794 accused of sedition in that he had circulated the Dundee paper (for which Palmer had been convicted), as a member of the Friends of the People, had circulated a seditious handbill, had been an active member of the Convention and had made seditious speeches and motions and after the Convention had been dispersed by a magistrate he had endeavoured to reassemble it. Cockburn argues that the prosecution of Skirving was chiefly a prosecution of the British Convention and certainly the indictment spells out the way the Convention had imitated French revolutionary styles:

... in the whole form and manner of their procedure, as well as in the principles it publicly avowed and promoted ...indicating the same rebellious maxims which have governed, and do still govern the proceedings of the convention of France, the public and avowed enemies of this country, and with whom this nation is at present at war. (40)

Cockburn gives much space to considering whether, on the view of the case taken by the public prosecutor and the courts, Skirving should not have been tried for the more serious, indeed the capital, crime of treason, and whether in the light of their views they were not acting improperly in preferring the lesser charges of sedition. In the event Skirving was found guilty by a unanimous vote of the jury and sentenced to transportation for fourteen years with Braxfield observing:

...as I have always considered sedition as the most dangerous crime that can be committed, I think we cannot discharge our duty to the country unless we inflict for that crime a severe punishment. (41)

In January 1794 Maurice Margarot, who had come to Scotland from

England as a delegate of the British Convention, stood trial for sedition. Margarot's behaviour during the trial was hardly well-judged. When asked by Braxfield whether he had counsel or wished to have an advocate appointed Margarot declared that he did not wish counsel but went on in a hit at Braxfield's accent that all he required was: '. . .an interpreter to make me understand what your Lordship says.' (42) This impolitic remark was equalled by his objection to the jurisdiction of the court because its nominal head, the Lord Justice-General, was not present. As the Justice-General was, of course, the Earl of Mansfield who was so stoutly to defend the Court's verdicts in the Muir and Palmer cases it is not clear that his presence would have done anything for Margarot's chances. One of the judges, Lord Abercromby, described Margarot's conduct thus:

> . . . from the moment he appeared at the bar, till the instant he was carried out, his own conduct was of the most indecent kind. (43)

The most serious clash between Margarot and his judges came when he accused Braxfield of pre-judging the case. When conducting his defence the following exchange took place:

Mr Margarot – Now, my Lord, comes a very delicate matter indeed. I mean to call upon my Lord Justice-Clerk, and I hope that the questions and answers will be given in the most solemn manner. I have received a piece of information which I shall lay before the court in the course of my questions. First, my Lord, are you upon your oath?

Lord Justice-Clerk – State your questions, and I will tell you whether I will answer them or not. If they are proper questions, I will answer them.

Mr Margarot – Did you dine at Mr Rochead's at Inverleith in the course of last week?

Lord Justice-Clerk – And what have you to do with that, sir?

Mr Margarot – Did any conversation take place with regard to my trial?

Lord Justice-Clerk – Go on, sir.

Mr Margarot – Did you use these words: What should you

think of giving him a hundred lashes, together with Botany Bay; or words to that effect?

Lord Justice-Clerk – Go on. Put your questions if you have any more.

Mr Margarot – Did any person – did a lady – say to you that the mob would not allow you to whip him? And, my Lord, did you not say that the mob would be the better for losing a little blood. These are the questions, my Lord, that I wish to put to you at present in the presence of the court. Deny them, or acknowledge them.

Lord Justice-Clerk – Do you think I should answer questions of that sort, my Lord Henderland? (44)

This rather remarkable scene, in which the presiding judge was being tried in his own courtroom by the accused, can have had few parallels. If Braxfield had said the words he was accused of then he had, at least, been injudicious and improper in discussing a forthcoming case, and at worst had disqualified himself. However Margarot was in the wrong in allowing the trial to go as far as it had before objecting to Braxfield's presence. Henderland and the rest of the bench gave as their opinion that Braxfield was not obliged to answer the questions as they did not relate to the charges in the trial – which was perhaps a somewhat narrow line to take.

Alexander Young, who had avoided jury service in the Margarot case, but nonetheless attended the trial, wrote of it that it:

. . . seemed to me to be more the trial of Lord Braxfield than of Margarot, and I must own that had I been the Judge I could never have preserved my temper, nor have acted with the same meekness and moderation that it appeared to me the Judges of the Court of Justiciary did on that occasion. They were all excellent men and when I recollect the character and conduct of the Lords Henderland and Swinton, who were my intimate friends, I think I may appeal to all who knew them, and many such are still living, that they were the most unlikely men in the world including their President the Justice Clerk to have inflicted Martyrdom even upon Criminals and yet they are now accused of having been despotic Judges, and those who were then tried by them are termed "The Scotch Martyrs". (45)

Margarot was something of a popular hero in Edinburgh. Young, who like most commentators has much less good to say of him than of Muir, Palmer and Gerald describes how he saw him:

> ... conducted by a great crowd of the lower class of the Citizenry of Edinburgh, carrying flags and Banners, with suitable inscriptions upon them. . .

The charges against Margarot, who had been one of the presidents of the Scottish meeting of the British Convention, and had participated in meetings which the indictment claimed to be of:

> ... a dangerous and destructive tendency, with a deliberate and determined intention to disturb the peace of the community, and to subvert the present constitution of the country; with which view they imitated, both in the form and tenor of their proceedings, that Convention of the People, the avowed enemies of this country, who at present usurp the government of France. (46)

Margarot was, unanimously, found guilty of the charges libelled and sentenced to fourteen years transportation. Cockburn notes:

> Both during his voyage to New South Wales, and while there, it has always been said, and I believe truly, that he behaved very ill, particularly to his companions in misfortune. (47)

In the midst of all these highly contentious political trials the Lord Justice-Clerk still found time to exercise his benevolent influence on behalf of his friends. On 6th February 1794 he writes from his Edinburgh home in George Square to Robert Graham of Fintry, one of the Commissioners of Excise, well known for his connections with Robert Burns, on behalf of a Lanark neighbour:

> My Dear Sir,
>   You'll remember that sometime ago I applied to you in favour of James Roy the son of a friend of mine at Lanark to be appointed an excise officer & you was so good as to say that you would endeavour to get him appointed. I have a

letter this day from his father telling me that his son has been depending upon it & has not been applying to any other business. As it must be a great loss to the young man to remain idle it will be a great favour done me if you can get that matter soon ended.

I was very sorry when I asked the favour of you to dine with me some time ago that you was oblidged to be in the country at the time. I want much to have a meeting with you. I beg you will do me the favour to dine here on Friday 21st February half past four o'clock & I am with much regard

My dear sir
Your most obedient humble servant
Robt. McQueen (48)

The James Roy that Lord Braxfield is exercising his influence on behalf of is, presumably, some relative of his Lanark contemporary General Roy, the great map-maker and founder of the Ordnance Survey.

Such domestic diversions aside the list of sedition trials continued. If, as almost all admit, Margarot was an egotistical, self-opinionated enthusiast then the next man in the list of sedition trials was a much more considerable and distinguished figure – Joseph Gerrald. His trial, in March 1794, commenced with his counsel lodging an objection to Braxfield presiding at the trial – on the grounds of his alleged assertion, made at the dinner at Mr Rochead's cited by Margarot, that members of the British Convention deserved transportation and public whipping. The Lord-Justice Clerk left the Chair, and Lord Henderland and his brethren debated the point before deciding that the objection was irrelevant. The court then proceeded with the case and, as the first step, found the libel, that is the charges preferred, relevant. Again in this case Cockburn suggests that, in the terms the indictment was presented and particularly as it was explained by the Crown, the matter seemed more a case of treason than of sedition; but this view excluded he feels that there were no irrelevancies such as would have warranted the court in refusing to place the matter before the jury.

Two members of the Jury were objected to by Gerrald – one William Rankine, the King's Tailor (as no King had been to Scotland and required a tailor's services there for a century and half this was hardly a very profitable position) on the grounds of his office, and William Creech, the bookseller and publisher, on the grounds of prejudice against the British Convention. Both objections were overruled.

The evidence was led for the Crown by the Solicitor General, Robert Blair. Dundas the Lord Advocate was in London on Parliamentary business. The evidence was intended to prove that Gerrald was a member of the Convention and had made speeches of a seditious nature therein. Gerrald, although represented by counsel, led no evidence and chose to make his own summing-up speech for the defence. This speech, which lasted for three and half hours, was even in the *Scots Magazine* , a journal not noted for its sympathy for the reform movement, described thus:

> . . . his speech, in point of language and delivery, fully
> justified the encomiums which had been paid to his
> eloquence and ability. (49)

It was however a lecture on the great reform topics of universal suffrage and annual parliaments and Cockburn criticises it as being:

> . . . far too short and casual on what ought to have been his
> great theme, the right, under the Constitution, of every one to
> recommend what the majority may think unconstitutional
> and dangerous reforms, provided the reformer be bucklered
> in honesty. (50)

It was during Gerrald's speech that he made the reference to Christianity being an innovation, the occasion for the Braxfield comment on Christ, discussed in Chapter 1, 'muckle he made o' that, he was hanget'. The evidence for the truth of this story is at best questionable. Cockburn gives an account of this incident in his work on the sedition trials. Gerrald had been arguing on the need for change in human institutions:

> Mr Gerrald – After all, the most useful discoveries in
> philosophy, the most important changes in the moral
> history of man, have been innovations. The Revolution was
> an innovation; Christianity itself was an innovation.

On this Lord Braxfield interrupted. Gerrald's reference to the

Revolution would be interpreted by Lord Henderland as a reference to the overthrow of the monarchy in the civil war – an interpretation which Gerrald did not deny, even though he perhaps could have been thought to have been referring to the much more acceptable "Glorious Revolution" of 1688. In any case the Justice-Clerk got in first with:

> You would have been stopped long before this, if you had not
>   been a stranger. All that you have been saying is sedition.
>   And now, my Lords, he is attacking Christianity.

Lord Henderland criticised Gerrald's comparison of the present situation with the Revolution and concluded:

> It is my duty to observe this; but I am for the panel going on
>   in his own way.
> Mr Gerrald – I conceive myself as vindicating the rights of
>   Britons at large: and I solemnly disclaim all intention of
>   attacking Christianity. I was merely stating the fact.
> Lord Justice-Clerk – Go on in your own way.
> Mr Gerrald – I think I may be allowed that at least.
> Lord Justice-Clerk – Go on, sir.
> Mr Gerrald – I should have been going on if your Lordship
>   had not interrupted me.

Which might be considered honours even. Cockburn goes on:

> No religiousness on the part of their Lordships could have
> accounted for this shocking perversion of what the prisoner
> said. But none of them were religious. Braxfield's very name
> made the pious shudder. And the very moment before he
> interrupted the panel he chuckled over a profane jest of his
> own, on our Saviour's success as an innovator – a jest too
> indecent to be recorded, but which transpired next day,
> because his brethren thought it too good to be kept to
> themselves, and has never been forgotten.

It is difficult not to feel a certain slight unease at Lord Cockburn's confident dismissal of the Justiciary Bench's total lack of religious faith. His assertion is not supported by any evidence and it seems unlikely that Lords Henderland, Swinton, Dunsinnan, Abercromby, Eskgrove, let alone Braxfield, ever discussed the state of their souls with the fifteen year old Cockburn. Lord Cockburn's work, which has become an unquestioned source for too many later writers, was severely criticised on its publication, and *The Law Magazine & Law Review* writer's dismissal of the 'muckle he made o' that, he was hanget' story is cited in Chapter 1.

Gerrald was sentenced to what had become the standard fourteen year term of transportation to Australia.

Lord Cockburn, in his consideration of the British Convention trials – Skirving, Margarot and Gerrald – reaches the revealing, and perhaps unexpected, conclusion:

> If I, with my present views, had been a juror on these Scotch convention trials, I would have been clear for convicting the prisoners of something, and of something serious. I never could have concurred in a general conviction on all the matter said to be seditious, but must have held some of it to be innocent and some absurd. . . As little, however, considering the times, could I have thought the prisoners entirely innocent. (51)

This is a most interesting conclusion, not least in its final sentence with its reference to 'considering the times' which recognises the stresses and inequities in the legal system which are likely to arise in a time of war. Later he comments:

> A correct trial, succeeded by a discriminating verdict, and ending in a rational and legal, though rather severe punishment, would have satisfied justice, and saved the court. (52)

These views, in which the lawyer's judgement overcomes the politician's prejudices and his innate distaste for Braxfield, are somewhat more balanced than many of the later commentaries on the "Scottish martyrs". Frequently these pass from justifiable strictures on the severity of the sentence and the evident prejudice of the judges to a less justifiable belief that there was no case to be answered. A contemporary legal view on this was given by Alexander Young – a Whig and a sympathiser with reform who successfully avoided what he saw as the distasteful duty of serving on the jury for the trial of Margarot. He records in his memoir of Lord Braxfield, after referring to the Margarot case:

> As I attended all the trials of Messrs Muir, Palmer and Gerald, I must acknowledge that my feelings with regard to these last were somewhat different and I earnestly wished that their punishment might be as lenient as possible, but I never had the smallest doubt that the Scotch law of Sedition was properly and fairly expounded and applied. It was at least that Law which I had learned as a man of Business, and seen practised on various occasions, and I solemnly declare that I never considered that the Judges could be blamed for the conduct at these Trials, and never heard insinuations thrown out against them, or could find anything in our best legal authorities, adverse to my understanding of the Law of Scotland on this head . . . (53)

However accurately the letter of the law was being applied there was, as ever, a political dimension to the administration of justice. The conduct of the courts was causing public and political controversy. The international situation and the national political situation both continued to deteriorate – the British Convention was implicated in a plan for armed insurrection and the Friends of the People were conspiring to seize the centres of power in Edinburgh and set up a provisional government. Attempts were being made to incite troops to mutiny. Arrests were made of two of those involved in these developments, Robert Watt and David Downie and charges of treason, as opposed to the non-capital charge of sedition, were preferred. Watt had, in the past, acted as a spy and informant for the Government, but his services had been dispensed with and he threw himself into conspiracy.

The High Court of Justiciary had, since an Act of 1709, administered a common British, that is in effect English, form of trial for high treason. There was however provision within this Act for matters to be taken out of the hands of the Lords of Justiciary and for a special Commission of Oyer and Terminer to be instituted – this had been done after the Jacobite risings and Robert Dundas, the Lord Advocate, now thought that this would be a good time to revive this practice. Writing to his uncle, Henry Dundas, in June 1794 he commented:

I would prefer a commission were it only for this reason that the President or Chief Baron would, in that way, fall to preside in place of the violent and intemperate gentleman who sits in the Justiciary, and whose present state of health and spirits is such as to afford no chance of his being more soberly inclined in his demeanour than he was last winter. (54)

'Violent and intemperate' might be thought a little rich coming from the man who had claimed that Thomas Muir's activities revealed: 'a wider range of diabolical mischief . . . than ever was seen in England, or any where else.'

The Commission was duly created and comprised nine judges – the Lord Justice Clerk and the other five Commissioners of Justiciary, the Lord Chief Baron and another Baron of the Court of Exchequer and the Lord President of the Court of Session, who presided.

On 14th August 1794 a Grand Jury of twenty-three was sworn and addressed at some considerable length by Lord President Succoth. The Grand Jury's function was not to try the case but to hear the Crown evidence and establish, in Succoth's words:

. . . whether such probable circumstances of guilt appear
against the prisoner, as to justify the sending of him to
another jury, who are appointed by law to hear the evidence
on both sides and to say whether the person charged be guilty
or not of the crime imputed to him. (55)

Succoth did not fail to make the seemingly obligatory reference to the blessings of the British Constitution and to the:

. . . admirable manner in which the powers of the state,
legislative and executive, are combined and balanced, whereby
the liberty of every individual is completely secured. . .

or to the French threat:

. . . we are engaged in war, with an inveterate, a cruel, and a
vindictive enemy; an enemy, whose object seems to be, to
spread desolation far and wide, whose leaders, if they ever

were in quest of liberty, have been very unsuccessful in
finding it . . .

and pondered that:

It is difficult to conceive, that British subjects, who are not
desperate or insane, should be so lost to all sense and duty; so
blind to every fair interest that men can have; or so
abandoned to wickedness; as to enter deliberately and
knowingly into the horrid conspiracy of destroying the
constitution of their country, and rising in rebellion against
their Sovereign.

Lord Succoth disclaimed any intention:

. . . to excite your passions against those who may have the
misfortune to be accused, so as to lead you to a hasty or ill-
founded opinion against them: on the contrary it is my duty
to admonish you against undue prepossessions, and to
request, that you may keep in view, that the presumption of
innocence is an essential and a valuable rule of criminal
jurisprudence, which rule is not in any degree weakened by
the atrocity of the crime.

This was certainly a somewhat more judicious statement than some of
Lord Braxfield's comments. The process of the Commission of Oyer
and Terminer by removing the question of determining whether there
was a case to answer from the discretion of the Lord Advocate, who in
all other situations exercised such powers, to the grand jury, gave a
definite benefit to the accused of having his case considered by two
separate and different juries before he could be convicted. As Succoth
commented:

. . . in cases of high treason, none of us will regret, that so high
and momentous a trust is committed to no individual whatever.

The prosecution was nominally headed by the Lord Advocate and the
Solicitor General but London had sent up a King's Counsel, John

Anstruther MP, together with William Dundas MP, Counsellor at Law (the Lord Advocate's younger brother) and Mr Knapp, Clerk of Arraigns to make sure matters went smoothly. True bills of high treason were returned by the Grand Jury against Robert Watt, wine merchant in Edinburgh and David Downie, goldsmith in Edinburgh.

Watt's trial came before the Commission on 3rd September and was heard before an English-style jury of twelve. Watt exercised his right of challenge and excluded nine of the jurors who were replaced by others from the assize list – this certainly marked a clear point of distinction between the Oyer and Terminer process and Braxfield's capricious refusal of challenges for cause in, for example, the Muir trial. The indictment against Watt covered a wide range of charges from raising rebellion against the King to planning to seize Edinburgh Castle, the Lord Justice-Clerk, Lords of Justiciary and Session, and the Lord Provost of Edinburgh, down to procuring pikes, spears and battle-axes and publishing 'wicked addresses, advising the subjects of the King to subscribe money.'

Henry Meikle in *Scotland and the French Revolution* concludes that the establishment of the Commission ensured that, for the first time since the wave of sedition prosecutions had begun, prisoners had a fair trial. The trial however resulted in the conviction of Watt and his execution. He was hung at the Tolbooth and afterward his head was cut off by the executioner and held up to view with the cry of "This is the head of a traitor."

Whatever special arrangements might be made for treason trials the other work of the Court of Session and the Court of Justiciary went on and Braxfield set out in September 1794 on the Northern Circuit. His first assize town was Inverness, where no criminal business awaited him. Part of Lord Braxfield's speech, on the unimprovable excellence of the British Constitution, was quoted above in Chapter 1, but he also alluded to the changes in the proceedings in cases of treason:

> These trials had led to a more particular consideration of the laws regarding high treason, than happily there had hitherto been occasion for in this country; and he had reason to apprehend that a mistaken idea had prevailed, which would be fatal to numbers, unless they were warned to guard against it. What his Lordship alluded to was, a belief which prevailed, that persons meeting together, and concerting measures for unhinging and undermining the government of

the country, are not guilty of a crime, unless they proceed to
acts of open violence, or rebellion against the King. But this
was directly contrary, not only to the spirit, but the enactment
of the statute of Edward III which is now the law of this
country in cases of treason. (56)

The Justice-Clerk urged his audience to pass on the message that
conspiracy could bring people into the scope of a charge of high treason
just as surely as active rebellion.

In 1795 Braxfield was to preside at what is often seen as a landmark
case in the consideration of the criminal responsibility of the insane;
the trial of Sir Archibald Gordon Kinloch. In fact there is an earlier
case, referred to in Chapter 3, in which a similar verdict was returned
but nonetheless the Kinloch case is of considerable novelty in its
circumstances and verdict and reflects creditably on the Scottish legal
system and the Lord Justice-Clerk.

Kinloch, who suffered from bouts of mental derangement, was
accused of shooting his brother, Sir Francis Kinloch at his home at
Gilmerton, Edinburgh. There was no question of the facts of the case
and the accused's counsel, David Hume:

> ... in a short speech, expressed with a degree of tenderness
> and feeling which greatly affected the Court, stated, that the
> unfortunate prisoner had long laboured under an insanity or
> furiosity of mind, in consequence of a violent fever contracted
> many years ago during his residence in the West Indies, in the
> service of his country. (57)

Hume concentrated on substantiating this defence of insanity. After a
well-considered summing up by the Lord Justice-Clerk the jury took
little time to return a unanimous verdict that Kinloch had killed his
brother but was at the time insane and deprived of reason. The verdict
of the Court, which echoed that of the 1747 case of Robert Spence, was:

> ... that the said Archibald Gordon Kinloch was not an object
> of punishment; but ordained him to be carried back to the
> tolbooth of Edinburgh, there to be confined all the days of his
> life; and authorised the Magistrates of Edinburgh, in case of
> his friends or others, finding caution to the satisfaction of the
> Court, and to the amount of £10,000, to deliver him over to

them, to be by them securely confined all the days of his life; and the above sum to be forfeited if he shall at any time be found at large. (58)

A curious case, which displays the ability of a jury of the period to listen to the Lord Justice-Clerk's charge and then make their own minds up, came to trial in the High Court in December 1795. James Niven had fired a cannon in Libberton's Wynd, Edinburgh. He had believed that the cannon was only loaded with powder, paper and tobacco. (Sadly, the reason for loading a cannon with tobacco does not emerge in the press account.) However there was a piece of metal in the cannon, which the Solicitor General, prosecuting, felt had probably been broken off the rammer, unknown to Niven. This metal projectile killed a Mr Knox, late gown-keeper to the Faculty of Advocates, and in consequence the Solicitor General invited the jury to return a verdict of culpable homicide.

> The Lord Justice-Clerk then summed up the evidence in a very accurate and candid manner; and after laying down the law with respect to murder, culpable homicide and casual homicide, left it entirely to the jury to return such a verdict as their own judgment should dictate to them. His Lordship agreed with Mr Solicitor General, that the pannel could not be found guilty of murder. He thought with Mr Solicitor likewise, that he was guilty of culpable homicide.
>
> The jury returned their verdict, finding, by a plurality of voices, the pannel not guilty; upon which he was dismissed from the bar. (59)

William Roughead gives an interesting account of what he characterises as Braxfield's last murder case, the trial of James McKean, in December 1796. Roughead, who was always anxious to paint a kindlier picture of Braxfield than that provided by Cockburn notes:

> In pronouncing sentence his Lordship, addressing the pannel "in a suitable and affecting manner," pointed out that the crime he had committed was such as to preclude him from all hope of mercy in this world, and therefore earnestly entreated him to make his peace with God, whose mercy

would, if he were truly penitent, be extended to him, great as his crimes had been.

It will be remarked that we have here no signs of the coarse and brutal exultation over convicted prisoners which Henry Cockburn would have us believe to have been upon such occasions the habitual manner of Lord Braxfield. (60)

1797 saw a number of trials associated with riots against the Militia Acts. The deteriorating military situation in the war with France had led the Government to introduce forced conscription by ballot. This was a highly unpopular move, exacerbated by the fact that the better off sections of the community could join the Volunteer movement (and be exempted from conscription) or buy themselves out of the ballot. Lists of eligible men were to be drawn up by parish schoolmasters and throughout Scotland many of these unfortunate functionaries found their homes ransacked and the lists forcibly seized. Tranent in East Lothian was a particularly active centre of anti-Militia demonstrations and eleven rioters were killed by cavalry brought in to restore order.

In October Lord Braxfield and the High Court were kept busy with the legal aftermath of these disorders. The first batch of cases, on the 9th, concerned four Berwickshire residents charged with mobbing and rioting and forcing a Deputy Lieutenant of the County to give up a militia list compiled by the parish schoolmaster of Eccles. One of the counsel for the accused was the young Walter Scott. One of the accused failed to appear, and the other three, two men and a woman, were found guilty and sentenced to fourteen years transportation.

Two days later Neil Redpath and Robert Mitchell stood trial for their involvement in the Tranent riots on 29th August. Redpath was defended by Walter Scott, Mitchell by John Clerk. Three of the Deputy Lieutenants of East Lothian gave evidence of how on the day appointed for correcting the militia lists several hundred people had gathered in the streets of Tranent and had stoned the house they were sheltering in.

The stones still continuing to pour in upon them, the cavalry were ordered to fire, which they accordingly did, but discharged their pistols in the air; this tended only to irritate the mob. The military at last had recourse to their carabines; upon which, after several people had unfortunately fallen . .

In fact twelve people were killed and perhaps twenty injured, and the action at Tranent was in fact considerably more of a massacre, with evidence of the troops involved being out of control, than the version presented in court would suggest:

> ... the mob dispersed, and the Deputy-Lieutenants finished
> the business of the meeting. The firmness of their conduct,
> and the humanity with which they acted, called forth the
> highest eulogiums from the counsel on both sides. (61)

Mitchell and Redpath were discharged, the jury finding the case against them not proven.

In the Spring of 1798 Lord Braxfield went on the Western Circuit to Stirling, Inveraray and Glasgow, on what would be his last Circuit journey. The breakdown in his health took place after this – he was unable to preside at the remarkable trial of Alastair MacDonnell of Glengarry for the murder of Captain McLeod arising out of a duel at Fort George, near Inverness. This took place at the High Court in August 1798 with Lord Eskgrove presiding. The Autumn 1798 circuit list does not include the Justice-Clerk, nor does the Spring 1799 list.

As a prudent lawyer Braxfield put his affairs in order. In August 1798 he nominated the trustees on his estate; his son-in-law William Honyman, his younger son John McQueen and James Marshall, Writer to the Signet, as his executors and he passed over the estate to these trustees. (62) He had already seen his elder son Robert Dundas appointed as Chief Clerk of Justiciary in May 1795 and in December 1798 he attempted to secure a post for his younger son John – an unsuccessful attempt which was discussed in Chapter 4.

On 30th May 1799, aged seventy seven, Robert McQueen of Braxfield, Lord Justice-Clerk of Scotland died. Friends and enemies recognised that an era was ending. Obituarists would describe him and attempt to sum up his character and his contribution:

> As a companion and a friend he was peculiarly beloved by
> such as stood in those relations to him. He had an openness of
> manners, and was so easy of access, that his friends were
> never disappointed when they wished to have his advice. His
> engaging, we may say fascinating manners, rendered him a
> most agreeable member of society. The company was always
> lively and happy of which the Lord Justice-Clerk was a

member. . . Lord Justice-Clerk was of middle size, and robust make; he was what is commonly expressed by the term hard-featured, but had a small quick eye and expressive countenance, impressive of mildness and intelligence. (63)

But the loss to his family and friends of this "agreeable member of society" was one thing – the political problem he created was quite another. A new Lord Justice-Clerk was required – and a vacancy would be created on the Justiciary Bench. The Justice-Clerk's position seems not have been a matter of debate – Eskgrove was the senior judge, he had been presiding in Braxfield's absence and was duly appointed. But the consequential vacancy excited the politicians and involved Robert Dundas in a flurry of letter writing.

Lord Advocate Robert Dundas to Henry Dundas, Edinburgh 30th May:

My dear sir, I arrived here this morning – your friends the Justice Clerk & Elder died within this hour, & about the same moment of time . . . as to the first I really think it requires some consideration. George Ferguson has just now stated to me his desire to accept a Double Gown – that tho' offered this three years ago, cannot perhaps now be acceded to. But he will not accept a single one. If the Duke of Portland does not wish to press Lord Cullen's appointment at present, I believe from all the circumstances that the nomination of David Hume to a Double Gown at once would be satisfactory to the Public and the best arrangement possible. If not then either Mr Tytler or Hume should be the single judge. I have wrote both to the Chancellor and the Duke of Portland . . .
R Dundas. (64)

Lord Advocate to Lord Loughborough, the Lord Chancellor, Edinburgh 31st May:

The Justice Clerk died yesterday morning & thereby another seat on the Bench of the Session is vacant.

The President with whom I have had a few minutes conversation, seems to think Mr Fraser Tytler the fittest at the top of the List. Mr George Ferguson, who is his junior, and

who three years ago declined accepting, informed me soon
after of his wish to accept a Double Gown, not a Single Gown.
If he had limited his Demand to one, I should humbly think
his Claim such as ought to be preferred. The Duke of Portland
wishes Lord Cullen to have the Seat in the Justiciary. But in
order to leave it entirely open to your Lordship to arrange
these vacancies in the way which appears most advantageous
to the Public I have wrote his Grace that untill I receive his
further directions on the subject I have avoided talking to
Lord Cullen on the matter at all – The President is very
desirous to have a good lawyer now on the Bench; and he is
right; And altho' I do not mean to recommend it, yet I feel it
my duty to throw out for your consideration whether David
Hume should not at once be brought forward both to the
Courts of Session and Justiciary, and that over all other
competition. If such a thing is judged adviseable my earnest
entreaty is that it should proceed from yourself, as clear of all
influence from personal application and originating in your
own opinion of the merits of the Individual. This however
would be a strong measure, & would offend Mr Ferguson,
Lord Cullen & others, and the easiest course on the whole
seems to be, if Geo. Ferguson persists in declining to accept
one Seat, to give Lord Cullen the Justiciary as the D. of
Portland wishes Mr Tytler the Seat in the Session . . . (65)

Lord Advocate to Duke of Portland, Home Secretary, Edinburgh 31st
May:

My Lord Duke
    The Lord Justice Clerk died yesterday morning and of
consequence another vacancy occurs on the Bench of the
Court of Session.

    If Mr. George Ferguson chooses to accept of that vacancy,
he from his Seniority & extensive practice at the Bar, seems
entitled to a preference. But as he probably will not accept it,
unless he is at the same time placed on the Bench of the
Justiciary I suspect that arrangement would fail. I have on this
occasion resolved not to talk to Lord Cullen on the subject I
had the honour of conversing with your Grace, till I receive
your further directions, that you may not be precluded from
adopting any arrangement which under all circumstances
you may judge most eligible & satisfactory . . . (66)

The result of all Robert Dundas's busy letter writing was that David Rae, Lord Eskgrove, was duly appointed as Lord Justice-Clerk. Robert Cullen, who had been a judge of the Court of Session since 1796, and was seen as the Duke of Portland's candidate, was given a Justiciary gown. There were in fact two vacancies on the High Court Bench – Lord Swinton had died at the beginning of the year and had not yet been replaced. The second vacancy was filled by the promotion from the Court of Session of William Honyman, Lord Armadale – the late Lord Braxfield's son-in-law.

CHAPTER 8

Summing-Up

*"He has carried more sound law with him
than he has left upon the Bench"*

> Braxfield, curiously enough, never found his Boswell. It is too
> late now for a complete biography; the material is
> unavailable. Extrinsic facts of his career are known, his
> character has become a legend, but of the man himself in his
> habit as he lived there is no adequate record. (1)

So wrote the most knowledgeable twentieth century writer on Braxfield
in an essay originally published in 1919. Oddly enough in the light of
William Roughead's reference to Braxfield lacking a Boswell it is to
James Boswell that we owe many valuable insights, the more significant
in that they were written for James Boswell's own eyes and by an
intelligent and active, if somewhat detached and critical, participant
in and observer of the Scottish legal world. The availability of the
Boswell diaries and letters, following their discovery in the 1920s and
1930s at Malahide Castle, near Dublin, and Fettercairn House,
Kincardineshire, makes some attempt at a life of Braxfield more possible
now than it was for Roughead in the early years of the century. Rather
than a biography Roughead wrote a series of excellent essays on
Braxfield and some of his cases, doing much to reclaim his reputation
from the attacks of Cockburn in the nineteenth century and some of
Cockburn's later followers. Roughead's interest in the man also resulted
in his volume in the *Notable British Trials* series on the Deacon Brodie

case. The other letters and documents quoted from earlier in the present book, which include sources that were not available to Roughead, also usefully, if tantalisingly, supplement our knowledge of the man. Nevertheless Roughead's assessment of the difficulties of writing a full account of Braxfield is still not too far short of the mark. More letters, a diary, more accounts of the man by his contemporaries would undoubtedly help to round out the portrait of the man.

Myth, however, requires fewer scholarly resources to ensure its survival. The popular, if erroneous, characterisation of Braxfield as a "hanging judge", which owes so much to transference from Stevenson's brilliant but fictional portrayal of Lord Justice-Clerk Weir of Hermiston, lives on, probably beyond hope of remedy. It is interesting to note that even Lord Braxfield's most powerful critic, Henry Cockburn, does not feature a delight in cruelty or a tendency to impose the most draconian punishments among his list of charges against Braxfield. True, he says that:

> It may be doubted if he was ever so much in his element as when tauntingly repelling the last despairing claim of a wretched culprit, and sending him to Botany Bay or the gallows with an insulting jest; over which he would chuckle the more from observing that correct people were shocked. Yet this was not from cruelty, for which he was too strong and too jovial, but from cherished coarseness. (2)

However Cockburn does not suggest, either in *Memorials of his time* or in his work on the sedition trials that Braxfield was in any way remarkable as being a more severe judge than his brethren. A verdict which Alexander Young, writing from a very different standpoint, confirms when he observes that:

> . . . in the trials of the men who are now termed The Scots Martyrs I do not remember that there was any difference of opinion betwixt him and the other Judges on the Bench. (3)

Nor indeed is there any evidence in the reported cases to suggest such a tendency to severity and indeed evidence was cited in Chapter 6 showing Braxfield successfully arguing for a more lenient sentence than that proposed by Lord Hailes.

It is, of course, difficult to read of a case like that of Archibald Stewart and Charles Gordon in 1785 and find a young man of fifteen being hung for shopbreaking and housebreaking and his accomplice being sentenced to whipping and banishment to the plantations for seven years without our twentieth century sensibilities being disturbed. Nonetheless it is surely a gross disservice to history to judge the eighteenth century by our modern standards. Hanging was, however distasteful it may be to us today, imposed in eighteenth century Scotland as a punishment for a wide range of crimes, even if the list of offences was shorter than in England.

As was noted in Chapter 3 William Creech recorded that in three successive years (1774, 1775 and 1776) there were no executions in Edinburgh. Further evidence on the comparative liberality of the Scottish jurisdiction comes from Andrew Coyle who notes:

> Over a twenty year period at the end of the eighteenth
> century, 134 Scots were sentenced to death and only 97 of
> these were actually executed. During the same period in
> London and the County of Middlesex, which together had a
> population about half the size of that of Scotland, 1910
> criminals were sentenced to death and 890 were executed. (4)

The Scottish courts were thus significantly less prone to apply the death penalty than were their English counterparts and Braxfield could hardly have presided over enough capital cases to warrant a reputation as a "hanging judge", if by such is meant a predilection for the death penalty or an exceptional readiness to resort to capital punishment in discretionary cases.

Braxfield could not have conscientiously discharged his duties as a judge in the criminal courts without recourse to the death penalty, any more than he could have acted as a prosecuting counsel if he had been intellectually or emotionally opposed to the death penalty. There is no evidence that, as a judge, he was more inclined to have recourse to it than any of his contemporaries. It was, after all Lord Justice-Clerk Glenlee who passed sentence of death on young Archibald Stewart and Lord President Succoth who passed sentence of death on the revolutionary conspirator Robert Watt, and it was the philosophical Lord Kames who "checkmated" the poisoner Matthew Hay. Kames, Glenlee, Succoth *et al* are not, however, remembered as "hanging judges" – they are not indeed remembered much at all outside a narrow field of specialists.

It is difficult to reconcile Cockburn's confident assertion that Braxfield delighted in sending culprits to the gallows or Botany Bay with 'an insulting jest' with the published accounts of cases. Deacon Brodie, who had little enough except a respectable family background to recommend him to anyone's favourable consideration, was given a brief homily on repentance and divine forgiveness and treated with dignified courtesy. The even less attractive murderer, James McKean, was sentenced after an equally appropriate exhortation to penitence and without any display of judicial spleen, spite or mockery.

It is, of course, the sedition trials which have ensured that Braxfield's name and ill-reputation have lived on. It cannot be denied that Braxfield acted very badly in these cases, displaying a fear of change, a distaste for the involvement of the broad mass of the population in the democratic process, a willingness to support the government in its repression of radicalism. But he was hardly alone in this. The fact that others shared his views and actions does not lessen any blame that might attach to Braxfield – but it surely does make him less of a unique monster-figure and more of a man of his time. Lord Abercromby, whom Cockburn describes as mild, respectable and honest, in trying Palmer for sedition felt called on to observe that:

> . . . the right of universal suffrage is a right which the subjects of this country never enjoyed; and were they to enjoy it, they would not long enjoy either liberty or a free constitution. (5)

George Mealmaker, tried for sedition at the High Court in January 1798, was, without much debate, sentenced to fourteen years transportation by a Bench presided over by Lord Eskgrove in the absence, due to illness, of Braxfield. This was a Bench which, since the trial of Gerrald, had lost through death Lords Henderland and Abercromby. These two judges had been replaced by Lords Craig and Methven but its tendencies remained the same. Craig and Methven, according to Cockburn, were: 'good, respectable men' (6) and he goes on to observe:

> Neither of them had any marked political intemperance; but neither were they superior to the prejudices which, in those days, affected the class to which they belonged.

Which is a fair and reasonable comment, but somehow Cockburn could never quite bring himself to extend the same degree of understanding to Braxfield.

Robert Dundas, Lord Advocate at the period of the sedition trials, commented to his uncle Henry on the 'violent and intemperate gentleman who sits in the Justiciary'. It was, however the Lord Advocate who, as the public prosecutor, determined the charges to be levelled against the radicals. It was the Lord Advocate, who with his Deputes conducted the Crown case in court. It was the Lord Advocate who spoke of Muir and 'diabolical mischief', and of Margarot and the Convention following the French down the path to revolution and bloodshed. Cockburn, deprecating such excesses, still managed to make some excuses for Robert Dundas. Few, he suggests:

> . . . could have exercised his half legal and half political office,
> in such times, without being excited into violence. (7)

Although the Lord Advocate was:

> . . . a person of no professional consideration, of very
> moderate ability, and a poor brisk speaker,

he had, to Henry Cockburn, this redeeming quality:

> . . . he was a gentleman; lively and amiable in private life, and
> with a singularly animated and engaging look and manner.

It is hard to resist the idea that Cockburn could forgive much to a gentleman, and equally hard to resist the idea that Robert McQueen did not meet his idea of a gentleman.

Cockburn starts his account of Braxfield thus:

> Strong built and dark with rough eyebrows, powerful eyes,
> threatening lips, and a low growling voice, he was like a
> formidable blacksmith. His accent and his dialect were
> exaggerated Scotch; his language, like his thoughts, short,
> strong, and conclusive. (8)

There is surely detectable in the language used a conscious, or

SummingUpSummingUp

unconscious, characterisation of the subject of this portrait as coming from the lower classes – 'strong', 'dark', 'rough', 'threatening', 'formidable blacksmith', 'exaggerated Scotch'.

Quite apart from the points made in Chapter 1 about the political gulf, generation gap and cultural divide between Cockburn and Braxfield it is possible to detect a certain distaste on the part of Henry Cockburn; who was conscious and proud of being a Cockburn of Cockpen, kinsman to the Dundases of Arniston, by birth, breeding and manners part of the dominant Midlothian legal establishment; for the coarse and country-bred Robert McQueen.

Robert Dundas, as Lord Advocate, had a half-legal, half-political role. Braxfield had, or should have had, a purely legal role and the Bench's independence of the political process should have been the citizen's best defence against the possible excesses and abuses of the state. Eighteenth century Britain did not however quite work that way. The framers of the American constitution could plan for the separation of powers and a system of checks and balances – the British state, lacking the benefits of a written constitution, was a much more complex, less clear-cut entity. Quite apart from what Cockburn describes as the prejudices of his class, Lord Justice-Clerk Braxfield was part of the structure of the state and there seems no good reason to doubt that he considered he was doing his plain duty to the state by his severity towards those who sought to alter the existing order of things. When appointments to high judicial office become the small change of party politics and patronage it is difficult to expect a clean line of separation between the executive and the judiciary. Add to this the fear of foreign inspired revolution and the actual reality of war and almost anything becomes possible and understandable, even if not forgivable.

If what Stevenson called 'a sneaking kindness for any unpopular person' is to be allowed, then, while one need not go all the way with Alexander Young, who concluded his *Memoir* and acquitted Braxfield of all charges by saying:

Now indeed the Justice Clerk is represented as having been an unprincipled despotic Judge and placed on the same level with Jeffaries (sic) and those who had formerly figured in that line, whilst the most atrocious falsehoods are daily circulated regarding his brutal conduct to Criminals in the Court where he presided, all which I solemnly declare, as far as I know, and I had the best cause of knowledge as to most of them; *as I shall answer to God* are false and utterly destitute of truth, (9)

one can at least attempt to see him in his context and see him in the round.

One can, for example, while condemning the narrowness of the Judge's political partialities, admire the physical and moral courage of the man. John Mowbray, writing to Alexander Young, with information for his *Memoir*, tells how during the trial of Maurice Margarot he had heard the public galleries threatening personal violence against the Lord Justice-Clerk. At the conclusion of the trial, about three or four in the morning, Braxfield, accompanied only by his servant James, left Parliament House and walked through the dark closes and streets of a January Edinburgh towards his home in George Square. Mowbray, fearing for the Justice-Clerk's safety followed him but was discovered by the old Judge as they left Hume's Close. When Braxfield challenged Mowbray, 'What brings you here at this time? This is not the road to your house.'

Mowbray explained that he had feared Braxfield might be attacked in view of the mass public support for Margarot and the unpopularity of the verdict and had wished to see him safely home. Braxfield's reply was worthy of Stevenson's indomitable Weir of Hermiston:

There is no danger, and I am only doing my duty, which I could not have done had I paid any regard to the mass of threatening letters I have received, but they gaed all the same gate.

It is also possible to feel that Braxfield was unfortunate in being called on to occupy the Justice-Clerk's chair in the times when he did and to agree with his contemporary James Ramsay that:

Nature surely did not intend the Justice-Clerk to be a statesman in perilous distracted times. He wanted those accommodating manners and that insinuating address which seem to wish for conciliation when harsh measures are necessary. . . The impetuosity of his temper – which scorned all disguise – and his hatred for the democrats, rendered him no safe counsellor. . . (10)

Ramsay, it should be remembered also spoke of Braxfield's faults being proportionate to his 'bright and useful endowments' – which all in all seems a not unreasonable assessment.

Whether Braxfield would have survived in the popular imagination if he had not lived 'in perilous distracted times' is an interesting question. His lasting reputation as a lawyer and a judge certainly was not enhanced by his conduct in the trials of Muir, Skirving, Margarot and Gerrald and had he retired on his seventieth birthday in 1792, before this series of trials, he could still have gone down in story and legend as the judge in the Deacon Brodie case, as the source of some pithy remarks, as a staunch defender of old ways, old manners and the old tongue. He would certainly have a place as a brilliantly successful, popular and highly regarded advocate. He would also undoubtedly have secured an honourable place as one of the leading figures on the Court of Session Bench of his day – Ramsay arguing that:

> In delivering his opinion, he set out and rested the cause on a
> fair principle of law, which he demonstrated in the clearest
> manner, to the great edification of his hearers. (11)

Even the censorious Henry Cockburn had, with whatever degree of reluctance, to acknowledge that:

> ... within the range of the Feudal and the Civil branches, and
> in every matter depending on natural ability and practical
> sense, he was very great... (12)

However it was his fate to preside over the High Court at a time of great difficulty and his inability to be anything other than a man of his time has darkened his reputation. It is not entirely clear however that a court presided over by Eskgrove, Abercromby, Henderland or any of the others would have been materially different in its attitudes and decisions.

It surely remains true that while Lord Braxfield's judicial indiscretions and shortcomings need to be deprecated, Robert McQueen's virtues need to be remembered, his adherence to a threatened Scottish identity and spirit applauded, his contribution to the Scottish bar and bench remembered. One of his judicial brethren, who surely was in a good position to judge, observed when the Lord Justice-Clerk died:

> He has carried more sound law with him than he has left upon the bench. (13)

– which is not the worst epitaph one could hope for.

Illustrious Martyr in the glorious cause
Of truth, of freedom, and of equal laws.

I.Kay 1793 125

Thomas Muir of Huntershill

Kay's caption to his portrait of Muir indicates the sympathy of many Scots with the reform cause. Muir was sentenced by Braxfield to fourteen years transportation for his conviction on a charge of sedition

NOTES

Chapter 1 Braxfield the Myth

1 Stevenson, Robert Louis: Weir of Hermiston, London 1911 p 45

2 Stevenson, Robert Louis: *op.cit.* p 24

3 Stevenson, Robert Louis: *op.cit.* p 28

4 Stevenson, Robert Louis: Some portraits by Raeburn *in* Virginibus Puerisque and other papers, London 1912 p 145-6

5 Quoted in Roughead, William: The real Braxfield in Riddle of the Ruthvens, Edinburgh 1936 p 47

6 Watt, Francis: The Book of Edinburgh Anecdote, Edinburgh 1913 p 16

7 Kay, John: Original Portraits, Edinburgh 1877 Vol. 1 p 169

8 Lockhart, Robert Gibson: Memoirs of the life of Sir Walter Scott, Vol. 3 p 342

9 Young, Alexander: Memoir of Robert Macqueen of Braxfield, Edinburgh University Library (EUL) Laing MSS. Div. ii. 113

10 Roughead, William: The Bi-Centenary of Lord Braxfield *in* Glengarry's Way and other studies, Edinburgh 1922 p 303

11 Stevenson, Robert Louis: Some Portraits by Raeburn *op.cit.* p 146

12 Cockburn, Henry: Memorials of his time, Edinburgh 1856 p 113–115

13 Cockburn, Henry: An examination of the Trials for Sedition . . . in Scotland, Edinburgh 1888 Vol. 1 p 86

14 Cockburn, Henry: Memorials of his time *op.cit.* p 114

15 *idem.* p 117

16 *idem.* p 111

17 Gray, W Forbes: Some Old Scots Judges, London 1914 p 105

18 Dictionary of National Biography

19 Cockburn, Henry: Memorials of his time *op.cit.* p 113

20 Cockburn, Henry: An examination of the Trials for Sedition . . . in Scotland, *op.cit.* Vol. 1 p 175–177

21 *Scots Magazine*: September 1794 p 586

22 Cockburn, Henry: Memorials of his time *op. cit.* p 116

23 *idem.* p 117

24 Roughead, William: The Bi-Centenary of Lord Braxfield *op. cit.* p 301

25 Cockburn, Henry: Memorials of his time *op. cit.* p 117

26 Cockburn, Henry: An examination of the Trials for Sedition . . . in Scotland *op. cit.* Vol. 2 p 84

27 Cockburn, Henry: Memorials of his time *op. cit.* p 117

28 Roughead, William: The Bi-Centenary of Lord Braxfield *op. cit.* p 300

29 Cockburn, Henry: Memorials of his time *op. cit.* p 115–116

30 Gray, W Forbes: *op. cit.* p 98–99

31 Cockburn, Henry: An examination of the Trials for Sedition . . . in Scotland
    op. cit. Vol. 1 p 80-81

32 *idem.* p 86–87

33 *idem.* p 85

34 *idem.* p 86

35 *idem.* p 86 (footnote)

36 *idem.* p 86

37 Scott, Walter: Letters of Malachi Malagrowther, 1826 2nd letter

Chapter Two Scotland in the Age of Braxfield

1 SRO (Scottish Record Office) SC1/16 Books of Sederunt of Lords of Council
    and Session

2 Johnson, Samuel: A journey to the Western Islands, London 1924 p 79

3 SRO GD51/1/193

4 *Scots Magazine*: May 1801

5 SRO GD51/6/1295

6 Campbell, Lord: Lives of the Lord Chancellors and Keepers of the Great Seal of
    England, vii 599

7 Walter Scott: Letter to Lord Montagu, 1822

8 Boswell, James quoted in Meikle, HW: Scotland and the French Revolution,
    Edinburgh 1912

9 London Magazine quoted in Boswell, James: Diaries – Boswell for the Defence
    1769–1774, London 1960 p 23

10 Quoted in Daiches, David et al: A hotbed of genius, Edinburgh 1986 p 1

11 Sinclair, James: Analysis of the Statistical Account of Scotland, Vol. 2
    Edinburgh 1826 p 226

12 NLS Robertson-Macdonald Papers, quoted in Ross, I S: Lord Kames and the
    Scotland of his day, Oxford 1971

13 Daniel Fellenberg to Lord Kames, 1762 quoted in Ross *op. cit.*

14 Boswell, James: Life of Johnson, 1953 p 627

15 SRO Register of Deeds RD2/277 ff79 *et. seq.*

16 Creech, William: Edinburgh fugitive pieces, Edinburgh 1815

17 John Mowbray: Letter to Alexander Young 17th March 1838, EUL Laing Mss.
    Div. ii 113

18 Ramsay, Dean: Reminiscences of Scottish Life and Character, Edinburgh 1872
    p 147

19 *Scots Magazine*: August 1761

20 *Scots Magazine*: July 1761

21 *Scots Magazine*: August 1761

22 Carlyle, Alexander: Autobiography, London 1910 p 199

23 Boswell, James: Diaries – London Journal 1762–63, London 1950 p 71–2

24 Illustration in Oldham, James: The Mansfield Manuscripts, Chapel Hill 1992
    Vol. 2 p 791

25 Boswell, James: Diaries – The English Experiment 1785–89, New York 1986 p68
26 SRO CS1/16 Books of Sederunt of Lords of Council and Session
27 Boswell, James: Diaries – The Ominous Years 1774–76, London 1963
28 Cockburn, Henry: An examination of the Trials for Sedition . . . in Scotland, Edinburgh 1888 Vol. 1 p 198
29 Wilson, Alexander: Address to the Synod of Glasgow and Ayr
30 Burns, Robert: The Tree of Liberty, c1793 *in* Poems and Songs, London 1969 p 721–2
31 *Caledonian Mercury*: March 10 1792
32 Cockburn, Henry: An examination of the Trials for Sedition . . . in Scotland, Edinburgh, 1888, Vol. 1 p 175-6
33 *idem.* p 211
34 Diderot & d'Alembert: Encyclopédie. art. Écosse, quoted in Meikle, Henry W: Scotland and the French Revolution, Glasgow 1912 p xix
35 Dorat-Cubières: Prophétie Républicaine, 1794 quoted in Meikle, Henry W: *op. cit.* p 167

Chapter 3 The Law

1 Articles of Union 1707, Acts of the Parliaments of Scotland (APS) Vol. xi p 411 *et. seq.*
2 National Library of Scotland (NLS) Advocates Mss 26.3.7 f137v. undated copy of opinion
3 Dalrymple of Stair, James: Institutions of the Laws of Scotland, 1681 Dedication
4 MacKenzie, George: Pleadings in some remarkable cases before the Supreme Court of Scotland, 1672 Preface
5 APS Vol. ix p 266 *et. seq.*
6 Quoted in Grant, F J: The Faculty of Advocates in Scotland 1532–1943, Edinburgh 1944, Intro.
7 APS Vol. ii p 8
8 *Scots Magazine*: March 1796
9 *Scots Magazine*: December 1790
10 Cockburn, Henry: An examination of the Trials for Sedition . . . in Scotland, Edinburgh 1888 Vol. 1 p 107
11 Creech, William: Edinburgh fugitive pieces, Edinburgh 1815 p 107
12 *Scots Magazine*: March 1788.
13 APS Vol. ii p 335
14 Young, Alexander: Memoir of Robert McQueen of Braxfield, EUL Laing MSS Div. ii 113
15 Carlyle, Thomas: Reminiscences, quoted in Edwards, Owen Dudley & Richardson, Graham: Edinburgh, Edinburgh 1983 p 158
16 Scott, Walter: Redgauntlet, Letter 13
17 Court of Session: Act of Sederunt 31 July 1674 quoted in Brunton, G & Haig, D: An historical account of the Senators of the College of Justice, Edinburgh 1836 p xlv
18 *Scots Magazine*: May 1785

19 *Scots Magazine*: May 1801
20 Boswell, James: Diaries – Boswell for the Defence 1769–1774, London 1960
    p 295
21 SRO Melville Papers GD 51/5/427/3 Robert Dundas to Duke of Portland
    31.5.1799.
22 Report by Lord Eskgrove to Lords Commissioners of Treasury in SRO
    Melville Papers GD51/5/426
23 Boswell, James: Diaries – Laird of Auchinleck 1778–1782, Edinburgh 1993
    p 185/6
24 *idem.* p 149
25 APS Vol. iii p 458
26 APS Vol. viii p 87–88
27 *Scots Magazine*: January 1791
28 Cockburn, Henry: Memorials of his time, Edinburgh 1856 p 344/5
29 Cockburn, Henry: An examination of the Trials for Sedition . . . in Scotland,
    Edinburgh 1888 Vol. 1 p 83
30 Report of the Judges of the High Court of Justiciary relating to the case of
    Thomas Muir and Thomas Fyshe Palmer, submitted to Henry Dundas,
    Home Secretary 27th December 1793, SRO RH/2/4/73 ff305 *et. seq.*
31 [Boswell, James] Letter to Robert McQueen, Lord Braxfield, on his promotion
    to be one of the Judges of the High Court of Justiciary, Edinburgh 1780
32 Young, Alexander *op. cit.*
33 Boswell, James *op. cit.*
34 Report by Lord Eskgrove to Lords Commissioners of Treasury in SRO
    Melville Papers GD51/5/426
35 Boswell, James: Diaries – The Laird of Auchinleck 1778–1782, Edinburgh 1993
    p239

Chapter 4 McQueen the Man

1 Malcolm, Charles A, ed: The Minutes of the Justices of the Peace for
    Lanarkshire 1707–1723, Edinburgh 1931
2 *Scots Magazine*: May 1801.
3 EUL: Morgan Transcripts of Edinburgh University Matriculation Records
4 Carlyle, Alexander: Autobiography, London 1910 p 47
5 Ramsay, James of Ochtertyre: Scotland and Scotsmen in the eighteenth century,
    Edinburgh 1888 p 380
6 *Scots Magazine*: May 1801
7 Boswell, James: Diaries – Laird of Auchinleck 1778–1782, Edinburgh 1993
    pp 239/240
8 SRO Books of Sederunt of the Lords of Council and Session CS1/13
9 SRO Register of Charters under Great Seal C2 Vol. 118 f86
10 SRO Agnew of Lochnaw Papers GD154/683/4
11 Young, Alexander: Memoir of Lord Braxfield, EUL Laing Mss. Div. ii 113
12 NLS The Watson Collection MS 588/1342
13 in Young, Alexander: Memoir of Lord Braxfield, EUL Laing Mss. Div. ii 113
14 SRO Edinburgh Commissary Court, Consistorial Processes CC8/6/53
15 SRO Melville Papers GD51/6/1295

16 SRO Melville Papers GD51/5/423/2

17 *Scots Magazine*: June 1801

18 Gray, W Forbes: Some Old Scots Judges, London 1914 p 120

19 Unattributed quotation in Gray, W Forbes: Some Old Scots Judges, London 1914 p 120

20 Cockburn, Henry: Memorials of his time, Edinburgh 1856 p 115

21 Ramsay, James: *op. cit.* p 390

22 Boswell, James: Diaries – The Ominous Years 1774–76, London 1963 p 238

23 Young, Alexander: *op. cit.*

24 Cockburn, Henry: *op. cit.* p 114

25 Young, Alexander: *op. cit.*

26 NLS MSS 90/14 Letter from Lord President to unknown correspondent, 16 March 1838

27 Boswell, James: Diaries – Laird of Auchinleck *op. cit.* p 279

28 Young, Alexander: *op. cit.*

29 Cockburn, Henry: *op. cit.* p 140

30 *idem.* p 134

31 Ramsay, James: *op. cit.* p 391

32 EUL: Laing MSS Div. ii 499/471

33 Ramsay, James: *op. cit.* pp 390/391

34 Young, Alexander: *op. cit.*

35 Ramsay, James: *op. cit.* p 390

36 *idem.* p 380

37 *idem.* p 392

38 SRO Lanarkshire Sasines RS42 XIX f160

39 Old Statistical Account: United Parishes of Wistoun and Robertoun, Edinburgh 1792

40 SRO Register of Deeds RD4/216 f205

41 SRO Register of Deeds RD2/216 f473

42 SRO Register of Deeds RD2/276 ff 606–637

43 Quoted in Buchanan, J W & Paton, H: History of Peeblesshire Vol. 3 Glasgow 1927 p 260

44 *Scots Magazine*: July 1799

45 Ramsay, James: *op. cit.* p 393

46 *Scots Magazine*: June 1801

47 Roughead, William: The Bi-centenary of Lord Braxfield *in* Glengarry's Way and other studies, Edinburgh 1922 p 306

Chapter 5 McQueen the Lawyer

1 *Edinburgh Magazine*: June 1799

2 SRO SC38/1/22

3 Pinkerton, J M: Minute Book of the Faculty of Advocates 1713–1750, Edinburgh 1980

4 *Scots Magazine*: May 1801

5 Roll of Edinburgh Burgesses, Edinburgh

6 Faculty of Advocates: Faculty Minutes 1751–1783

7 Ramsay, James of Ochtertyre: Scotland and Scotsmen in the eighteenth century, Edinburgh 1888 p 382

8 Boswell, James: Diaries – Boswell for the Defence 1769–1774, London 1960 p 233/4

9 Boswell, James: Diaries – The Ominous Years 1774–1776, London 1963 p 224

10 NLS Saltoun Papers MS 17549 f85

11 NLS Saltoun Papers MS 17550 f124

12 Ramsay, James *op. cit.* p 381

13 SRO Justiciary Records Books of Adjournal JC3/32

14 *Scots Magazine*: Jan 1755

15 Ridpath, George: Diary, Edinburgh 192. p 100

16 NLS Stuart Stevenson Papers – Castlemilk Muniments MS 5326 no. 59

17 Faculty of Advocates: Faculty Minutes 1751–1783

18 NLS Saltoun Papers MS 16763 ff111–129

19 Addison, Joseph: Sir Roger on the Bench, *Spectator* July 20th 1711

20 NLS Saltoun Papers MS 16764 f14

21 NLS Saltoun Papers MS 16764 f1

22 Roughead, William: The Bi-centenary of Lord Braxfield *in* Glengarry's Way and other studies, Edinburgh 1922 p 286

23 Faculty of Advocates: Faculty Minutes 1751–1783

24 Boswell, James: Diaries – Boswell in search of a wife 1766–1769, London 1957 pp 201–202

25 Boswell, James & Maclaurin, John: Court of Session Garland *in* Robert Chambers: Traditions of Edinburgh, Edinburgh 1868 p 139/40

26 Boswell, James: Diaries – Boswell for the Defence 1769–1744 p 222

27 *idem.* p 295

28 NLS Dickson autographs MS 9657 f4

29 NLS Advocates MSS 26.3.7. f137v

30 Ramsay, Dean: Reminiscences of Scottish Life and Character, Edinburgh 1872 p 201

31 Meston, MC *et. al.* The Scottish Legal Tradition, Edinburgh 1991 p 98

32 NLS MS 3835 f14v

33 NLS MS 20003 ff77 & 144–158

34 *Scots Magazine*: March 1770

35 *Scots Magazine*: April 1770

36 *Scots Magazine*: May 1770

37 *Scots Magazine*: March 1770

38 *Scots Magazine*: April 1770

39 Boswell, James: Diaries– Boswell in search of a wife 1766–1769 *op. cit.* p 35

40 *Scots Magazine*: May 1801

41 Stewart, Angus: *in* Stair Society Miscellany 3, Edinburgh 1992 p 203

42 Ramsay, James: *op. cit.* p 381/383

Chapter 6 Braxfield the Judge

1 *Scots Magazine*: May 1801

2 Fry, Michael: The Dundas Despotism, Edinburgh 1992 p 59

3 Dictionary of National Biography, William Murray, 1st Earl of Mansfield
4 Boswell, James: Diaries – Boswell in Extremes 1776–1778, London 1971 p 58/9
5 *idem.* p 64
6 SRO CS1/16 Books of Sederunt of the Lords of Council & Session 1776–1784
7 Roughead, William: The real Braxfield *in* The Riddle of the Ruthvens,
　　　Edinburgh 1936 p 37
8 Ramsay, James of Ochtertyre: Scotland and Scotsmen in the eighteenth century,
　　　Edinburgh 1888 p 384/5
9 Lyell, W D: The real Weir of Hermiston *in* Juridical Review Vol. XVI 1904 p134
10 Cockburn, Henry: Memorials of his time, Edinburgh 1856 p 113
11 Young, Alexander: Memoir of Robert McQueen of Braxfield EUL Laing MSS
　　　Div. ii 113
12 Boswell, James: Diaries – Boswell in Extremes *op. cit.* p 102
13 Ramsay, Dean: Reminiscences of Scottish Life and Character, Edinburgh 1872
　　　p 151
14 *idem.* p 153
15 [Boswell, James] Letter to Robert Macqueen, Lord Braxfield, on his
　　　promotion to be one of the Judges of the High Court of Justiciary,
　　　Edinburgh 178
16 Boswell, James: Diaries – Laird of Auchinleck 17.8.1782, Edinburgh 1993 p202
17 *idem.* p 211
18 *idem.* p 212/3
19 *idem.* p 226/7
20 *idem.* p 288
21 *idem.* p 382
22 *idem.* p 389
23 SRO Sinclair of Freswick papers GD136/147
24 NLS Saltoun Papers MSS 16766 f1
25 *Scots Magazine*: March 1785
26 Scottish Civil List 1761 *in* Murdoch, Alexander: The people above . . .
　　　Edinburgh 1980 145/6
27 Fry, Michael: *op. cit.* p 144
28 quoted in Fry, Michael: *op. cit.* p 144
29 Boswell, James: Diaries – The English Experiment 1785–89, New York 1986
　　　p 179
30 *Scots Magazine*: May 1801

Chapter 7 Lord Justice-Clerk

1 SRO Justiciary Records Book of Adjournal JC3/34
2 *Scots Magazine*: February 1788
3 *Scots Magazine*: March 1788
4 Annual Register 1788
5 Roughead, William: Trial of Deacon Brodie, 3rd ed, Edinburgh 1931 p 123
6 Gibson, John S: Deacon Brodie, Father to Jekyll and Hyde, Edinburgh 1993
7 Roughead *op. cit.* p 79
8 *idem.* p 87
9 *idem.* p 102/3

10 *idem.* p 112
11 *idem.* p 127
12 *idem.* p 132
13 *idem.* p 174
14 *idem.* p 177 *et. seq.*
15 *idem.* p 197
16 *idem.* p 200
17 *idem.* p 207
18 *idem.* p 209
19 Roughead, William: The Bi-centenary of Lord Braxfield *in* Glengarry's Way and other studies, Edinburgh 1922 p 299
20 Roughead, William: Trial of Deacon Brodie, 3rd ed, Edinburgh 1921 p 209
21 Cockburn, Henry: Memorials of his time, Edinburgh 1856 p 127
22 Cockburn, Henry: An examination of the Trials for Sedition . . . in Scotland, Edinburgh 1888 Vol. 1 p 85
23 Letter quoted in Meikle, Henry: Scotland and the French Revolution, Glasgow 1912 p 94
24 Cockburn, Henry: *op. cit.* p 95
25 *idem.* p 105
26 *idem.* p 106
27 *Scots Magazine*: September 1793
28 Cockburn *op. cit.* p 165
29 *Scots Magazine*: September 1793
30 *Scots Magazine*: October 1793
31 Cockburn, Henry: *op. cit.* p 178
32 *Scots Magazine*: October 1793
33 SRO Home Office Correspondence RH2/4/73 f285
34 SRO Home Office Correspondence RH2/4/73 f303-4
35 SRO Home Office Correspondence RH2/4/73 f305 *et. seq.*
36 SRO Home Office Correspondence RH2/4/73 f315
37 Cockburn, Henry: *op. cit.* Vol. 2 p 145
38 *Scots Magazine*: July 1794
39 *Scots Magazine*: May 1794
40 Cockburn, Henry: *op. cit.* Vol. 1 p 235
41 *idem.* p 291
42 Roughead, William: The Real Braxfield *in* The Riddle of the Ruthvens, Edinburgh 1936 p 50
43 Cockburn, Henry: *op. cit.* Vol. 2 p 25
44 *idem.* Vol. 2 p 28/9
45 Young, Alexander: Memoir of Lord Braxfield, EUL Laing MSS Div. ii 113
46 Cockburn, Henry: *op. cit.* Vol. 2 p 2
47 *idem.* Vol. 2 p 32
48 SRO Microfilm of Graham of Fintry Papers RH4/119/11
49 *Scots Magazine*: March 1794
50 Cockburn, Henry: *op. cit.* Vol. 2 p 79
51 *idem.* Vol. 1 p 268
52 *idem.* Vol. 1 p 269
53 Young, Alexander: *op. cit.*

54 Home Office Scottish Correspondence quoted in Meikle, Henry W: Scotland and the French Revolution, Edinburgh 1912 p 150/151

55 *Scots Magazine*: September 1794

56 *Scots Magazine*: September 1794

57 *Scots Magazine*: July 1795

58 *Scots Magazine*: August 1795

59 *Scots Magazine*: December 1795

60 Roughead, William: The Hanging of James M'Kean *in* Glengarry's Way and other studies, Edinburgh 1922 p 271

61 *Scots Magazine*: October 1797

62 SRO Register of Deeds RD2/276/f435 and RD2/277/ff79 *et. seq.*

63 *Scots Magazine*: June 1801

64 SRO Melville Papers GD51/5/427 /1

65 SRO Melville Papers GD51/5/427 /2

66 SRO Melville Papers GD51/5/427 /3

Chapter 8 Summing-up

1 Roughead, William: The Real Braxfield *in* The Riddle of the Ruthvens, 1936 p 33

2 Cockburn, Henry: Memorials of his time, 1856 p 115/6

3 Young, Alexander: Memoir of Lord Braxfield, EUL Laing MSS Div. ii, 113

4 Coyle, Andrew: Inside – Rethinking Scotland's Prisons, Edinburgh 1991 p 23

5 Cockburn, Henry: An examination of the Trials for Sedition . . . in Scotland, Edinburgh 1888 Vol. 1 p 198

6 *idem.* Vol. 2 p 152

7 *idem.* Vol. 2 p 91

8 Cockburn, Henry: Memorials of his time, Edinburgh 1856 p 115

9 Young, Alexander: *op. cit.*

10 Ramsay, James of Ochtertyre: Scotland and Scotsmen in the Eighteenth Century, Edinburgh 1888 p 388/9

11 *idem.* p 385

12 Cockburn, Henry: Memorials of his time, Edinburgh 1856 p 113

13 Ramsay: *op. cit.* p 393

LAST SITTING of the OLD COURT of SESSION 11 of JULY 1808

J. KAY. 1808   300

The Last Sitting of the Old Court of Session

Kay's engraving shows the "hale fifteen" sitting together for the last time in 1808. After this time the Court that Braxfield knew was divided into two – the Inner and the Outer House

INDEX